In Search of Healing

In Search of Healing

Collected papers *from the*
Annual Conference *of the*
Society for Pastoral Counselling Research

Edited by
Augustine Meier

The Society for Pastoral Counseling Research
Ottawa, Ontario
2003

Cover: Caroline Gagnon
Layout: Caroline Gagnon

Business Office:
Society for Pastoral Counselling Research
Augustine Meier
223 Main Street
Ottawa, Ontario, Canada
K1S 1C4

Phone: (613) 236-1393 Ext. 2258 or (613) 739-3056
E-mail: ameier@ustpaul.ca or ameier@sympatico.ca

National Library of Canada Cataloguing in Publication

In search of healing : collected papers from the annual conference of the Society for Pastoral Counselling Research, 1994 to 1999 / Augustine Meier, editor.

Includes 2 papers in French.
Includes bibliographical references.
ISBN 0-9732721-0-4

1. Pastoral counseling—Congresses. I. Meier, Augustine, Date-
II. Society for Pastoral Counselling Research

BV4335.I5 2003 253'.5 C2003-901194-1

Printed in Canada

Contents

Part Three: Healing in Practice

Part Four: Healing in Research

Acknowledgments

Editing and publishing a book requires the collaboration and generosity of many people. The author wishes to express his gratitude to the following persons:

To Anne Chevalier, Director of Production, Novalis and Anne Louise Mahoney, Managing Editor, Novalis, for their generous giving of their time and for their advice, suggestions and help in the entire publication process; and to graphic artist Caroline Gagnon, for designing the cover and for doing the layout of the book.

To Jack McCann, for his suggestions for the earlier versions of the English chapters; to Madeleine Thériault and Lise Chevrette, for their suggestions for the earlier versions of the French chapters; and to Suzanne Nussey, for her meticulous editing which improved the quality of the book.

To the contributors to this book, whose eagerness, collaboration and patience made the task of editing the book a satisfying and rewarding experience.

To the Executive of the Society for Pastoral Counselling Research, for entrusting me with the task of editing and publishing the papers presented at the annual conferences. Your encouragement and interest were much appreciated.

To my daughter Molisa Meier, for formatting chapters of the book, and to my wife, Micheline Boivin, and Molisa for their support and accepting the many evenings and weekends I was away from home while working on the book.

Contributing Authors

Bernell Anstey, M.Ed., is currently an itinerant school counsellor in the Saskatoon (East) School Division in Saskatchewan where she provides individual and group counselling to students of all grade levels and consultation to school staff and families. In addition, she conducts psychoeducational assessments and has authored psychoeducational test reviews in the Canadian Journal of School Psychology.

Micheline Boivin, M.A., is a certified clinical psychologist working with traumatized children and their parents at the Programme Enfance-Famille-Jeunesse du Centre local des services communautaires de Gatineau, Québec. She has co-authored articles on psychotherapy, published in refereed journals, presented workshops on child sexual abuse and the use of puppets in child therapy, and co-presented advanced workshops on the use of mental imagery in psychotherapy.

Frank Landino, M.A., is currently a family counsellor with The Elizabeth Fry Society in Vancouver. He has supervised a group home for ex-convicts and post-psychiatric patients at Horizon House in Ottawa and for several years worked as a child-care worker with Children's Aid Society.

Claude Mailloux, Ph.D., is a Professor at the Faculté de théologie, d'éthique et de philosophie de l'Université de Sherbrooke where he teaches spiritual anthropology and pastoral counselling. His research interest is the anthropological dimension of the human person and his research method is praxology. He presented a workshop with Denis Vasse on the topic "Le désir dans l'oeuvre de Denis Vasse" to a group called "Psychanalyse et anthropologie,"Lyons, France, 2002. One of his most recent publications is "Spiritualité en mal d'intégration: Comment une anthropologie psychoreligieuse fondamentale permet-elle de comprendre le problème?" dans Léandre Boisvert, *Spiritualité en crise. De l'éclatement à l'intégration.*

Augustine Meier, Ph.D., is a certified clinical psychologist in private practice, a Professor in the Faculty of Human Sciences, Saint Paul University, and an Adjunct Research Professor in the Department of Psychology, Carleton University, Ottawa. He teaches a course and provides advanced training in object relations therapy and self psychology. He taught graduate courses in psychotherapy and psychopathology and trained graduate students in individual counselling. He has co-authored articles on psychotherapy and psychopathology in refereed journals and co-presented advanced workshops on the use of mental imagery in psychotherapy and on theme-analysis. He is co-author of the book, *The Challenge of Forgiveness.* Professor Meier is the Founder and former President of The Society for Pastoral Counselling Research.

Marie-Line Morin, Ph.D., is a Professor of Pastoral Counselling at the Faculté de théologie, d'éthique et de philosophie de l'Université de Sherbrooke, Québec. Her research interests relate to the concept of fundamental value and its various applications to pastoral counselling as well as to the integration of psychology, theology and spirituality in the context of clinical work and the field of spiritual anthropology. One of her most recent publications is "Pour une écoute en profondeur, la Valeur, fondamentale," 2001.

Beverly Anne Musgrave, PhD., is an Assistant Professor in Pastoral Counselling and Spiritual Care, Graduate School of Religion and Religious Education, Fordham University, Bronx, New York. She has a clinical Practice in Pastoral Counselling, in New York City. Professor Musgrave is a founder and former president of Partners In Healing and a Fellow in the American Association of Pastoral Counsellors.

Peter Sanders, M.Th., L. Past. Th., is a Lecturer in the Faculty of Human Sciences, Saint Paul University, Ottawa. His interest and research areas are religious education and practical theology.

John Shea, Ph.D., is an Associate Professor of Psychology and Pastoral Counselling in the Graduate School of Religion at Fordham University, Bronx, New York. His interests are human development, with a special focus on the psychological and religious dimensions, and understanding and furthering therapeutic change. He is a Fellow in the American Association of Pastoral Counsellors.

Lucille Smelzter-Legault, M.A., is a counsellor in the Employee Assistance Program with Family Service Centre of Ottawa, and Mental Health Program at Family Services, Ottawa, Ontario.

William J., Sneck, S.J., Ph.D., is Adjunct Professor of Psychology and Pastoral Counselling at Loyola College, Baltimore, and Associate Director of the Jesuit Center for Spiritual Growth, Wernersville, PA. He has published on the integration of spirituality and psychology, especially Jungian.

Peter L. VanKatwyk, Ph.D., is a Professor in Practical Theology and the Director of Pastoral Counselling Programs at Waterloo Lutheran Seminary at Wilfrid Laurier University, Waterloo, Ontario. He is a Supervisor in the Canadian Association for Pastoral Practice and Education and an Approved Supervisor and Clinical Member of the American Association for Marriage and Family Therapy. Administrative positions that he held include Executive Director of the Cambridge Interfaith Pastoral Counselling Centre, Ontario and Director of Training at the Kitchener Interfaith Pastoral Counselling Centre. In addition to articles published in refereed pastoral counselling journals, he is co-author of the book, *The Challenge of Forgiveness*. Peter VanKatwyk is a former President of The Society for Pastoral Counselling Research.

Loretta Wiseman, a graduate of Teacher's College, Saskatoon, Saskatchewan, is currently working in a multigrade classroom in the Prairie Rose School Division, Alberta. In her teaching career (interrupted to raise her family), she taught students in elementary school and has worked with students having both physical and learning handicaps.

Introduction

This past year has made us painfully aware that the reality of the human condition includes the experience of tragedy, suffering, death, loss, and woundedness. We have also been reminded that people transcend these adversities and find the courage to pick up the pieces and carry on. It is within our human and spiritual nature to come to terms with these realities, to integrate them and then to move on with our lives. In our own way, we find a way to heal ourselves from these terrifying experiences and in the process arrive at a state of tranquility and inner harmony so as to be able to courageously continue with our lives. We have been given the hope that people are able to find healing in the midst of these tragedies.

Healing from different experiences of suffering and loss is the theme of *In Search of Healing*. The book contains stories of persons who experienced tragedy and the loss of loved ones and how they found healing from these painful experiences. *In Search of Healing* presents counselling approaches used by professionals to aid the healing process. Lastly, methods to evaluate the usefulness of the healing approaches are presented and critiqued.

Healing from adversities was one of the themes of the Annual Conferences of the Society for Pastoral Counselling Research which was founded in 1994. The Society, through its annual conferences, fosters the exchange of experiences and ideas between pastoral counselling and health care professionals and researchers, and supports the development of theoretical and research models and treatment of human problems such as healing from tragedies.

This book comprises papers presented at the annual conferences of the Society between the years 1994 and 1999, inclusive. All who presented papers at any of the first six annual conferences were invited to submit their manuscripts for inclusion in the book. The papers accepted for this book have been revised and their contents have been brought up to date. In addition to these papers, two authors were invited to submit papers on the topic of healing. The submitted and invited papers underwent a peer review before being accepted for this publication.

The theme of the book is healing and how persons turn to resources within themselves or to resources available in the community to bring about healing from tragedy and loss experiences. One of the available community resources is pastoral counselling. Some chapters in this book focus on the meaning and nature of pastoral counselling as a healing process, others focus on how pastoral counselling can bring healing to specific settings, and the remainder focus on research methods designed to track the healing process. The informal tone of the chapters was preserved. This was the flavour of the papers presented at the first annual conferences. Two chapters written in French have been included as the Society is bilingual in nature.

The book is divided into four parts: inaugural address, theory, practice and research. The first part, "Inaugural Address," comprises one chapter that presents the address given at the Founding of the Society. Chapters 2 to 7 comprise the second part, "Healing In Theory." Here the authors distinguish between pastoral counselling, psychotherapy and spiritual direction, present the ontogenesis and development of empathy, describe how differentiation facilitates the healing process, and investigate how desires and fundamental values relate to the healing process. Chapters 8 to 13 comprise the third part, "Healing in Practice." This part describes the process of healing from tragedy and death in the family, shows how pastoral counselling is applied in a secular setting to address spiritual and religious issues, and presents the approaches of two professionals in helping children and adults heal from the emotional wounds caused by sexual abuse. The last part, "Healing in Research," comprises three chapters that present three different qualitative research methods to study human phenomena including depression, religious experiences and fundamental values. The three research methods are useful to gain a better understanding of human phenomena that are not well known and to study phenomena in depth.

Part One: Inaugural Address

(1) Chapter 1 comprises the inaugural address given by Augustine Meier at the founding of the Society for Pastoral Counselling Research. The chapter describes the circumstances that led to the birth of the Society and outlines its purpose and objective. Professor Meier distinguishes between formal and informal research and underlines the unique quality of pastoral counselling research. He also points out the importance for the profession of pastoral counselling to develop its own theoretical models, research methods, and body of knowledge.

Part Two: Healing in Theory

(2) Chapter 2, written by William Sneck, distinguishes between pastoral counselling, secular therapy, and spiritual direction. The author offers implications for conceptualizing and practicing each form of service.

(3) The topic of Chapter 3 is empathy and intimacy. The author, Beverly Musgrave, provides novel definitions for both empathy and intimacy. The body of this chapter provides an in-depth exploration of the cognitive and affective components of empathy and their relationship to intimacy. The specific importance of multi-dimensional empathy is defined and clarified from various perspectives. The relationship of intimacy to empathy is briefly explored.

(4) John Shea, in Chapter 4, considers empathy in relation to human development. From a review of the literature, he offers a working definition of empathy. Next, Professor Shea offers a definition of an adult self and describes six characteristics of self. The author then shows how empathy for the self and empathy for the other are essential to an adult self. Finally, the chapter takes a brief look at the development of empathy, and the relation of empathy to both adult morality and adult religion.

(5) Peter VanKatwyk, in Chapter 5, presents a family process model of pastoral care for those who experience a death in the family. Death in the family often impairs the family's ability to

function and impedes the family members in the tasks of ongoing life. Professor VanKatwyk correlates the levels of self-differentiation between individuals and their families with the family grief process and with the style of pastoral care. He gives special attention to the spiritual dimension in the family grieving process and how this process can be further facilitated through pastoral care and counselling.

(6) In Chapter 6, Marie-Line Morin presents the role of fundamental values in family systems therapy. In the first part, the author presents research results where fundamental values were identified in clients' discourse using a phenomenological method of analysis. Professor Morin draws a parallel between fundamental values and foundational concepts of the systems approach. In the second part, she conceptualizes a family systems approach that integrates fundamental values. She presents data from a case study to support her theory.

(7) Chapitre 7 présente les premiers résultats de recherche qui ont émergé de l'étude de l'œuvre de Denis Vasse entreprise par Claude Mailloux. Deux techniques se complètent au niveau de l'analyse et du traitement des données. La collecte des données s'effectue à l'aide d'une grille de forme qui enregistre la relation existant entre deux concepts reliés au désir. Ensuite, les données sont interprétées à partir d'un concept clé pris à même le texte vassien. Cet exercice permet de construire une synthèse théorique où l'on découvre le désir comme une dynamique qui est à l'œuvre à la fois dans la structuration psychique et dans l'expérience religieuse. À l'inverse du besoin qui réclame son dû, le désir demeure ouvert. Il engage la personne dans le mouvement de sa vie.

> (Chapter 7 presents the results from Claude Mailloux's theoretical study of Denis Vasse. Combining two research techniques, the author explored part of Vasse's work. First, the author developed a grid to collect and organize data and to show how the data were related to two concepts derived from Vasse's concept of desire. Second, he interpreted the data using a key concept drawn from Vasse's works. From these data, the author constructed a theory of desire where desire is understood as a dynamic at play

in the psychic structuring processes as well as in religious experience. Unlike need which requires satisfaction, desire remains an open search. Desire is the dynamic that engages persons in their own life).

Part Three: Healing in Practice

(8) Loretta Wiseman, in Chapter 8, narrates her healing from her son's tragic burn. She describes her experiences in caring for her son both when he was in the hospital and after he was discharged from the hospital. She draws a parallel between the stages of her own healing experience and the stages outlined by Kübler-Ross.

(9) Bernell Anstey, in Chapter 9, examines her journey as a researcher conducting grief therapy with a bereaved client after the death of her own father. Autoethnography was utilized to investigate her experience as a bereaved counsellor counselling a bereaved client and to specifically examine how her capacity as a bereaved counsellor was facilitated or impeded by counter-transferential interactions between the client and herself. This chapter highlights the challenges that she confronted as a bereaved counsellor and how the insight gained from confronting these challenges was therapeutic and facilitative in her journey of healing.

(10) Chapter 10 focuses on the function of healing as central to the cure-of-souls tradition of pastoral care and counselling, and describes two prominent but opposing styles of healing in ministry. The author, Peter VanKatwyk, proposes an interactional model of pastoral care which integrates the two healing styles of compassion and competence through the principle of differentiation. The author demonstrates how the two models of healing styles can be integrated to form an interactional pastoral counselling model. This model draws from the perspective of social constructivism as practised in narrative therapy and from the theory of natural systems as applied to the role of the pastor.

(11) In Chapter 11, Lucille Smelzer-Legault relates how she brought pastoral counselling to the work place. To clarify her per-

sonal practice of pastoral counselling, she broadened the meaning of pastoral counselling. Using her experience in the work place, the author demonstrates how she has been pastoral to those who sought her help.

(12) Micheline Boivin nous entretient, au chapitre douze, de l'importance d'ouvrir nos yeux et d'être attentifs aux signes de détresse qu'un enfant, ayant été exploité sexuellement, donne à son entourage, de bien les décoder, de comprendre l'enfant, et de lui tendre la main dans ses besoins d'être cru, protégé et aidé. Dans ce chapitre truffé d'exemples cliniques, Micheline Boivin indique en premier lieu, les signes de détresse qui alertent notre oeil et notre coeur dépisteurs; en deuxième lieu, les aspects faisant l'objet d'une évaluation; et, en troisième lieu, l'approche et le processus thérapeutiques. La méthode de la thérapie par le jeu avec l'enfant est expliquée et illustrée d'exemples.

> (Micheline Boivin, in Chapter 12, draws our attention to the importance of opening our eyes to the signs of distress that a child who has been sexually abused manifests, to decode these signs, to understand the child, and to extend a hand to him/her who needs to be believed, protected and helped. In this chapter, filled with clinical examples, Micheline Boivin indicates, first, the child's signs of distress that alert our vigilant eyes and compassionate heart; second, the dimensions to be assessed; and third, the therapeutic approach and process. The use of play therapy with a child is explained and illustrated).

(13) Frank Landino, in Chapter 13, shares his experiences in working with adult survivors of sexual abuse. The author's counselling office comprised various sites where he assisted his clients. The author narrates the long-term after-effects of the abuse. In the last part of the chapter, Frank Landino reveals how he suffered from burnout, from which he found a way to extricate himself.

Part Four: Healing in Research

(14) A qualitative research method that uses case notes to study counselling issues is the topic of Chapter 14. This method is referred to as a thematic analytic research method. Augustine Meier proposes a discovery-oriented research method that studies the pastoral counselling experience in terms of themes. The author proposes a method to writeup case notes that are amenable to analysis using the thematic method. The research method is illustrated by applying it to an adult male client suffering from depression. The author proposes that this method could be used by practitioners who are unable to carry out formal research.

(15) The topic of Chapter 15 is the appropriation of peak religious experiences through the use of metaphors. In this chapter, Peter Sanders defines religious peak experiences, presents three different theories regarding metaphor and summarizes four therapeutic approaches to the use of metaphors. In the last part of the chapter, Professor Sanders summarizes the results from a qualitative research wherein the participants were asked to report their life experience prior to, during, and after a peak religious experience and to construe these time periods in terms of a metaphor.

(16) In Chapter 16, Marie-Line Morin presents internal validation data for the *Fundamental Value Questionnaire* designed to identify a person's fundamental values. Fundamental values were identified using an existential phenomenological research method. Clinicians and researchers can use *The Fundamental Value Questionnaire* to identify, without requiring a great amount of time, a subject's or client's fundamental values.

In Search of Healing covers a broad array of topics on the theme of healing. It is the hope that the reader will find the content of this book informative, interesting and inspiring.

Augustine Meier
April 2003

Part One

Inaugural Address

Chapter 1

The Research Challenges for the Profession of Pastoral Counselling*

Augustine Meier, Ph.D.

I am very pleased to be with you today to celebrate the founding of the Society for Pastoral Counselling Research. This, hopefully, will be a historic moment for all of us connected with the profession of pastoral counselling.

I am very pleased, as well, that you, Claudette Dubé-Socqué, Director of the Institute of Pastoral Studies, were able to free yourself from administrative responsibilities and officially welcome us to this first annual conference of The Society for Pastoral Counselling Research.

In the name of the organizing team, whose names are identified on the inside cover of the program, we express our thanks to all of you who have offered to participate in our program by presenting a paper. Finally, we express our appreciation to everyone for being here to take part in this year's proceedings.

According to the program the title of my address is to be "The Society for Pastoral Counselling Research: Research Goals and

---

*Inaugural Address presented at the Founding and First Annual Conference of the Society for Pastoral Counselling Research held at Saint Paul University, Ottawa, Ontario, May 5-7, 1994.

Professional Implications." I have changed the title to, "The Research Challenges for the Profession of Pastoral Counselling." I have done this to better reflect the content of my address this morning, and to better reflect the theme of this year's proceedings, "Sharing Experiences and Models of Pastoral Counselling."

Introduction

Over the past fifty years, pastoral counselling has made little progress in establishing itself as a unique and viable profession, and it has made even less progress in establishing itself as a discipline (Meier, 1990b; Meier, Boivin & Aylward, 1986). Pastoral counselling has not developed any theoretical models specific to its experience (Meier, 1990a, 1990b), and it has done little research (Meier & Weber, 1992). Pastoral counselling has relied almost exclusively on the theoretical models from theology and psychology. For example, in the 1940s, pastoral counsellors relied on psychoanalysis and client-center therapy, in the 1960s and 1970s, they relied on the active therapies such as transactional analysis and systems theory, and in the 1980s they relied on the neo-Freudian models such as object relations theory. There was a similar shift in terms of the theological models adopted across the same years. In short, pastoral counselling has relied on other disciplines for its theoretical models, methods of assessment and methods of intervention (Meier, Boivin, Aylward, 1986).

To establish itself as a viable and valid profession and discipline, pastoral counselling must develop its own theoretical models, establish its assessment and treatment methods, devise methods of research particular to it, and become engaged in research (Meier, 1994a, 1994b). We cannot leave this kind of activity to individual efforts or to chance. It is important that the research activity become a collective interest and a collective enterprise.

To encourage the collective research interest and the collective research enterprise of pastoral counsellors, and to offer a forum wherein they can discuss their experiences, discoveries, models and research activities, we are forming the Society for Pastoral Counselling Research. The purpose of the society is to offer a forum for pastoral counsellors to share and exchange, with their colleagues, in a formal way, their emerging ideas, thoughts, and models regarding the practice of pastoral counselling.

Beginnings of SPCR

I would like to relate two anecdotes that influenced the founding of the Society for Pastoral Counselling Research.

First, when I became a full-time professor at Saint Paul University about twelve years ago, there seemed to be a lot of discussion on what it meant to be pastoral. I heard this discussion at faculty council meetings and at one of our annual one-day reflection days. What impressed me was that everyone seemed to have his or her own notion as to what it meant to be "pastoral." Following these discussions, I was left with the impression that no one really knew what the term meant. After teaching and training students for about two years, I was told by another professor that I was not pastoral in my approach. And yet I received the opposite message from my students. For example, during my training sessions, students would say, "Gus, that is pastoral." Nevertheless, my faculty colleague continued to tell me indirectly, and sometimes not so indirectly, but always politely, that I was not pastoral in my teaching and training.

I reached a point where I could no longer tolerate hearing the word pastoral and to receive remarks about being or not being pastoral. I thought that it was time to take the bull by the horns. Consequently three of us, that is, Micheline Boivin, Colette Aylward and myself, undertook a comprehensive review of the literature on pastoral counselling. We were particularly interested in what it meant to be pastoral and what was meant by pastoral counselling. But this initial research question took us far afield, and we ended up reviewing theoretical models, training methods, research activities, and so on. We presented our first paper at the annual colloquium of the Group for Research in Pastoral Studies (Meier, Boivin, & Aylward, 1986). After the presentation, my colleague came up to me and said, "Gus, now you are being pastoral." Needless to say, this professor made no further remarks regarding me being pastoral in my training and teaching of students. I must add, I am thankful to my colleague for having challenged me.

The second anecdote relates to my attendance for the past five years at the annual conferences of the Society for Psychotherapy Research and the annual conferences of the Society for the Exploration of Psychotherapy Integration. These conferences, which are international in scope, have taken place in different countries including Canada, the United States, England, France, and South America. Often a professor with his or her students would form a symposium and present their research findings at these conferences. For example, on one occasion Laura Rice and her graduate students from York University have presented their research. On another occasion, Jeremy Safran and his students from Adelphi University presented research being conducted at the university's counselling centre. Last June, at the annual conference of the Society for Psychotherapy Research held in Pittsburgh, Les Greenberg and his students from York University, Toronto, presented their findings on the "unfinished business" research. As I sat there and listened to these groups present their research, I said to myself, "I wish that the students in my research seminar could be present to hear this." I also said to myself, "The students in my research seminar could do an equally good presentation."

Upon my return home from this conference, I was riding my bicycle along Colonel By Drive on a sunny Sunday morning and reflecting on the Pittsburgh experience, the idea struck me that the graduates from the Pastoral Counselling Program at Saint Paul University did not have an association or society which they can call their own, nor did they have a forum they could attend on a regular basis. I didn't know if creating such an association was a dream, if it was real, or both. I then explored the possibility of founding a Society for Pastoral Counselling Research. I shared this idea with Micheline Boivin, and with professors, including Claudette Dubé-Socqué, and the response was positive and encouraging. I also shared this idea with former graduate students, and the response again was positive and encouraging (Meier, 1993b). Lastly, I spoke to the first- and second-year students enrolled in the pastoral counselling programs. Their response was more then positive and encouraging; they were eager to get the society under way.

These two sets of experiences, then, merged, and out of them was born the Society for Pastoral Counselling Research. Thus, conceptually, began the Society for Pastoral Counselling Research.

Purpose and Objectives of SPCR

We can ask ourselves the question — why do we need a society for pastoral counselling research? What purpose will the society play in the development of the pastoral counselling profession?

To answer the first of these questions, we can say that the Society for Pastoral Counselling Research is designed to serve several objectives and goals. One of these is to provide a forum wherein pastoral counsellors may share and exchange experiences and ideas emerging from their work. Currently, pastoral counsellors do not have a learned society that they can call their own. They do not have a society which they can attend to share their common experiences. Pastoral counsellors often feel alone and isolated. In order to feel that they were part of a professional organization and to nourish themselves intellectually, pastoral counsellors, in the past, found themselves going to conferences for psychologists, social workers, guidance counsellors, chaplains, and criminologists. As helpful as these experiences are, they do not meet the unique interests and needs of pastoral counsellors. There does not exist, to my knowledge, a society for pastoral counsellors which has as its primary focus the sharing of new experiences, theoretical models and research activities. The Society for Pastoral Counselling Research attempts to respond to this need. The society provides a forum wherein the pastoral practitioners will be able to share, exchange and test out ideas and models. These exchanges will foster a greater understanding of the pastoral phenomena. This understanding will then be expressed in terms of theoretical and research models, and treatment approaches specific to the pastoral counselling profession.

A second purpose of the society is to encourage continued research on the part of the pastoral counsellor. By sharing his or her research experiences with colleagues at the annual conference, the pastoral counsellor researcher will maintain his or her enthusiasm and interest in research. The counsellor will find a support group that has similar interests and needs.

Thirdly, the formation of a society specific for Pastoral Counsellors would go a long way to establish Pastoral Counselling as a profession and as a discipline. It would add a research dimension, now badly lacking, to the practice and profession of pastoral counselling.

The profession of pastoral counselling will continue to remain relevant and effective only if it is grounded on research (Meier & Weber, 1992). Pastoral counselling cannot be divorced from theory and research. Research, theory, and the practice of pastoral counselling are integrated: they form one unit. All three domains are needed to enrich each other. The activities of the society's members would add credibility to the profession of pastoral counselling.

Research in General

I would now like to speak more specifically about research — research in general, and research within the context of pastoral counselling.

As you have already observed, the name of the society is "The Society for Pastoral Counselling Research." Research, therefore, is an essential component of the society's goals. How are we to understand research in this context?

When we think of research, we often think of it in terms of formulating and testing hypotheses, choosing a research method, gathering empirical data, and statistically analyzing the data. We think of finding evidence to verify an hypothesis. We think of verification. And yet research is far more then either one of these taken separately, and it is far more then all of these taken together.

The word, research, means to re-search, to seek, to explore, to uncover, and to find. An important component of research, therefore, is to discover or to understand. This line of thinking is consistent with that of Les Greenberg (1991). He satirically comments on how the western world has come to adore scientism and the gods of "control," "statistical significance," "random sampling," "generalizability," and "power," and how we have come to minimize the value of understanding (p. 5). Yet, as Greenberg points out, understanding is the beginning of all meaningful research. Without understanding, research is but an empty shell. Research, therefore, as defined in the context of the Society for Pastoral Counselling Research, is understood in its broadest sense and includes both understanding and verification.

How can we proceed to understand a phenomenon about which there is little known, such as an adult's experience of childhood abuse, the phases of the counselling process, and the development of personal and interpersonal competency? Or how can we proceed to understand in a new way, a phenomenon that seems already to be well understood, such as obsessive- compulsive neurosis, the resolution of conflicts, and the therapeutic alliance?

We could turn to one of several methods to obtain this type of understanding. We could use a case study method, or we could use any one of the qualitative research methods. Regardless of which method we use, it will be important that we approach the phenomenon by using a phenomenological and discovery-oriented research method (Meier, 1990a). Some of the prominent researchers in the field of psychotherapy, such as David Rennie (Rennie, Phillips, & Quartaro, 1988), Robert Elliott (1984, 1986), and Les Greenberg (1991) recommend these approaches. By using such approaches one sees anew the phenomenon being studied, that is, one broadens one's understanding of the phenomenon. A phenomenological and discovery-oriented approach allows us to see the whole of the phenomenon, rather than a small part, as is the case when a quantitative research method is used (Meier & Weber, 1992).

I would like to ask yet another question: how might we proceed to use the counselling experience to better understand a phenomenon such as the phases of the change process. We who are counsellors want our clients to change. At times, when the clients do not change fast enough, we become impatient, frustrated, pushy and/or critical of ourselves. We expect that clients change; we are interested in the change process. How might we go about studying the change process and how might we go about understanding the change process?

One way to better understand the change process is to listen to the client, to observe what goes on within therapy, and to reflect upon the counselling process. Obviously we do not want to direct the unfolding of the change process. We want to facilitate the natural process of unfolding. We might decide to use a self-discovery approach to counselling, so that all of the truth that is there will have a chance to emerge (Meier & Boivin, 1987; Meier, Boivin & Driscoll, 1987). As we listen to the client, observe what is happening, and reflect upon the counselling experience, we will become aware of important client events or moments. We will notice that something new occurs with each passing session. We observe a pattern that is forming and taking shape. We then formulate our observations in terms of a model.

However, by developing an initial model of change, our work is not yet completed. We need to apply this initial model of change to other counselling experiences. In this activity, we might extend, refine, or revise the model. After having applied this model to a number of experiences with different clients, we are then ready to finalize a model which describes the phases of the change process.

Micheline Boivin and myself, for example, have developed a seven-phase model of the change process using a procedure similar to the one described above (Meier & Boivin, 1983; 1992). We have operationalized the seven phases, and four groups of research seminar students have, over the past eight years, tested out the adequacy of the seven phases to describe the counselling experience, and analyzed, phase by phase, the process in working through a psychological theme (Anderson et al., 1994; Aylward et al, 1986; Bluger et al., 1984; Charlebois et al., 1985; Meier & Boivin, 1992).

Pastoral Counselling Research

Now, I would like to talk about research within the context of pastoral counselling. Let me begin by asking the question: In what way is research in pastoral counselling different from the research that I just finished describing? That is, in what way is pastoral counselling research different from psychological counselling research, educational counselling research, or from psychiatric research, to mention only a few areas of research?

I think that the major difference between pastoral counselling research and other non-pastoral forms of counselling research lies at the level of the understanding that guides the research. That is, the difference does not lie at the level of the research techniques being used, but at the level of understanding or theory that guides pastoral counselling research. Therefore, when we talk about research, we have to differentiate the understanding or theory that guides the research from the method or technique used to test an aspect of the understanding. Research always implies an understanding and a method of investigation.

A psychologist, for example, brings to the research enterprise a theory that is derived from an understanding of the intellectual, perceptual, emotional, social, and interpersonal dimensions. A psychiatrist would add a biological understanding. These professions have, over the years, developed theoretical models to guide their research. Therefore psychologists, sociologists, and theologians conduct research using data-based or empirically based models. They have a well-established viewpoint with which to understand the data.

Unlike psychologists, psychiatrists, theologians, social workers, or criminologists, pastoral counsellors do not have ready-made theoretical models that can be applied to the pastoral experience and to research. Pastoral counsellors do not have models that come directly from the pastoral counselling experience. Currently, pastoral counsellors come to the experience with models from different disciplines. They have models from psychology, theology, sociology, etc. But they do not have a model that describes fully the pastoral counselling experience. At present, pastoral counselling researchers are handicapped, because they do not possess models specific to the pastoral experience.

The first stage, then, in developing research programs specific to pastoral counselling is to develop models that emerge from an understanding of the pastoral counselling experience. This experience is characterized by client statements concerning beliefs, faith, values, meanings, emotions, and yearnings. The targets of these statements are relationships, persons, the deity, physical well-being and so on. The pastoral counsellor, in his or her practice, is interested in the person's whole experience and in the person's entire concerns. The pastoral counsellor's approach to counselling is holistic.

How might we use these pastoral counsellor-client experiences to develop new models? I have written about this topic in great length in an earlier paper, "Future Directions in Pastoral Counselling I. Constructing Theoretical Models" (Meier, 1990a). I will summarize here only the gist of that paper. As I have already mentioned, in order that pastoral counsellors can conduct research specific to their profession, they must first develop theoretical models specific to the pastoral experience. How might this be done? For guidance we can turn to the innovators in psychological counselling such as Carl Rogers, Aaron Beck, Margaret Mahler, B.F. Skinner, and Sigmund Freud. Each of them used client experiences as a data base to develop new models (see Meier, 1990a, pp. 139-141).

For purposes of illustration, I will use the example of Freud who, as a medical student, was assigned patients suffering from hysteria. At that time no one understood the phenomenon of hysteria, and there was no known treatment for hysteria. Through the use of free association Freud helped clients to talk out their feelings. He observed that as clients talked about their feelings they were freed from their disabling symptoms. Beginning with the data generated by these clients, Freud developed an innovative theory to understand their phenomena. Over time the initial hypothesis was elaborated to form a theory that included concepts such as the unconscious, trauma, repression, unacceptable ideas, defenses, decoupling, and so on. He put all of this together to explain that, because of an unacceptable experience as a child (e.g. being sexually abused), the hysteric repressed both the content (memory) and the affect of the experience from the mind. However, the feeling decoupled (broke loose) from the memory and expressed itself in anxiety. The anxiety, in turn, was dealt with through conversion phenomena such as paralysis, blindness, etc. Thus Freud developed a new theory — psychoanalysis — to explain the origin and treatment of hysteria. He built this theory on his observation of clients as they worked through their symptoms. From these observations emerged a new understanding of hysteria.

In order that pastoral counselling may develop into a discipline and a science, it too must begin afresh and develop its own theories using as a basis the pastoral counselling experience of both the counsellors and the clients. To do less than that means that pastoral counselling will remain a profession, an applied science, not a theoretically based science that generates its own concepts, has a specific body of knowledge, a research methodology, and treatment methods.

It is important that the understanding and the theories emerge from the pastoral counselling experience. For this reason it will be important for the counsellor to allow the clients to speak for themselves and to bring forth their own concepts and explanations. The counsellor will listen carefully to the words of the client to detect therein the abstract system that the client implicitly refers to when making sense out of his or her experience. The counsellor will use this material to begin to formulate a hypothesis to understand the experience as presented by the client. In later sessions, and with other clients who bring forward a similar problem or difficulty, the counsellor will test out the initial hypothesis. From these observations the counsellor may begin to form a theory which at first is descriptive, but which later becomes more abstract, yet always related to the initial clinical material.

In order to grasp the fullness of the client's communications, it will be necessary to develop a new vocabulary. The vocabulary will not be that of theology nor that of psychology, nor that of any existing system. The language will be that of the client who encapsulates his or her experiences in theological, psychological, philosophical, and sociological concepts at one and the same time. The counsellor will listen in a new way, which surmount the artificial walls created by the theoretical systems, to the client's statements. Out of these observations will emerge new concepts, a new language, and a new theory that will be specific to the pastoral experience.

It is the theoretical models developed from such a process that will make the difference for pastoral counselling. Although pastoral counselling today borrows models from other disciplines in order to understand and help the client, it will be models that emerge directly from the pastoral experiences that will be instrumental in the development of pastoral counselling as a discipline and in guiding significant pastoral counselling research. This is not to minimize the importance of current pastoral counselling models or current pastoral counselling research. The point is that the contemporary models and research efforts are not enough. More is needed.

Challenges for SPCR Members

What then are the challenges that lie ahead for the Society of Pastoral Counselling and its members? I think that for the next five to ten years, our great challenge will be to develop theoretical models that encapsulate the counselling experiences. Without the development of these models, there cannot be research specific to the pastoral counselling experience. The counsellor's attempts to make sense out of pastoral experience, to articulate it and organize it in terms of a model, will be vital in the early stages of research in pastoral counselling. It provides the backbone to the more formal research activities.

Secondly, all of us who are engaged in the practice of pastoral counselling are challenged to reflect upon our experiences, to put these experiences into words, to systematize these experiences and express them in terms of emerging models. We are challenged to put our thoughts and insights down on paper, and then share these with our colleagues at the annual conferences of the Society for Pastoral Counselling Research. It is through this activity and sharing of ideas that models specific to the pastoral counselling experience will emerge.

Conclusion

In concluding my address, I would like to underline the fact that the Society for Pastoral Counselling Research is your society. Embrace the society, make it your own. Ask yourselves: what can

I give to the society? Its future rests with you. In working together as a team, the society will prosper and move forward. The society has experienced a strong beginning, assuredly, the best is yet to come.

References

Anderson, J., Laronde, M., Kennedy, M., Leblanc, P., McGuinty, E., & Walsh, S. (1994). *Patterns of change emerging from an analysis of therapeutic themes.* Ottawa, Ontario: St. Paul University. Unpublished M.A. Research Project.

Aylward, C., Cooke, M., Coughlin, L., Favretto, A., Fullerton, M., & Stasiuk, J. (1986). *An empirical investigation of the counselling phases and their characteristics in short-term counselling.* Ottawa, Ontario: St. Paul University. Unpublished M.A. Research Project.

Bluger, T., Doughty, G., Gingrich, F., Hare, W., & Melanson, M. (1984). *A theoretical and empirical investigation of the phases in psychotherapy.* Ottawa, Ontario: St. Paul University. Unpublished M.A. Research Project.

Charlebois, J., Chong, M., McMurdo, C., & Stauber, M. (1985). *The empirical investigation of the phases of the counselling process and their characteristics.* Ottawa, Ontario: St. Paul University. Unpublished M.A. Research Project.

Elliott, R. (1984). A discovery-oriented approach to significant change events in psychotherapy: Interpersonal process recall and comprehensive process analysis. In L.N. Rice & L.S. Greenberg (Eds.), *Patterns of change, intensive analysis of psychotherapy process.* New York: Guilford Press, 249-286.

Elliott, R. (1986). Interpersonal process recall (IPR) as a psychotherapy process research method. In L.S. Greenberg & W.M. Pinsof (Eds.), *The psychotherapeutic process: A research handbook.* New York: The Guilford Press, 503-527.

Greenberg, L.S. (1991). Research on the process of change. *Psychotherapy Research, 1*(1), 3-16.

Meier, A. (1990a). The application of hermeneutics to psychotherapy practice, theory and research. In Adrian Visscher (Ed.*), Pastoral studies in the university setting*, Ottawa, Ontario: Ottawa University Press, 109-135.

Meier, A. (1990b). Future directions in pastoral counselling I. Constructing theoretical models. *Pastoral Sciences, 9*, 131-152.

Meier, A. (1993a). Toward an integrated model of competency: Linking White and Bandura. *Journal of Cognitive Psychotherapy: An International Quarterly, 7*(1), 35-47.

Meier, A. (1993b). *Society for pastoral counselling research*, Ottawa, Ontario: Saint Paul University. Letter written to Graduate Students.

Meier, A. (1994a). *Future directions in pastoral counselling: III. Professional training.* Paper presented at the 10th symposium of the Group for Research in Pastoral Studies, Laval University, Quebec, Canada, June 2-4. (Since published as, Future directions in pastoral counselling: Training professionals to meet the changing needs of the believing community (1995), in G. Routhier (Ed.), La paroisse en eclats. Laval University: Novalis, 219-236)

Meier, A. (1994b). *Professional portrait of the practicing pastoral counsellor.* Paper presented at the founding and first annual conference of the Society for Pastoral Counselling Research held at St. Paul University, Ottawa, Ontario, May 5-7. (Since published as, Professional portrait of the practicing counsellor and directions for the future (1996), *Pastoral Sciences, 15*, 61-86)

Meier, A., & Boivin, M. (1983). Towards a synthetic model of psychotherapy. *Pastoral Sciences, 2*, 137-176.

Meier, A., & Boivin, M. (1987). Self-discovery approach to counselling. *Pastoral Sciences, 6,* 145-168.

Meier, A. & Boivin, M. (1992). *A Seven-phase model of the change process and its research and clinical application.* Paper presented at the 8th annual conference of the Society for the Exploration of Psychotherapy Integration, San Diego, California, April 2-4.

Meier, A., Boivin, M., & Aylward, C. (1986). The pastoral counsellor: Yesterday and today. *Pastoral Sciences, 5*, 19-46.

Meier, A., Boivin, M., & Driscoll, E. (1987). Self-discovery approach to counselling: An interdisciplinary perspective. *Les Cahiers de Recherches en Sciences de la Religion, 8*, 95-135.

Meier, A., & Weber, W. (1992). Future directions in pastoral counselling: II. Qualitative and quantitative research. In Marc Pelchat (Ed.), *Empirical approaches in theology*, Quebec, Canada: University of Laval, 157-182.

Rennie, D.L., Phillips, J.R., & Quartaro, G.K. (1988). Grounded theory: Approach to conceptualization in psychology. *Canadian Psychology, 29*, 139-150.

Smeltzer-Legault, L. (1991). Pastoral care to parents with a disabled child. In Jacques Gagne (Ed.), *The exploration of the future in pastoral studies.* Quebec, Canada: Laval University, 77-85.

Part Two

Healing in Theory

Chapter 2

Distinguishing Pastoral Counselling from Secular Psychotherapy and Spiritual Direction*

William J. Sneck

Distilling twenty-five years of providing therapy, pastoral counselling, and spiritual direction, and of supervising master's and doctoral-level interns in the same three helping relationships, the author attempts a theoretical articulation comparing and contrasting the similarities and differences among these professions. An implicit/explicit relationship with God, the Numinous, one's "Higher Power," (or the absence or such a "Higher Power") experienced by client and/or counsellor constitutes the major distinguishing characteristic among the three. Implications for conceptualizing and practicing each service are offered.

The "turf," the "territory" of pastoral counsellors, secular psychotherapists, and spiritual directors overlaps. All three sets of helping professionals claim to assist in matters of the mind, heart, spirit, soul. Persons seeking help from one or other of these practitioners may have more or less clarity about their wants and needs, and about the ability of those consulted to provide assistance.

---

*Revision of a paper presented at the 5th Annual Conference of the Society for Pastoral Counselling Research, Waterloo Lutheran Seminary, Waterloo, Ontario, May 16, 1998

Similarly, those sought out may have different degrees of training, and provide differing levels of comfort in dealing with the possible array of issues presented by the visitors to their offices.

Consider these situations: A middle-aged man suffering from depression feels that seeing a therapist indicates a character weakness or moral flaw. He has read that many people today are consulting spiritual directors, and so seeks out assistance from a professional whose focus and training are not relevant to the problem. Again, a pastoral counsellor is working for several months with a client concerning career issues. More and more of their time together, however, is taken up by the client's discussion of her prayer-life and what God might be saying about entering religious life. Should the pastoral counsellor consider referring the client to a spiritual director while continuing (or not?) with the client?

The present discussion attempts a theoretical articulation comparing and contrasting the similarities and differences among the three professions of pastoral counselling, secular psychotherapy, and spiritual direction, with the hope that light may be shed for both help-seekers and providers who find themselves in situations like those sketched above.

Diagram 1 attempts to illustrate, in what is hopefully not too schematic and simplistic a fashion, some elementary differences in the activities and assumptions of three seemingly overlapping professions. It is important at the outset to discern how, theoretically at least, these approaches to care of the spirit do and do not resemble each other.

Counselling

Before beginning to present the different fields of endeavor, I remind the reader that even between two of them, therapy and counselling, scholars and writers disagree. Some authors (e.g., Patterson, 1986) hold that there is no real distinction between counselling and therapy since practitioners of both fields deal with the same problems and to the same degree of depth. "Counsellors" simply get paid less than "therapists," and may not have the same sorts of advanced degrees (e.g. M.A., or M.S. instead of

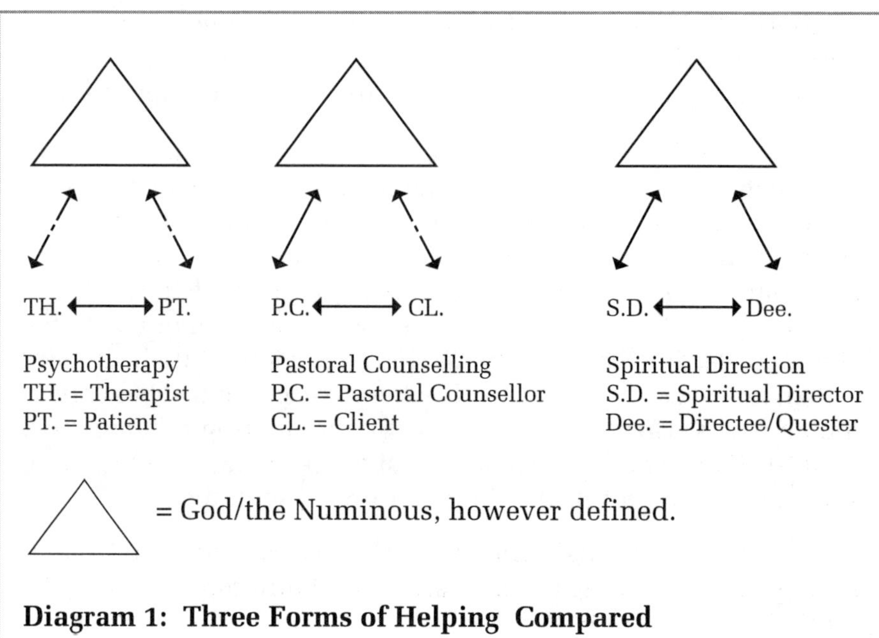

Diagram 1: Three Forms of Helping Compared

M.D. or Ph.D., though the Ph.D. and Ed.D. are given in counselling!). Yet even educated lay folk presume that "counsellors" deal with real but less severe problems, e.g., those having to do with work, relationships, developmental issues, etc., while "therapists" handle more severe situations like "breakdowns" or anything requiring hospitalizations. Our own discussion here will not resolve or even take sides in this debate, but rather will focus on another dimension entirely, namely, the three way relationships involving God, the professional, and the help-seeker.

Psychotherapy

The horizontal arrow in Figure I connecting Therapist and Patient suggests that the work of psychotherapy is done within the dyadic relationship established between them. Perhaps the relationship involves no more than thirty seconds a month as a psychiatrist writes out a prescription while inquiring how things are. Perhaps the relationship consumes an hour a day for five days a week over five years as a patient lies on a couch free-associating while a Freudian analyst sits out of sight. Maybe the relationship requires a patient to report back to the therapist about how many agreed-upon activities in their behavioural contract the patient has completed. The point is that the dyad — and the "patient" may be a group or an organization as well as an individual — focuses the healing/wellness process.

The broken lines connecting God/the Numinous (however defined) suggest that Therapist and Patient may or may not enjoy a conscious relationship or interchange with the deity through prayer, church or denominational membership, spiritual quest. Similarly, the patient may or may not choose to bring spiritual quest issues into therapy depending on their salience to his/her growth and on his/her sense of acceptance of such topics by her therapist. More than likely, the therapist will not allude to the numinous dimension unless invited to do so by the patient.

Pastoral Counselling

Again the horizontal line in the above diagram which connects Pastoral Counsellor and Client implies that, as in Psychotherapy, much of the work is done within their dyadic relationship. Just as within Psychotherapy, a variety of activities may quite legitimately be engaged in by counsellor and client depending on the theoretical orientation of the former and the type of presenting problem of the latter.

Notice, however, the solid line connecting Pastoral Counsellor and the Numinous. This line indicates that the counsellor has a consciously established relationship with the Numinous, and furthermore, that the counsellor will exercise his/her profession — which the counsellor will consider a "ministry" in some form — within the context of that numinous relationship. How that occurs concretely will vary from counsellor to counsellor, but the following may suggest the texture of this mutuality: pastoral counsellors will probably pray for and about their client; they will invoke the "Spirit's" guidance on their sessions and on the lives of both them and their clients; they may pray with the client during sessions, but that will depend on the comfort-level of the client, and on whether or not they agree to such a step; they may couch their interventions (questions, comments, advice, etc.) in Biblical terms or on ethical directives drawn from them or their client's religious tradition, etc.

Notice that as in the Psychotherapy diagram, the line connecting "Client" and "the Numinous" in the Pastoral Counselling schematic is broken. This implies that the client may or may not have religious/spiritual issues to deal with in counselling depending on the presence/absence of a relationship with the numinous in his life, and whether or not such a relationship is involved in the dynamics of his problem. In any case, by calling oneself a pastoral counsellor, the helping professional in effect says to the client, "'God-talk' may, but need not, be spoken here, but expect some kind of religious or spiritual context and overtones in what we say and do here."

Spiritual Direction

In the schematic, solid lines connect all the players: Numinous, Spiritual Director, and Spiritual Directee. The inter-relationship is triadic rather than dyadic, that is, Spiritual Director and Quester consciously relate to the Numinous however they define Him/Her/It, and make such a relationship of the Directee the main focus of their interaction. (Hence the circle around the God-Directee arrow.) Like the Psychotherapist and Pastoral Counsellor, the Director and Directee may talk about home-life, work-life, personal/group problems and challenges, hopes and fears, etc., but the real topic is the Quester's relationship with the Numinous and how that relationship impacts the rest of life. Both during and outside of sessions, the Director and Directee seek the help of the Numinous for the life of the Directee, and from some theoretical basis or other claim an ability to interpret the will of the Numinous in the Directee's life.

This abstract language is quite deliberately employed so as to cover the widest possible range of Director/Directee pairings. A concrete example is an American Indian Shaman who might invoke the gods to bring physical healing and peace of mind to a sufferer from his tribe. A New Age Astral Guide may counsel her disciple that the stars suggest a particularly appropriate wedding date. A Russian Orthodox Starets might guide a young monk in praying the "Jesus-Prayer." A Protestant Spiritual Director of the Ignatian Exercises might reflect together with her Roman Catholic priest-Directee about his prayer-experiences during an eight-day "Retreat." (Lest the last example seem to be outlandish, it is provided from the author's own life.) In all of these cases, Director and Directee share a religious or spiritual tradition involving not merely "theology," that is, a more-or-less systematized explanation of creed, code and cult, but more vitally, a way of interacting with the Numinous that also is governed by a set of principles called a "spirituality."

Their spirituality suggests ways of approaching the Numinous, of discerning its intentions, and of responding to its directives. Again, we may put this more concretely: the Shaman may suggest a nocturnal dance or may interpret a dream; the Astral Guide may consult her charts; the Starets will judge from his own and others' frequent repetition of the "Jesus Prayer" whether or not his devotee has the psychological stamina to enjoy this method; the Ignatian Director will weigh the consolations and desolations of her Directee as he seeks to make a decision about his ministry that will fulfill God's Will.

The examples cited have been ecumenical, and the principles and definitions quite broad (if a bit abstract) so as to include the widest possible audience of potential help-seekers/providers.

Thus to return to the examples with which this discussion began: the depressed gentleman who consults a spiritual director needs to be instructed in the very first session that if he wishes to continue, he will need to concentrate on his prayer-life and relationship with God. Meanwhile, he can be gently asked about how he plans to deal with his depression. Depending on the place of religion or spirituality in the client's life, the spiritual director can refer to a pastoral counsellor or a secular psychotherapist after helping him explore his prejudice against the whole counselling enterprise. Such a goal may not be able to be accomplished in a few sessions, but what is crucial is that a directee not believe he is receiving spiritual direction if he is subtly seeking a substitute form of counselling from a more socially-acceptable caregiver.

The case of the career-counselling argues for both pastoral counselling and spiritual direction in tandem. Presumably, a pastoral counsellor will have had more experience and training in sorting through career issues, and a spiritual director likewise will have had more background in discerning prayer experiences. Ideally, the client could continue working with her pastoral counsellor, begin sharing her prayer-journey with a spiritual director, and give her permission for mutual consultation by both professionals as they seek to assist her in charting her course.

After twenty-five years of offering therapy, pastoral counselling, and spiritual direction, and of supervising master's and doctoral level interns in the same three helping relationships, the author has devised the diagrammed paradigm, and found it useful in sorting out perceptions and expectations of both clients and supervisees. His hope is that readers will also find it easy to understand, work from, and teach.

References

Barry, W. A. & Connolly, W. J. (1982). *The practice of spiritual direction.* San Francisco: Harper & Row.

Estadt, B. K. (1983). Profile of a pastoral counsellor. In B. K. Estadt, M. Blanchette, & J.R. Compton (Eds.), *Pastoral counselling.* Englewood Cliffs, NJ: Prentice-Hall.

Patterson, C.H. (1986). *Theories of counselling and psychotherapy* (4th ed.). New York: Harper Collins.

Chapter 3

The Ontogenesis of Empathy: The Heart of Intimacy*

Beverly Anne Musgrave

As historical studies of empathy (Gladstein, 1984; Gladstein & Associates, 1987; Hickson, 1985; Marks & Tolsma, 1986; Reed, 1984; Bohart & Greenberg, 1997) have clearly demonstrated, the various theoretical perspectives — namely, the aesthetic, the sociological and the social-psychological, the developmental and the counselling and psychotherapeutic — have defined and measured empathy using different parameters, resulting in confusion, inconsistency and ambivalence. It logically follows that there will be a lack of consistency in terminology (Musgrave, 1989). Gladstein (1987) identified eighteen different types of empathy. The one word "empathy" has within it two separate aspects of one psychological experience: the affective and the cognitive.

In this chapter I explore some of the historical perspectives of empathy and focus on how this mercurial variable is at the heart of intimacy. First, I offer a definition of empathy and give a brief overview of its roots. Second, I focus on the multidimensional approach to the subject. Third, I briefly examine the relationship between empathy and intimacy.

---

*Revision of a paper presented at the 6th Annual Conference of the Society for Pastoral Counselling Research, Saint Paul University, Ottawa, Ontario, May 15, 1999

Empathy Defined

For the purpose of this paper I define empathy as the ability to tolerate the tension of being truly open to the experience of another person, while simultaneously attempting both to understand the subjective world of the other and to remain a differentiated self.

This definition evolved out of several years of empathy research and reflects three aspects that are central to an in-depth appreciation of the subject. First, empathy is defined from a multidimensional perspective that includes both the affective and the cognitive. Second, it reflects the challenge that is integral to being empathic, namely, the ability to tolerate anxiety. Third, it distinguishes empathy from fusion and sympathy, and includes the ability to remain a differentiated person. With this definition I plan to explore some of the historical perspectives on empathy out of which this definition evolved, and will look briefly at the interface of empathy and intimacy.

Affective Empathy: A Historical Perspective

Affective empathy has its roots within the aesthetic, the social-psychological and the counselling and psychotherapy literature. The concept of sympathy and empathy are deeply intertwined in this literature, resulting in a confusion that still exists today (Gladstein, 1984).

Sympathy can be traced to eighteenth-century moral philosophy (Smith, 1976). Sympathy was conceptualized by Smith (1976), Spencer (1870), and McDougall (1908) as having a largely, though not entirely, passive character. The emphasis was on the ways an observer comes to feel what another feels or is moved by another's experience.

Empathy, in contrast, comes from the German term *Einfuehlung,* initially used in aesthetic literature (Lipps, 1923). In contrast to sympathy, empathy was conceptualized as a more active way in which an observer comes to feel what another feels or is deeply moved by another's experience. This understanding of empathy is largely an epistemology, a way of knowing in which artists and poets gained access to their subject. In this sense it referred to the tendency of the observers to project themselves "into" that which they observed, typically some physical object of beauty. This experience occurs, for example, when we stand silent before a great painting and find ourselves drawn into the imagery and are moved beyond ourselves into sacred space and time. Such an experience is reflected in the literature on contemplative prayer and mysticism.

Lipps (1923) first delineated the empathic process as involving projection in terms of inanimate objects. Later, he saw it as strictly a mental activity that was affective and usually very brief, spontaneous, unconscious and occurring between one person and another person or an object. Although Lipps was not the first person to use the term *Einfuehlung*, his detailed and extensive writings (1923, 1926) led others (Listowel, 1933; Racer, 1935) to identify him as the creator of the concept. The term empathy was first used by Titchener (1909) as a translation of Lipps' *Einfuehlung.* Several central ideas that evolved from the aesthetic empathy theory reappeared in empathy literature much later, namely, self-actualization, projection, motor-mimicry, and emotional mimicry (Borke, 1971; Hoffman, 1977; Rogers, 1951; Stotland, 1969). It was the work of Lipps (1923) and Scheler (1970) that initiated our confusion between the terms "empathy" and "sympathy" (Gladstein, 1984).

In contrast to the aesthetic writers, sociological and social psychological thinkers wrote only tangentially about the empathic process (H. Allport, 1908; G. Allport, 1937; Baldwin, 1897; Cooley, 1902, 1930; Cottrell, 1942; Heider, 1958; McDougall, 1908; Mead, 1934; Wandt, 1897). The social psychological theorists are responsible for creating two branches of empathy research: role taking and emotional reaction. The role taking theoretical stream led immediately into empirical research. However, the emotional reaction theoretical stream remained dormant until mid 1960 (Gladstein, 1984).

From the psychotherapy and counselling literature, the works of Freud (1921, 1923), Reik (1948), Rogers (1951), Stewart (1956), and Sullivan (1947) are significant in our tracing the development of the concept of affective empathy. Freud (1921) wrote very little concerning identification and empathy, but his statements have impacted most of the empathy literature. His concept of identification process is reflected in the works of Kohut, Reik, Stewart and Sullivan. Kohut (1977, 1978, 1984a, 1984b) viewed empathy as crucial not only to psychoanalysis but also to human relations in general. Kohut's focus on empathy as central to human experience seems to sum up its importance and clinical relevance and hints at its significance for intimacy.

Of the psychotherapeutically-oriented writers, Rogers is significant because he describes the counsellor's role with such phrases as "empathic attitude" and "empathic understanding" (Rogers, 1957, pp. 91-103). He believed that empathy consists of behaviour that is active, deliberate, and conscious. Freud and Rogers relied almost exclusively on their clinical experience in organizing their ideas on empathy. Freud's identification theory evolved independently from the views of Cooley, Lipps, McDougall, Scheller, and Worringer, all of whom were contemporaries. In the same way, Rogers' "empathic understanding communication construct" did not benefit from these writers nor from Cottrell and Mead (Gladstein, 1984).

It is precisely this lack of integration that led to the confusion regarding the theoretical bases of empathy, and this in turn facilitated the fragmented process of inquiry and research that is prevalent in our present-day literature. However, the richness of the historical perspective of affective empathy is central to our understanding.

Although affective empathy research has a long history dating back at least two centuries, as noted in the writings of Hume (1751/1957) and Smith (1759/1976), there is , however, a paucity of empirical research on affective empathy specifically. The considerable confusion regarding both definitions and measures is particularly pertinent to affective empathy research. At first glance, it appears that some empirical work may have focused on affective empathy. On closer inspection, however, one finds a cognitive theoretical structure, with or without cognitive measures, to be part of that research. The fact that this has not been clearly stated has added more confusion to the empirical empathy literature.

Cognitive Empathy: An Historical Perspective

The concept of cognitive empathy evolved out of the sociological, social-psychological, and the developmental psychological literature. The theoretical writings of Baldwin (1897), Cooley (1902), and Mead (1934,1970) support the position that a unique aspect of social cognition and judgment that differentiates human from subhuman functioning is "role-taking," or the ability to take the perspective of another.

Cooley (1902) said that it is through observation and imitation that the child learns the meaning of "my," "mine," and "me," thus learning to differentiate self from others. He was the first sociologist to focus on empathy as an age-related process that evolves from infancy through adulthood. Mead was a friend of Cooley's, and their mutual influence on each other is obvious in their writings. Cooley's influence is notable in Mead's reflections on the age-related sympathy process. With his definition of "sympathy" in explicit role-taking terms, Mead influenced Cooley's thinking. Although Mead never used the term "empathy", we can see in his work (1926, 1970, 1972) the origins of role-taking theories that emerged later in the empirical literature. Defining empathy as the capacity to take the role of another person with whom one interacts or "putting yourself in her place," Mead stated that relevant internal and interpersonal images would be acquired with the accumulation and organization of experiences. Mead noted that role-playing activity provides the means for developing these interpersonal images and that subsequently it facilitates the ability to understand another's behaviour in certain situations. As Deutsch and Madle (1975) pointed out, it was in Mead's (1934) work on "role-playing" that such factors as intelligence were studied in order to determine what might enhance the acquisition of empathy. Mead's findings supported other investigators (e.g., Gates, 1923; Walton, 1936) who found a positive relationship between intelligence and age with an ability to identify correctly the intended emotional expressions depicted in a series of pictures.

Like Mead, Piaget never used the term "empathy." However, his theory of egocentrism, which postulates that one emerges in successive stages from embeddedness in one's own point of view in order to take the point of view of another, is central to the concept of cognitive empathy. Piaget (1955) focused on the importance of socialization in the process of developing reciprocal relationships. Socialization includes the ability to see things from another person's point of view and not only from one's own point of view. However, social adaptation, or the movement from egocentrism, is not a single process. It entails, as noted previously, several successive stages of emergence from embeddedness in one's own perspective. These stages of emergence can be characterized generally as a movement of differentiation toward "recentration," which is a recovery of a new centre or a new way of adapting to the world (Kegan, 1982). The differentiation itself consists of an emergence from embeddedness in one's own point of view (Schachtel, 1959) or a "decentration," which is the emergence from embeddedness in, or the loss of, an old centre (Piaget, 1955). This concept of differentiation is central to one's ability to be empathic, either cognitively or affectively empathic.

The early empirical research in cognitive empathy has typically focused on children; relatively few studies have been conducted with adults. The literature and research on cognitive empathy have been closely tied to broader interests in the development of social perception or social cognition (Feshback, 1973), perspective-taking (Flavell, Botkin, Fry, Wright & Jarvis, 1968), moral development and role taking (Piaget, 1950; Kohlberg, 1969), the relationship between perspective taking and pro-social behaviour (Underwood & Moore 1982), and altruism and empathy (Coke, Batson, & Davis 1978). Selman's (1980) model of perspective taking follows the Piagetian tradition. Empathy scales developed by Kerr & Speroff (1954), Hogan (1969), and the work of Hoffman (1977) and Iannotti (1975) gave the research in cognitive empathy interesting perspectives from which new understandings could develop.

The present writer holds a position similar to that of Goldstein and Michaels (1985), namely, that both non-egocentrism as Piaget used the term, and role taking or perspective taking as Shantz,

Wellmen & Siber (1983) called it, are very important cognitive processes that influence quantitatively and qualitatively how a person will comprehend another's emotional experience. However, just as non-egocentrism does not by itself determine role taking ability, so non-egocentrism and role taking are not the only cognitive processes that influence empathy. Rather, they are highly significant factors in the ability to be cognitively empathic.

The Multidimensional View of Empathy

I have pointed out that both affective and cognitive empathy have been researched and theorized by several disciplines: sociological, social psychological, developmental psychology, counselling and psychotherapy. It was also noted that the various disciplines defined and operationalized empathy differently, often without referring to one another. Over the years, two distinct ways of researching empathy have developed: (1) Defining and measuring either affective or cognitive empathy in isolation from one another, and (2) Defining and measuring empathy as a unitary construct.

Recently we have witnessed an increase in affective empathy research and, concomitantly, an increased movement toward and integration of the affective and cognitive components of empathy. There is a growing consensus that these two research traditions comprise an interdependent system in which each influences the other but neither one can ever be fully understood as long as research efforts concentrate on one aspect to the relative exclusion of the other (Berger, 1980, 1987; Deutsch & Madle, 1975; Feshbach, 1978; Gladstein & associates, 1987; Hickson, 1985; Hoffman, 1977; Marks & Tolsma, 1986). Some fairly recent evidence demonstrates the predictive superiority of taking into account both the affective and the cognitive aspects of the empathic process (Coke & Bateson, 1978; Davis, 1982, 1983c; Hoffman, 1975, 1977; Feshbach, 1975,1978; Iannotti, 1979; Eisenbers, Shea et al., 1991). This multidimensional approach clearly defines the different types of reactions that can be called empathic, thus enabling us to explore the systematic similarities and differences between the types and their implications for behaviour.

Two important multidimensional models of children's empathy are those of Hoffman (1975, 1982) and Feshbach (1975, 1978, 1980, 1982). It is important to note that, although cognitive role taking is seen as important in Hoffman's model, it operates in the service of the affective empathy response to the other person rather than for the purpose of furthering cognitive understanding of the other person's experience. He has described a form of cognitive role taking that works together with a form of affective relational response which, taken as one, becomes an interdependent or single phenomenon of empathy. Thus, he may be regarded as laying the groundwork for a multidimensional perspective of empathy.

Feshbach (1975, 1978, 1980, 1982) has developed another major model of empathy. His is a "three-factor" model which contains two distinct cognitive components and an affective component. It should be noted that, although they are (distinctly) multidimensional, the models of Hoffman and Feshbach both conceptualize empathy as being primarily affective rather than cognitive.

Keefe (1976), on the other hand, presented a third model in which cognitive understanding is central to the empathic experience. In Keefe's model, cognitive involvement goes beyond the affective identification and role-playing and includes more complex judgments directed inward toward the observer's own affective process. Furthermore, the Keefe model presents empathic behaviour as a sequential process, moving from stimulus perception to affective reverberation, to cognitive mediation, and finally, to communication. The models of Hoffman and Feshbach do not specify such a sequential process for each individual component of empathy. Neither do they include empathic communication as an inherent part of the empathic process.

Scheler (1970) and Rogers (1951, 1957, 1961) both made reference in their work to the complexity of empathy which includes both the affective and cognitive component. It is important to note the two best-known scales that came out of this position, namely, the Truax Accuracy Empathy Scale (Truax & Carkhuff, 1967) and Carkhuff's Empathic Understanding Interpersonal Process Scale (1969), derived from the earlier Truax scales, measure the counsellor's cognitive and affective empathic verbal response to clients. The Barrett-Lennard Relational Inventory (1978) also followed from Rogerian theory. These scales are alike in the fact that they have a fulfillment/phenomenological frame of reference. They differ with respect to the inclusion or the exclusion of the client's subjective experience as a component in defining the empathic experience.

Several writers (Davis, 1980, 1983a; Gladstein, 1983, 1984; Gladstein & Associates, 1987; Golstein & Michaels, 1985; Hoffman, 1975, 1982; Iannotti, 1975, 1979) have pointed out the necessity and the importance of researching empathy as a multidimensional construct. However, since empathy has generally been defined and researched exclusively as either an affective or a cognitive construct, and since few researchers have focused on the multidimensional importance of empathy in adults, it is not surprising to note that there is limited research on empathy from that point of view.

It was not until 1980 that an individual difference measure of empathy, one that provided separate assessment of cognitive perspective-taking ability as well as emotional reactivity, was developed. The Interpersonal Reactivity Index (IRI) of Davis (1980,1983b, 1983c) is a multidimensional perspective empathy scale. The instrument takes as its starting point the notion that empathy consists of a set of separate but related constructs and seeks to provide measures of dispositional tendencies in several areas. The instrument contains four, seven-item subscales, each tapping a separate facet of empathy. Davis (1983c, 1996) reported evidence for the validity of the four subscales and their relationship with indices of emotionality, social style, self-esteem and sensitivity to others. Franzoi, Davis & Young (1985) conducted research on the effects of private self-consciousness and perspective-taking (cognitive empathy) using the IRI measure. Davis, Hall, Young & Warren (1980) investigated the multidimensional view of empathy through an examination of affective reaction to an arousing stimulus.

As noted throughout this review, there is confusion concerning the nature of empathy. This confusion can be traced directly to diverse literature — aesthetic, sociological, social-psychological, developmental, counselling , and psychotherapeutic — on the subject. Many writers do not make sufficient reference to the other empathy scholars nor do they specify adequately the theory of empathy from which their own orientation evolves.

Given this history of empathy literature, it is understandable that the integrative research on cognitive-affective dimensions of empathy may be sparse. This, however, forms a compelling rationale for conceptualizing a multidimensional perspective of empathy. This more inclusive perspective of empathy is central to the understanding and the practice of intimacy.

Empathy at the Heart of Intimacy

If empathy is multidimensional, affective and cognitive, requiring one to be a differentiated "self-in-relation," then empathy is not merely a way of relating, but a fundamental way of knowing oneself and the other, developing a sense of "I am I" and "you are you" and "I am in relation to you." Relationship, according to Surrey (1985), "is the experience of emotional and cognitive intersubjectivity: the ongoing intrinsic inner awareness and responsiveness to the continuous existence of the other or others, and the expectation of mutuality in this regard" (p. 4). This relationship between two differentiated entities describes a relational view of empathy and points to intimacy as the heart of empathy. The working definition for this paper is as follows:

> Intimacy is the process of extending oneself actively in trust to listen to and to respond to another, the process of allowing one's inner spirit to be touched by the inner spirit of another; it is simultaneously the process of entering into relationship transcending itself and becoming a "self-in-relation," open to both the affective and the cognitive world of the other, and, at the same time, remaining a differentiated self.

The ability to be a differentiated "self-in-relation" (not fused), to be touched by the spirit of the other, and the ability to tolerate the tension of being open to another's experience — taking another's perspective when different from one's own, actively working at appreciating the depth and the uniqueness of the richness of the other, while remaining differentiated — is a specific way of being empathic and possibly going "beyond empathy" into intimacy (Mahrer, 1996; Mahrer, Boulet & Fairweather, 1994). Intimacy, like empathy, has intrinsic healing capacities, where growth can occur. Intrinsic to development within relationships is Surrey's (1985) concept of "relationship authenticity." She describes it as "the challenge of relationship which provides the energy for growth — the need to be seen and recognized for who one is and the need to see and understand the other with ongoing authenticity." Empathy, according to Jordan (1997), diminishes one's sense of isolation, and enhances the experience of interpersonal effectiveness; being responded to increases one's sense of connectedness and relational competence. Jordan was referring to the role of empathy as central to the process of relational psychotherapy.

I propose that it is true for all in-depth relational intimate communications. The relational dance of empathy and intimacy is one of cooperation, trust, and honest communication, as each person opens his/her inner spirit to be significantly touched by the other, becoming a new "self-in-relation" available to both the affective and cognitive world of the other, while remaining a differentiated self, an empathic self. Empathy is at the heart of intimacy.

References

Allport, F. H. (1908). *An Introduction to social psychology.* Boston : Luce Publishers.

Allport, F.H. (1937). *Personality : A psychological interpretation.* New York : Holt Publishers.

Baldwin, J.M. (1897). *Social and ethical interpretation in mental development.* New York: Macmillan.

Barrett-Lennard, G. T. (1978). The relationship inventory: Later developments and adaptations. *JSAC Catalogue of Selected Documents in Psychology, 8*, 68.

Berger, D. M. (1987). *Clinical empathy.* Northvale, NJ: Jason Aronson, Inc.

Borke, H. (1971). Interpersonal perception of young children: Egocentrism, or empathy? *Developmental Psychology, 5,* 263-269.

Carkhuff, R.R. (1969 *). Helping and human relations, (Volumes I & II).* Vol. 1: Selection and Training; Vol. II : Practice and research. New York: Holt, Rinehart and Winston, Inc.

Coke, J. S., Batson, C. D., & McDavis, K. (1978). Empathic mediation of helping: A two-stage model. *Journal of Personality and Social Psychology, 36*(7), 752-766.

Cooley, C. H. (1902). *Human nature and the social order.* New York: Charles Scribner's Sons.

Cooley, C. H. (1930). *Social theory and social research.* New York: Henry Holt.

Cottrell, L. (1942). The analysis of situational fields in social psychology. *American Sociological Review, 7,* 374.

Davis , M.H. (1983a.) . The effects of dispositional empathy on emotional reactions and helping : A multidimensional approach. *Journal of Personality and Social Psychology, 51* (2).

Davis M. H. (1983b). Empathic concern and the Muscular Dystrophy Telethon: Empathy as a multidimensional construct. *Personality and Social Psychology Bulletin, 9*(2), 223-229.

Davis M. H. (1983c). Measuring individual differences in empathy: Evidence for a multidimensional approach. *Journal of Personality and Social Psychology, 44*(l), 113-126.

Davis M.H. (1996). *Empathy : A social psychological approach.* Colorado: Westview Press, Inc.

Davis, M. H. (1980). A multidimensional approach to individual differences in empathy. Abstracted in the *JSAS Catalog of Selected Documents in Psychology, 4,* 85.

Davis, M.H., Hall, J. G. , Young, R.D. & Warren, G.G. (1980). Emotional reactions to dramatic film stimuli: The influence of cognitive and emotional empathy. *Journal of Personality and Social Psychology, 52*(1), 126-133.

Deutsch, F., & Madle, R. (1975). Empathy: Historic and current conceptualizations, measurement, and a cognitive theoretical perspective. *Human Development, 18,* 267-287.

Eisenberg, N., Shea, C.L. , Carlo, G., & Knight, G.P. (1991). Empathy-related responding and cognition: "Chicken and the egg" dilemma. In W. Kurtines & J. Gewirtz (Eds.), *Handbook of moral behavior and development. Vol. 2. : Research,* Hillside N.J. : Lawrence Erlbaum Associates, 66-88.

Eisenberg-Berg, N., & Mussen, P. (1978). Empathy and moral development in adolescence. *Developmental Psychology, 14,* 185-186.

Feshbach, N. D. (1973). *The relationship of child-rearing factors on children's aggression, empathy and related positive and negative social behaviors.* Paper presented as part of NATO conference on Determinants and Origins of Aggressive Behavior: Monaco.

Feshbach, N. D. (1975). Empathy in children: Some theoretical and empirical considerations. *Counseling Psychologist, 5,* 25-30.

Feshbach, N. D. (1978). Studies of empathic behavior in children. In B. Maher (Ed.), *Progress in experimental personality research.* New York: Academic Press.

Feshbach, N. D. (1980). *The psychology of empathy and the empathy of psychology.* Presidential Address presented at the Meeting of the Western Psychological Association: Honolulu.

Feshbach, N. D. (1982). Empathy, empathy training and the regulation of aggression in elementary school children. In R. M. Kaplan, V. J. Konecni, & R. Novoco (Eds.), *Aggression in childhood and youth.* Alphen den Rigin, the Netherlands: Wijhoff/Noordhoff International Publisher.

Flavell, J. H., Botkin, P.J., Fry, C.L., Wright, J.W., & Jarvis, P.E. (1968). *The development of role-taking and communication skills in children.* New York: Wiley.

Franzoi, S. , Davis, M.H. & Young, R.D. (1985). The effects of private self-consciousness and perspective taking on satisfaction in close relationships. *Journal of Personality and Social Psychology, 48*(6), 133-154.

Freud, S. (1921). *Group psychology and the analysis of the ego.* London: Hogarth Press. 69-143.

Freud, S. (1923). *New introductory lectures on psychoanalysis.* In J. Strachey (Ed. & Trans.), New York: W. W. Norton.

Freud, S. (1933). In J. Strachey (Ed & Trans.), *New introductory lectures on psychoanalysis.* New York: W.W. Norton. (First published in 1923).

Gates, G. S. (1923). An experimental study of the growth of perception. *Journal of Education Psychology, 14,* 449-461.

Gladstein G.A. (1983). Understanding empathy: integrating counseling, developmental and social psychological perspectives. *Journal of Counseling Psychology, 4,* 467-482.

Gladstein, G. A. & Associates (1987). *Empathy and counseling: Exploration in theory and research.* New York: Springer-Verlag.

Gladstein, G. A. (January, 1984). The historical roots of contemporary empathy research. *Journal of the History of the Behavioral Sciences, 20,* 38-59.

Goldstein, A. P. & Michaels, G. Y. (1985). Empathy: Development, training and consequences. Hillside, NJ: Lawrence Erlbaum Associates.

Heider, F. (1958). *The psychology of interpersonal relations.* New York: Wiley.

Hickson, J. (1985). Psychological research on empathy: In search of an elusive phenomenon. *Psychological Reports, 57*, 91-94.

Hoffman, M. L. (1975). Sex differences in moral internalization. *Journal of Personality & Social Psychology, 32,* 720-729.

Hoffman, M. L. (1977). Empathy, its development and prosocial implications. In C. B. Keasey (Ed.), *Nebraska symposium on motivation* (Vol. 25). Lincoln, NE: University of Nebraska Press.

Hoffman, M.L. (1982). Toward a theory of empathic arousal and development. In M.Lewis & L.A. Rosenblum Eds., *The development of affect.* (pp. 227-256). New York : Plenum Press.

Hogan, R. (1969). Development of an empathy scale. *Journal of Counseling and Clinical Psychology, 33,* 307-316.

Hume, D. (1957/1751). *An inquiry concerning the principles of morals.* New York: Liberal Arts Press.

Iannotti, R. J. (1975). The nature and measurement of empathy in children. *The Counseling Psychologist, 5*(2), 21-24.

Iannotti, R.J. (1979). The Elements of Empathy. Paper presented at the Biennial meeting of the Society for Research in Child Development, San Francisco.

Jordan, V. J. (1997). Through Mutual Empathy. In A. C. Bohart & L. Greenberg (Eds.) *Empathy reconsidered: New directions in psychotherapy.* Washington DC: American Psychological Press. 343-348.

Keefe, T. (1976). Empathy: The critical skill. *Social Work, 21*, 10-14.

Kegan, R. (1982). *The evolving self: Problems and process in human development.* Cambridge, MA: Harvard University Press.

Kerr, W. A., & Speroff, B. G. (1954). Validation and evaluation of the empathy test. *Journal of General Psychology, 50,* 369-376.

Kohlberg, L. (1969). Stages and sequence: The cognitive-developmental approach to socialization. In D. A. Goslin (Ed.), *Handbook of socialization theory and research.* Chicago: Rand McNally Co.

Kohut, H. (1977). *The restoration of the self.* New York: International Universities Press.

Kohut, H. (1978). *The search for the self* (Vols. 1 and 2). New York: International Universities Press.

Kohut, H. (1984). *How does analysis cure?* Chicago: The University of Chicago Press.

Kohut, H. (1984). In retrospection, empathy and the semicircle of mental health. In L. Lichtenberg, M. Bornstein & D. Silver (Eds.), *Empathy I.* Hillsdale, NJ: The Analytic Press.

Lipps, T. (1923). Empathy, inner imitation of sense feelings. In Rader, *Esthetics.* New York: Holt. This paper was published in German in 1903; English translation by Rader and Max Schertel.

Lipps, T. (1926). H. C. Sanborn (Trans), *Psychological studies.* Baltimore: The Williams and Wilkins Co.

Listowel, W. A. (1933). *A critical history of modern aesthetics.* London: George Allen & Unwin.

Mahrer, A.R. (1996). *The complete guide to experimental psychotherapy.* New York : Wiley Publishers.

Mahrer, A.R. , Boulet, A.B., & Fairweather, D.R. (1994). Beyond empathy: Advances in the clinical theory and methods of empathy. *Clinical Psychological Review, 14,* 183-198.

Marks, S. E., & Tolsma, R. J. (1986). Empathy research: Some methodological considerations. *Psychotherapy, 23*(1), 4-20.

McDougall, W. (1908). *An introduction to social psychology.* Boston: Luce.

Mead, G. H. (1934). *Mind, self and society.* Chicago: University of Chicago Press.

Mead G. H. (1970). Social consciousness and the consciousness of meaning. In H.S. Thayer (Ed). , *Pragmatism: The classic writing.* New York : American Library.

Musgrave, B. (1989). *Individual differences in empathy: Social and emotional antecedents in the family of origin.* Doctoral Dissertation.

Piaget, J. (1932). *The moral judgment of the child.* New York: Harcourt, Brace, & World.

Piaget, J. (1950). *The psychology of intelligence.* New York : Harcourt & Brace.

Piaget, J. (1955). In M. Gabian (Trans.), *The language and thought of the child.* Cleveland: Meridian Books. (Originally published in 1923).

Piaget, J. (1955/1923). In M. Gabian (Trans). *The Language and thought of the child.* Cleveland : Meridian Books.

Piaget, J. (1969). *Judgment and reasoning in the child.* Totowa, NJ: Littlefield, Adams & Co.

Rader, M. M. (1935). *A modern book of aesthetics: An anthology.* New York: Holt.

Reed, G. (1984). The antithetical meaning of the term "empathy" in psychoanalytic discourse. In I. Joseph Lichtenberg, M. Bornstein & D. Silver, (Eds.), *Empathy,* New Jersey : Lawrence Erlbaum associates, Publishers .

Reik, T. (1948). *Listening with the third ear.* New York: Grove Press.

Rogers, C. R. (1951). *Client-centered therapy.* Boston: Houghton Mifflin.

Rogers, C.R. (1957). The necessary and sufficient conditions of therapeutic personality change. *Journal of Counseling Psychology, 21*, 91-103.

Schachtel, E. G. (1959). *Metamorphosis: On the development of affect, perception, attention, and memory.* New York: Da Capo Press.

Scheler, M. (1970). *The nature of sympathy.* Hamden, CT: Shoestring Press. (Original German version published in 1913).

Selman, R. L. (1980). *The growth of interpersonal understanding: Developmental and clinical analyses.* New York: Academic Press.

Shantz, M., Wellman, H. M., & Silber, S. (1983). The acquisition of mental verbs: A systematic investigation of the first reference to mental state. *Cognition, 14*, 301-321.

Smith, A. (1976). *The theory of moral sentiment.* Indianapolis, IN: Liberty Classics. (Originally published in 1759).

Spencer, H. (1870). *The principles of psychology.* London: William & Norgate.

Stewart, D. (1956). *Preface to empathy.* New York: Philosophical Library.

Stotland, E. (1969). Exploratory studies in empathy. In L. Berkowitz (Ed.), *Advances in experimental social psychology* (Vol. 4). New York: Academic Press.

Sullivan, H. S. (1947). *Conception of modern psychiatry.* Washington, DC: White Foundation.

Surrey, J. (1985). The "Self-in-Relation": A Theory of Women's Development. The Stone Center, Wellesley College. *Work in Progress 13.*, 1-6.

Titchener, E. (1909). *Elementary psychology of the thought process.* New York : MacMillian.

Traux, C., & Carkhuff, R. (1967). *Toward effective counseling and psychotherapy.* Chicago: Aldine Press.

Underwood, B., & Moore, B. (1982). Perspective-taking and altruism. *Psychological Bulletin, 91*, 143-173.

Walton, W. E. (1936). Empathic responses in children. *Psychological Monographs*, 48(213), 40-67.

Worringer, W. (1967). *Abstraction and Empathy: A contribution to the psychology of style.* New York: International Universities Press.

Wundt W. (1897). *Ethics: An Investigation of the Laws of the moral life (Vol. I*). New York: MacMillan.

Chapter 4

The Development of Empathy: Adulthood, Morality and Religion*

John Shea

In this chapter I want to look at empathy in relation to human development, especially as empathy functions in adulthood. First, I will look at some understandings of empathy in the literature and then come to a working definition of empathy. Second, I will make a clear connection between empathy and the functioning of an adult self, and offer two ways of looking at how empathy develops. Finally, I will briefly sketch the relation of empathy to adult morality and to adult religion.

Toward a Working Definition of Empathy

There are almost as many definitions of empathy as there are persons trying to define this human phenomenon. Let me mention some of these definitions as we work towards a definition of empathy that will relate this phenomenon to adulthood, to morality and to religion.

Empathy according to Greenson (1967), means "to share, to experience the feelings of another human being" (p. 368). Kohut

*Revision of a paper presented at the 6th Annual Conference of the Society for Pastoral Counselling Research, Saint Paul University, Ottawa, Ontario, May 15, 1999

(1984) sees empathy as "the capacity to think and feel oneself into the inner life of another person" (p. 82). Rogers (1959), in what has become a classical definition, says: "The state of empathy, or being empathic, is to perceive the internal frame of reference of another with accuracy and with the emotional components and meanings which pertain thereto as if one were the other person but without ever losing the 'as if' condition" (p. 210). Feshback (1997) states that "empathy can be conceived of as an interaction between any two individuals with one experiencing and sharing the feeling of the other" (p. 34). Staub (1987) says "a general (and therefore inaccurate) definition of empathy might be apprehending another's inner world and joining the other in his or her feelings" (p. 104). Zahn-Waxler and Radke-Yarrow (1990) point out that "empathy refers to the experiencing of another's affective or psychological state and has both affective and cognitive components" (p. 108). Miller and Stiver (1997) see empathy as "the capacity to feel and think something similar to the feelings and thoughts of another person that exists in all people" (p. 27).

From these different definitions we can say, for our working definition, that empathy is one person feeling — with an attitude of care and concern — what the other person feels as if one were the other person; it involves sensing the emotions, the attitudes, the way of seeing things, the way of relating, and the meanings the other person senses.

Three aspects of this definition can be highlighted. First, feeling is not just emotion, but it is a felt sensing, a felt knowing. It is as Rogers (1959) says, "an emotionally tinged experience together with its personal meaning." (p. 198). In other words, the feeling of the person that empathy is trying to grasp has both emotion and cognition within it. Second, the attitude of care and concern is essential to empathy. Farley (1996) notes that "empathy not only feels with another but would cease the other's suffering and promote the other's well-being" (p. 296). Third, empathy is a paradox; one has to feel what the other feels as if one were the other person, and at the same time one has to remain separate from the other person as well.

The Relation of Empathy to the Adult Self

A few years ago, in an effort to understand adult religion, I worked out a definition along with six characteristics of what I call an "adult self." Let me outline briefly what this adult self looks like. Then I will make the case that empathy is intrinsically and essentially related to human adulthood.

The Adult Self

The adult self is best defined as an identity in a mutuality of relating. This self is "a single whole system" (Souvaine, Lahey & Kegan, 1990, p. 234), a cohesive gestalt in which all the parts function for the good of the whole. As Meissner (1984) explains, it is a self with "a consistent and coherent sense of personal identity" (p. 18). Jung (1981) calls this adult self a "psychic whole that is capable of resistance and abounding in energy" (p. 169). Geertz's (1975) understanding of the person in the West as "a dynamic center of awareness, emotion, judgment, and action organized into a distinctive whole" (p. 49) is a good description of the adult self. The adult self may not be a perfect whole, but it is clearly a functioning whole.

At the same time, the adult self is necessarily a self-in-relatedness. "The human person," as McDargh (1986) insists, "is born with a primary and irreducible need for the confirmation and affirmation of relationship" (p. 255). In adulthood, it seems, identity can be realized only in relationship with others whose identity and freedom are also recognized and respected. The adult self lives only in some kind of real relating of one adult self to another. As Jones (1991) remarks: "the dynamics of selfhood are the dynamics of interconnection" (p. 64). The adult self cannot exist without relationships of solicitude, love, and mutual understanding.

There are six characteristics that give a fuller description of the adult self: (1) the adult self is a body-self, (2) the adult self is rooted and disclosed in feeling, (3) the adult self is a felt sense of depth, (4) the adult self has its own clear boundaries, (5) the adult self exists in intimacy, and (6) the adult self is its own responsible process of experiencing.

The adult self as a body-self

The primary characteristic of the adult self is that it is a body-self. The adult self is embodied; it is "a self that finds its anchor in its own body" (Ricoeur, 1992 , p. 319). This means that the body is owned by the self and the self is at home in the body. Self and body are united. To experience the self is to experience the body, and to experience the body with its memories and its struggles and its desires and its limits is to experience the self. Although our culture has long harboured a "suspicion of embodiment" (Leder, 1990, p. 128), the truth is that it is only in and through the body-self that we can fully be ourselves and fully engage reality.

The adult self is rooted and disclosed in feeling

"Individuality," as James (1985) insists, "is founded in feeling" (p. 128). Nelson (1983) shows the relatedness of feeling when he defines it as "the wholeness of the human response to reality" (p. 10). Marcel (1952) makes the connection between feeling and the body clear with his understanding that it is "the act of feeling which is at the root of the affirmation I am my body and is its necessary foundation" (p. 259-260). Heron (1992) observes that "feeling is deeply and deliciously paradoxical. It unites us with what is other while telling us that it is other and that we are other to it. It celebrates unity in diversity, identification with what is different without loss of personal distinctness" (p. 93).

The adult self is a felt sense of depth

Living in the fullness of the body, there is a "pervasive inner sense of self," a felt sense of inwardness within the self (Elhard, 1968, p. 137). "We are," says Taylor (1989), "creatures with inner depths, with partly unexplored and dark interiors" (p. 111). Blasi (1988) speaks of "deep, preconscious, feelings of rootedness and well-being, self-esteem, and purposefulness" (p. 227). Meissner (1984) speaks of "an inner feeling of worth, trustworthiness, autonomy, and capability" (p. 229). In the religious tradition this depth is often understood as "interiority" or the inner dimension of the person. Some see this depth as the place of "soul" because the essence of the human is there (Moore, 1992). Some call this depth the "heart" because it is a living centre of striving and courage (Hillman, 1992). Some understand this depth as the locus of the "spirit" because aliveness, purpose, and resolve are celebrated there (Scheler, 1962).

The adult self has its own clear boundaries

"There is," says Jung (1981), "no personality without definiteness, wholeness, and ripeness" (p. 171). With "firm self-delineation" (Erikson, 1980, p. 134) this self now has its own dimension and place, especially with others. It has become a coherent self and it knows who it is and who it is not. It knows where its own body-self ends, so to speak, and where the other body-self begins. The adult self is able to see the other as "a Thou in his or her own right"(Jacobi, 1984, p. 64). This sense of having clear boundaries comes from the awareness of feeling and depth, from the sense of being fully in the body.

The adult self exists in intimacy

The boundaries of the adult self which are clear and definite are, paradoxically, quite penetrable at the same time. It is the very penetrability of these boundaries — evidenced in such qualities as openness, availability, self-forgetfulness, understanding, and love — which makes intimacy possible. Erikson (1963) understands intimacy in terms of "ethical strength," as the capacity to commit oneself to "concrete affiliations and partnerships" (p. 263) For Erikson, this ethical strength is seen in sexuality. What he calls "true genitality" is really possible only on the basis of intimacy (Erikson, 1963, p. 264).

The adult self is its own responsible process of experiencing

"To have a sense of responsibility," says Meissner (1984), "is to have a sense of inner reality and identity" (p. 237). Experiencing is now a lived-body response; it is boundaried and coherent; it has a centre, a depth, and a focus. There is a clear difference between a sense of self which has experiences and a sense of self which really is its experiencing. The latter, the adult self, is an ongoing process, a body-self which in feeling and in depth maintains a continuity with the past, a meaning for the present, and a direction for the future (Marcia, 1988, p. 217). In an adult self, ongoing experiencing and the ability to respond go together.

Empathy and the Adult Self

An adult self, as an identity in a mutuality of relating, needs empathy in order to be itself. Mutuality is only possible on the basis of some real understanding of the feeling of the other and of the feeling of the self. Full mutuality is only possible because of empathic knowing, an empathic knowing of the other and an empathic knowing of the self. In this empathic knowing, moreover, the self and the other are united, but they are not merged. It is the nature of empathy, as Vettesen (1994) observes, that it "leaves intact the distinctness and unique identity of the person who empathizes as well as that of his or her addressee" (p. 118). Deigh (1995) makes much the same point when he says that "it is distinctive of empathy that it entails imaginative participation in the other's life without forgetting oneself" (p. 759).

In the "self-in-relation" understanding of human development — and in particular women's development — articulated by those involved at the Stone Center for Developmental Services and Studies at Wellesley College in Massachusetts, empathy is seen as a "crucial feature of development" (Surrey, 1991). "The assumption is," says Surrey (1991), "that the self is organized and developed through practice in relationships where the goal is the increasing development of mutually empathic relationships" (p. 54). Jordan (1997) speaks of "mutual empathy" as a way of human development. As she says, "mutual empathy enhances dialogue, a sense of connection, and the experience of human community for all participants" (p. 344).

Unfortunately, the nature of this mutual empathy is not always that well understood. As Jordan (1991) puts it, empathy is "often construed as a mysterious, contagion-like, and primitive phenomenon or dismissed as a vague and unknowable subjective state" (p. 69). Jordan (1991) continues: "Empathy, however, is a complex process, relying on a high level of ego development and ego strength and, in fact, may provide a good index of both of these" (p. 69). This is the case I am making here; the adult self and empathy go together.

Empathy is essential and intrinsic to the first three characteristics of the adult self. Self-empathy and the ability to be empathic with others is only possible in a body-self. If the adult self is rooted and disclosed in feeling, so is empathy; the very definition of empathy is that it is rooted and disclosed in feeling. If the adult self is a felt sense of depth, so is empathy; the very definition of empathy is that it is a felt sense of depth. Self empathy and the ability to be empathic with others are rooted and disclosed in feeling. Self empathy and the ability to be empathic with others are a felt sense of depth. They are, in Barrett-Lennard's (1997) words, "a respectful inner listening" which is able "to take seriously whatever signals arise internally" (p. 108). The adult self as a body-self with feeling and depth is only possible in empathy.

Empathy is also essential and intrinsic to the adult self as a self with its own clear boundaries and a self that is able to exist in intimacy. It is self-empathy, that is, the ability of the self to own its own feeling and to own its own depth, which allows the boundaries of the self to form. At the same time, it is empathy for the other, recognizing the other's feeling and depth, that allows the boundaries of the other to form. It is empathy that allows for the boundaries of the self and the boundaries of the other. Empathy and clear boundaries go together. And, of course, empathy is at the heart of intimacy. Jordan (1997) says: "In empathy I am present, vulnerable, open, responsive, and concerned" (p. 343-344). In this quote "intimacy" could replace "empathy;" empathy defines intimacy. "Without empathy," as Jordan (1991) says, "there is no intimacy, no real attainment of an appreciation of the paradox of separateness within connection" (p. 69). Empathy, clear boundaries, and intimacy go together in an adult self.

Finally, if to have "a sense of responsibility is to have a sense of inner reality and identity" (p. 237), as Meissner (1984) says, then self-empathy and empathy for the other are what allows for the sense of responsibility that is possible for an adult self. It is empathy that allows for the body-self in its feeling and depth and with its clear boundaries and intimacy to respond as itself to reality. And it is at this point that the question of empathy in relation to morality and religion can be entertained.

The Development of Empathy

Now that the case has been made that empathy is intrinsically and essentially related to psychological adulthood, it is easier, perhaps, to look at the question of how empathy develops. Two ways of thinking may be helpful. First, if empathy is so intrinsic and essential to adult development, then whatever fosters adult development would seem to foster empathy. In other words, as we are growing up, if we are respected as emerging body-selves, if our feeling and what is in the direction of depth is honoured, if our boundaries are respected by others who respect their boundaries, if we can experience intimacy as we need to, and if we are honoured for the ways in which we are becoming our own responsible process of experiencing, then we will be experiencing empathy from others and we will have every chance to develop self-empathy and empathy for the other.

Second, there is in the work of Selman (1980, pp. 37-40) on "perspective taking" a way of seeing what the development of empathy is like. Selman, who is interested in the development of social cognition and who sees his work as an outgrowth of the work of Piaget (1948), has developed five age-related levels or stages of the structure of perspective taking. Let us look very briefly at these five levels in terms of the "concepts of persons" and "concepts of relations" described in *The Growth of Interpersonal Understanding* (Selman, 1980).

Level O: Undifferentiated and Egocentric Perspective Taking (about Ages 3 to 6)

Concepts of persons: undifferentiated. At this level, young children do not clearly differentiate physical and psychological characteristics of persons.

Concepts of relations: egocentric. Selves and others are clearly differentiated only as physical entities, not psychological entities. Thus subjective perspectives are undifferentiated and that another may interpret the same situation differently is not recognized.

Level 1: Differentiated and Subjective Perspective Taking (about Ages 5 to 9)

Concepts of persons: differentiated. At Level 1, the key conceptual advance is the clear differentiation of physical and psychological characteristics of persons. As a result, intentional and unintentional acts are differentiated and a new awareness is generated that each person has a unique subjective covert psychological life.

Concepts of relations: subjective. The subjective perspectives of self and other are clearly differentiated and recognized as potentially different. However, another's subjective state is still thought to be legible by simply physical observation.

Level 2: Self-reflective/Second-person and Reciprocal Perspective Taking (about Ages 7-12)

Concepts of persons: self-reflective/second-person. Key conceptual advances at Level 2 are the growing child's ability to step mentally outside himself or herself and take a self-reflective or second-person perspective on his or her own thoughts and actions and on the realization that others can do so as well.

Concepts of relations: reciprocal. A new two-way reciprocity is the hallmark of Level 2 concepts of relations. It is a reciprocity of thoughts and feelings, not merely actions. The child puts himself or herself in another's shoes and realizes the other will do the same.

Level 3: Third-person and Mutual Perspective Taking (about Ages 10 to 15)

Concepts of persons: third-person. Persons are seen by the young adolescent thinking at Level 3 as systems of attitudes and values fairly consistent over the long haul, as opposed to randomly changeable assortments of states as at Level 2. The critical conceptual advance is toward ability to take a true third-person perspective, to step outside not only one's own immediate perspective, but outside the self as a system, a totality.

Concepts of relations: mutual. The third-person perspective permits more than the taking of another's perspective on the self; the truly third-person perspective on relations which is characteristic of Level 3 simultaneously includes and coordinates the perspectives of self and other(s), and thus the system or situation and all parties are seen from the third-person or generalized other perspective.

Level 4: In-depth and Social-Symbolic Perspective Taking (about Ages 12 to Adult)

Concepts of persons: in-depth. Two new notions are characteristic of Level 4 conceptions of persons. First, thoughts, motives, or feelings are understood to be psychologically determined, but not necessarily self-reflectively understood. In this view, there are more complicated interactions within a person that cannot always be comprehended by the "observing ego" of Level 3. Thus, we see, whether or not it is so named, the generation of a notion of the unconscious in individuals. Second, there emerges at Level 4 a new notion of personality as a product of traits, beliefs, values, and attitudes, a system with its own developmental history.

Concepts of relations: societal-symbolic. The individual now conceptualizes subjective perspectives of persons toward each other (mutuality) as existing not only on the plane of common expectations or awareness, but also simultaneously at multidimensional or deeper levels of communication. For example, in a dyad, perspectives can be shared at the level of superficial information, of common interests, or of deeper unverbalized feelings and communication (Selman, 1980, pp. 37-40).

Although Selman (1980) is writing from the point of view of social cognition and although he frames development as the ability to move away from a position of egocentrism, the levels of perspective taking he describes do have some similarities with the description of empathy in relation to the adult self. As one progresses through the levels there is a move from the person as physical to the person as psychological, from the person as exterior to the person as interior; there is the understanding that the thoughts and feelings of the self and the thoughts and feelings of the other are increasingly important and increasingly differentiated; there is the understanding that mutuality becomes more and more the social reality; there is the understanding that the depth of the self and the depth of the other emerge as the most significant aspects of the self and the most significant aspects of mutual relating; and there is the sense that this personal depth can be felt and communicated, even if it is not always able to be adequately verbalized. The development of perspective taking as described by Selman does throw some light on what the development of empathy looks like.

Empathy, Adult Morality, and Adult Religion

In this final section of the chapter I want to make the case that empathy is intrinsically and essentially related to adult morality and to adult religion. In other words, without self-empathy and empathy for the other, a morality that is adult and a religion that is adult cannot be realized.

What seems to be the case is that adult morality is dependent upon the realization of an adult self. In fact, adult morality has the same structure as an adult self. Adult morality has for its structure a self which is "an identity in a mutuality of relating." As inherently a mutuality of relating, an adult morality is only possible on the basis of self-empathy and empathy for the other. Adult morality depends on one person as a body-self with feeling and depth recognizing the other person as a body-self with feeling and depth. Adult morality depends on one person with clear boundaries and the ability to relate in intimacy trying to find the other person and trying to respect the other person in his or her need for intimacy. Adult morality is really one person relating in mutuality as his or her own responsible process of experiencing. To be responsible to the self is to be responsible to the other, and to be responsible to the other is to be responsible to the self. Empathy and morality go together in adulthood.

The same seems to be true for adult religion. What seems to be the case is that adult religion is dependent upon the realization of an adult self. In fact, adult religion has the same structure as an adult self. Adult religion has for its structure a self which is "an identity in a mutuality of relating." As inherently a mutuality of relating, adult religion is only possible on the basis on self-empathy and empathy for God. Adult religion depends on a person as a body-self with feeling and depth recognizing God as somehow a body-self with feeling and depth. Adult religion depends on a person with clear boundaries who is able to relate in intimacy trying to find a God with clear boundaries who is able to relate in intimacy. In fact, adult religion depends on mutual empathy. Adult religion is really the self in empathy and love with God finding God in empathy and love with the self. To be responsible to the self is to be responsible to God, and to be responsible to God is to be responsible to the self.

In this presentation, empathy is defined as one person feeling - with an attitude of care and concern - what the other person feels as if one were the other person; it involves sensing the emotions, the attitudes, the way of seeing things, the way of relating, and the meanings the other person senses. This understanding of empathy is intrinsically and essentially related to adulthood defined as an identity in a mutuality of relating, and this understanding of empathy is intrinsically and essentially related to all the characteristics of an adult self. Adulthood and empathy necessarily go together.

Empathy is a developmental reality: it develops as an adult self develops. A comparison of empathy with Selman's notion of perspective taking suggests that this development is along the lines of a shift from seeing the person as physical to seeing the person as psychological, a shift from seeing the person as exterior to seeing the person as interior. There is the understanding that the thoughts and feelings of the self and the thoughts and feelings of the other are increasingly important and increasingly differentiated. There is the understanding that mutuality becomes more and more the social reality. There is the understanding that the depth of the self and the depth of the other emerge as the most significant aspects of the self and the most significant aspects of mutual relating. The development of empathy is the development of adulthood.

Finally, adult morality, understood as an identity in a mutuality of relating, has the same structure as an adult self, suggesting that an adult morality is only possible on the basis of self-empathy and empathy for the other. Likewise, adult religion, understood as an identity in a mutuality of relating, has the same structure as an adult self, suggesting that adult religion is only possible on the basis on self-empathy and empathy for God.

References

Barrett-Lennard, G. T. (1997). The Recovery of empathy — Toward others and self. In A. C. Bohart and L. S. Greenberg, (Eds.), *Empathy reconsidered: New directions in psychotherapy*, Washington, D.C.: American Psychological Association.

Blasi, A. (1988). Identity and the development of the self. In D. K. Lapsley and F. C. Power (Eds.), *Self, ego, and identity: Integrative approaches*, New York: Springer-Verlag.

Deigh, J. (1995). Empathy and universalizability. *Ethics, 105*(July).

Elhard, L. (1968) Living faith: Some contributions of the concept of ego-identity to the understanding of faith. In P. Homans (Ed.), *The dialogue between theology and psychology*, Chicago: University of Chicago Press.

Erikson, E. H. (1980). The problem of ego identity. In E.H. Erikson, *Identity and the life cycle,* New York: Norton.

Erikson, E.H. (1963). *Childhood and society.* New York: Norton.

Farley, E. (1996). *Divine empathy: A theology of God.* Minneapolis: Fortress Press.

Feshback, N.D. (1997). Empathy: The formative years: Implications for clinical practice. In A. C. Bohart and L. S. Greenberg, (Eds.), *Empathy reconsidered: New directions in psychotherapy*, Washington, D.C.: American Psychological Association.

Geertz, C. (1975). On the nature of anthropological understanding. *American Scientist, 63.*

Greenson, R.R. (1967). *The technique and practice of psychoanalysis, Volume 1.* New York: International Universities Press.

Heron, J. (1992). *Feeling and personhood: Psychology in another key.* London: Sage.

Hillman, J. (1992). *The thought of the heart and the soul of the world.* Dallas, Texas: Spring Publisher.

Jacobi, M. (1984). *The analytic encounter: Transference and human relationship.* Toronto: Inner City Books.

James, W. (1985). *The varieties of religious experience.* Cambridge: Harvard University Press.

Jones, J. W. (1991). *Contemporary psychoanalysis and religion: Transference and transcendence.* New Haven: Yale University Press.

Jordan, J. V. (1997). Relational development through mutual empathy. In A. C. Bohart and L. S. Greenberg, (Eds.), *Empathy reconsidered: New directions in psychotherapy*, Washington, D.C.: American Psychological Association.

Jordan, J.V. (1991). Empathy and self boundaries. In J. V. Jordan, A. G. Kaplan, J. B. Miller, I. P. Stiver, & J. L. Surrey (Eds.), *Women's growth in connection: Writings from the Stone Center.* New York: Guilford.

Jung, C. G. (1981). The development of personality: *Collected Works, 17.* Princeton, Bollingen: Princeton University Press.

Kohut, H. (1984). *How does analysis cure*? Chicago: University of Chicago Press.

Leder, D. (1990). *The absent body.* Chicago: University of Chicago Press.

Marcel, G. (1952). *Metaphysical journal.* Chicago: Regnery.

Marcia, J.E. (1988). Common processes underlying ego identity, cognitive/moral development, and individuation, in D. K. Lapsley & F. C. Power (Eds.), *Self, ego, and identity: Integrative approaches*, New York: Springer-Verlag.

McDargh, J. (1986). God, mother and me: An object relational perspective on religious material. *Pastoral Psychology, 34*(4).

Meissner, W. W. (1984). *Psychoanalysis and Religious Experience*, New Haven, Yale University Press.

Miller, J.B. & Stiver, I.P. (1997). *The healing connection: How women form relationships in therapy and in life.* Boston: Beacon Press.

Moore, T. (1992). *Care of the soul: A guide for cultivating depth and sacredness in everyday life.* New York: Harper Collins.

Nelson, J. (1983). *Between two gardens: Reflections on sexuality and religious experience.* New York: Pilgrim.

Piaget, J. (1948). *The moral judgment of the child.* Glencoe, IL: Free Press.

Ricoeur, P. (1992). *Oneself as another.* Chicago: University of Chicago Press.

Rogers, C.R. (1959). A theory of therapy, personality, and interpersonal relationships as developed in the client-centered framework. In S. Koch (Ed.), *Psychology: A study of a science, Vol. III,* New York: McGraw-Hill.

Selman, R.L. (1980). *The growth of interpersonal understanding: Developmental and clinical analyses.* New York: Academic Press.

Souvaine, E., Lahey, L. L., & Kegan, R. (1990). Life after formal operations: Implications for a psychology of the self. In C.N. Alexander, & E.J.Langer (Eds)., *Higher stages of human development: Perspectives on adult growth,* New York: Oxford.

Staub, E. (1987). Commentary of Part I. In N. Eisenberg & J. Strayer, (Eds.), *Empathy and its development,* New York: Cambridge University Press.

Surrey, J.L. (1991). The self-in-Relation: A theory of women's development. In J. V. Jordan, A. G. Kaplan, J. B. Miller, I. P. Stiver, & J. L. Surrey (Eds.), *Women's growth in connection: Writings from the Stone Center.* New York: Guilford.

Taylor C. (1989). *Sources of the self: The making of the modern identity.* Cambridge: Harvard University Press.

Vettesen, A.J. (1994). *Perception, empathy, and judgment: An inquiry into the preconditions of moral performance.* University Park, Pennsylvania: Pennsylvania State University Press.

Zahn-Waxler, C. & Radke-Yarrow, M. (1990). The origins of empathic concern. *Motivation and Emotion, 14*(2).

Chapter 5

Healing Through Differentiation: A Pastoral Care and Counselling Perspective*

Peter L. VanKatwyk

As a pastoral counsellor I have often been asked what is unique about being "pastoral" in counselling. What makes counselling *pastoral counselling*? Most times, I am sure, curiosity prompts the question. It is a good question; a question that has gathered a rich and varied literature, through generations, of caring in religious communities. At others times I wonder whether the question, rather than indicating polite interest, reflects critical doubts about whether pastoral counselling is really all that different from other forms of counselling and therapy. Such an inquiry of suspicion questions whether current pastoral counselling practice is still rooted in and informed by the cure-of-souls religious traditions.

Pastoral counselling as a specialized expression of pastoral care extends a healing ministry to those in distress or crisis. This broad use of the term "healing" connects us simultaneously with the historical roots of pastoral care and the current heightened sensitivity to lives saturated with stress and scarred by trauma.

*Revision of the keynote address given at the 3rd Annual Conference of the Society for Pastoral Counselling Research, Saint Paul University, Ottawa, Ontario, May 10, 1996

What does it mean to see healing as the heart of pastoral care and counselling?

The Gospel accounts focus on Jesus' healing-miracles as authentic signatures of God's works. When Jesus heals a blind man he refutes his disciples' diagnostic perspective on the past: "who sinned, this man or his parents, that he was born blind?" With a perspective on the future, human disabilities and suffering become opportunities for healing as the marker events of God's presence : "he was born blind so that God's works might be revealed in him" (John 9:3,4 NRSV).

In the Early Church the emphasis on healing of the total person remained the touchstone of pastoral care. Later, the intimate unity of body and soul slowly separated into a hierarchical configuration in which the body represented the manifold ills and afflictions of this world, and the soul symbolized one's eternal destiny in the world to come. In the same line, the Reformers emphasized the message that the real miracle of healing is not so much one of the body but of the soul.

This pastoral distinction between body and soul became further entrenched in the modern period through the rise of the medical model, which claimed specialization in the physical reality of the body, leaving other dimensions of the human condition to be addressed by nonmedical specialities of care. The medical model described the process of healing as the diagnosis of disease agents to be eradicated through clinical means. Psychotherapy inherited some of the legacy of the medical model's orientation around pathology, and in time developed a matching clinical terminology following the dialectics of diagnosis and treatment. As illustrated in Adler's prototypical departure from Freudian biological drive theory, psychotherapy also reached beyond the medical model by adopting more holistic and health oriented-therapy approaches (Mosak, 1989).

In the last few decades, new paradigms have evolved which go beyond linear cause and effect connections and question the orderly and analytical ways in which we have presumed to know ourselves and our world. Systems thinking promoted circular models of equal reciprocity which invite playful interchanges between cause and effect, physical and spiritual functioning, individuals and their social contexts. Current social constructivist and narrative metaphors go beyond both the medical model and systems thought by redefining the role of the "healer" and the process of the healing interaction. Translated into pastoral ministry, care-receivers become co-authors of the "good news" and co-creators of the "new life" of preferred life and spirit enhancing realities.

The current focus on the extent and diversity of stress and its treatment has provided a new appreciation for the pastoral tradition of the "cure of souls." There is a return to the roots of pastoral care where the concept of soul embraces the total person. This holistic understanding of healing includes the physical, psychological, social, ecological and spiritual dimensions in the multiple relationships which constitute the communal contexts that define our separate identities. The literature of pastoral care and counselling demonstrates a growing awareness that a family system context is essential to the ministry of healing, as human households constitute the settings for the realization of reconciliation, justice, and forgiveness. This emphasis on a relational understanding of healing is expressed with special urgency for those most vulnerable in our world; it promotes social action and ecological stewardship in securing a place for people in threatened and fragile environments.

Theories and practices of healing in the Western world are profoundly influenced by seemingly escalating and frequently debilitating stress levels experienced in today's living conditions. Adults as well as children are increasingly at risk of losing a safe place and sense of protection in the world. The media expose all of us to what used to be reserved for only the few directly involved in such catastrophic events as accidents, natural disasters, crime, AIDS, child abuse, rape and other acts of violence, and the ugly faces of discrimination and dissolution of communities in various types of "ethnic cleansing." Stress studies have opened new windows on the complexities and consequences of hurt. The word "trauma" has been reserved for those hurts that overwhelm and disrupt human abilities to adjust and go on with life. *Post-Traumatic Stress Disorder* (American Psychiatric Association, 1994) has become a common medical label which covers the absorbing stories of wounds that persist, stubbornly resisting natural healing processes.

It is remarkable how pronounced the term "healing" has become in psychotherapy, especially in current self-help literature. Today pastoral counselling can no longer presume a special claim on the word. However, the "healing" metaphor carries for many people spiritual or religious connotations, whether or not it is experienced in the context of pastoral care and counselling. Such is the case in a "tale of psychotherapy" told by the existential psychotherapist Irvin Yalom (1989) in a story entitled *I Never Thought it Would Happen to Me*. It is about an older woman grieving the loss of her husband, followed less than two years later by a brutal purse snatching. Left with the post-traumatic stress symptoms of overwhelming feelings of isolation and preoccupation with her safety, she came to therapy. The robbery went beyond her purse and touched her place in the world: "That sense of specialness, of being charmed, of being the exception, of being eternally protected; all those self-deceptions that had served her so well suddenly lost their persuasiveness. She saw through her own illusions, and what illusion had shielded now lay before her, bare and terrible. Her grief wound was now fully exposed" (Yalom, 1989, p. 149). This I take as a religious understanding of trauma, transcending the traumatic event to touch upon our very place in the universe. In a parallel process spiritual healing in therapy also will transcend particular pains and touch the deeper woundedness in need of "cures of the soul". In this chapter I will introduce two prominent but contrary models of healing in pastoral care and counselling, set apart by radically different styles of care: the one of compassion, the other of competence. While healing has wide ecological and socio-political system dimensions, for the sake of clarity my lens will be narrow in focus, mainly observing the healing process in individual care. I will describe these two models as stereotypes polar opposites, each offering a crucial but limiting perspective on healing. Rather than polemical sketches, the two models will be presented as educational toys, to be played with towards the construction of an interactional model in motion. This "mobile" of healing is not a pure model, stripped from what was wrong with each of the two preceding models, but represents the unique merits in each model and enacts the potential of a relationship between the two. At best the mobile resembles that extraordinary couple relationship that is resilient enough to hold the tension of differences without divorcing into absolutizing and competitive claims.

The Compassion Model

The first uniquely pastoral response to human suffering which has shaped a model of care can be captured in the word compassion. In compassion the caregiver is deeply touched by a person's pain and moved in spirit and action to sharing and alleviating the suffering. Through compassion the caregiver participates in and identifies with the suffering. Attachment theory (Bowen, 1978) describes the evolutionary, deeply innate dynamics initially observed in parent-child interactions where helpers are drawn close in physical space by those who signal their pain and distress as they feel abandoned, threatened and insecure.

The compassion model (Figure 1) rests on a powerful base in the wounded person's experience of pain, which generates the gravitational pull that draws the helper through empathic identification. This base line in the wounded person is represented by a line of interaction between "suffering" and "knowing" the wound. Knowing is found in the ongoing process of naming, interpreting and representing the wound through such narrative and symbolic expressions as story, lamentation, prayer, and symptom. The knowing and suffering interaction keeps the wound, though dated in precipitating events in the past, hurting in the present and projected through anticipation into the future.

The caregiver in the compassion model becomes connected with the suffering primarily through what the wounded person "knows" and tells about the wound. The bridge of empathic involvement is the connecting link with the suffering person. The expertise of the compassionate caregiver is the empathic imagination shaped by the inner knowledge of the suffering person. The knowing and suffering are reciprocally related: the knowledge of the wound informs and shapes the suffering as much as the suffering informs and shapes the knowledge. Compassion is in knowing and feeling the wound. In compassion, knowing is loving, with the erotic intensity that unites. Yalom (1989) expresses empathy to the grieving widow when he says: "When you say you never thought it would happen to you, I know just what you mean. It's so hard for me, too, to accept that all these afflictions — ageing, loss, death — are going to happen to me too" (p. 150).

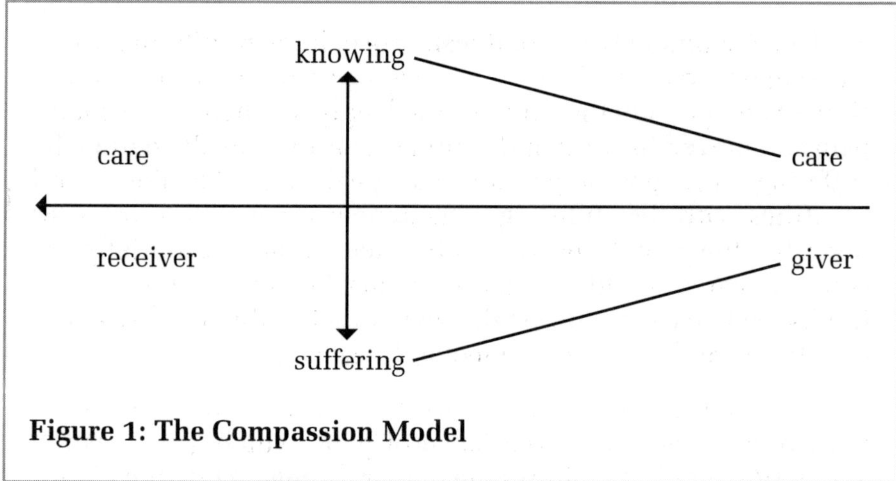

Figure 1: The Compassion Model

The compassion model embodies a profoundly pastoral approach. The ministry of presence is one of "being with" in empathic solidarity and understanding. *Pastoral* presence goes beyond empathy in pointing to the God who remembers us. In the Christian tradition the ministry of presence is *incarnational* presence, modelled after the image of the Christ who identified himself with our sufferings unto death. The incarnation encompasses the full range of human experience but culminates in ultimate suffering. The crucifixion surrounds us with the stark images of trauma: the bloody torture to death, the rejection and loneliness of the cross, the abandonment by God.

The traumatic dimensions in suffering dramatize both the intrinsic genius and the hazards of the compassion model. Trauma represents suffering in escalating intensity which increasingly cripples and disrupts the person's orientation and functioning in life. Trauma is the wound that enlarges itself through the persistence of intrusive thoughts, dreams, images and flashbacks. As wounding approximates traumatic proportions, the suffering person will lose the ability to name the pain, paralyzed by what cannot be grasped or expressed. Trauma is the pain that breaks the connection between knowing and feeling the suffering. Greg Mogenson (1989) in his book *God is a Trauma* describes how trauma in its overwhelming claims on the psyche functions as a God: "Just as God has been described as transcendent and unknowable, a trauma is an event which transcends our capacity to experience it. Compared to the finite nature of the traumatized soul, the traumatic event seems infinite, all-powerful, and wholly other" (pp. 1-2). Trauma in this demanding, God-like impact creates and organizes life after its own image.

According to a triangle diagram, as presented in Figure 1, the more traumatically charged the suffering, the more compassion will be generated and the closer the caregiver will be drawn into the cycle of trauma incapacitation. The identification with overwhelming suffering in the wounded person will heighten empathy transference in sensitizing and activating the caregiver's own woundedness. This reciprocal process will increasingly put the caregiver at risk of the debilitating impact of what has been aptly labelled "compassion fatigue," or, with a theological ring, "vicarious traumatization."

The Competence Model

The second model of pastoral healing, the competence model, shares with the compassion model a similar triangle diagram. The contrast between the two models is that the two triangles interact as mirror images. The compassion model focuses on the wounded person while the competence model focuses on the therapist as the basis of gravitation that organizes the energy field of healing and directs the pull in the therapy interaction. In the compassion model empathy propels the caregiver into the inner dynamics of knowing and suffering in the wounded person. In the competence model, the lure of the therapist's expertise propels the careseeker into the dynamics of outer resources offered through the caregiver.

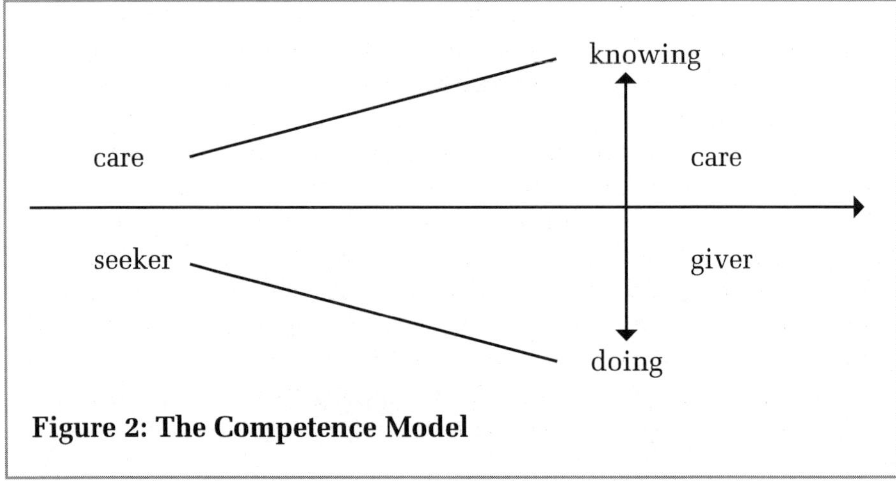

Figure 2: The Competence Model

The competence model (Figure 2) provides the wounded person, or group of persons, with a point of connection outside the troubled and, in traumatized lives, flooded inner world of "not knowing" and the resulting helplessness and hopelessness of mindless suffering. The caregiver offers outer perspectives and resources in order to facilitate the wounded to go beyond the confines of private suffering. As a trained professional the caregiver draws from her or his pastoral image and tradition, clinical wisdom and ministry expertise to provide new and authoritative perspectives of "knowing" and "doing" in addressing the woundedness. Yalom (1989) goes beyond empathy and, informed by his existentialist perspective, tells his grieving patient:

> You must feel that if Albert were alive, this would never have happened to you. So the robbery brings home the fact that he's really gone. You knew that before, I know. But part of you didn't. Now you really know that he's dead. He's not in the yard. He's not out back in the workshop. He's not anywhere. Except in your memories. (Yalom, 1989, p. 150) (Also see Freedman & Combs, 1996)

The "knowing" in the wounded is not just mirrored but expanded, confronted, or edited by the "knowing" and "doing" of the caregiver. In clinical psychology the "knowing" and "doing" of the caregiver is often expressed in the link between "diagnosis" and "treatment." Diagnosis presents the "objective" knowledge of suffering, the knowledge that maintains clinical distance by reflecting extensive case study research with generalized profiles of the symptoms of distress. Treatment is guided by the link that ties diagnostic criteria to the clinical research of preferred outcomes and interventions of choice. While it is tempting to draw damning contrasts between "clinical" knowledge and "pastoral" wisdom, it is remarkable to note the similarities between the classical method of pastoral care and the modern clinical model. Pastoral care and counselling in the classical tradition emphasized the contents of the "objective" message from the sacred scriptures and traditions of care while minimizing the more "subjective" process of empathic understanding in the pastoral relationship. The ministry of preaching eclipsed the ministry of listening in the classical mode. Chrysostom, generally considered the greatest preacher of antiquity, provides an example of a pastor who never really leaves the pulpit in his pastoral care and counselling. In a "letter to a young widow" he excuses himself for not writing to her earlier on account of the fact that she could not hear him in the time of her acute grief, "but when the troubled water has begun to subside, and the fury of the waves is abated, one can spread the sails of conversation" (cited by Volz, 1990, p. 157). In the same vein Luther's pastoral grief ministry strategy stressed moderation and control of one's grief. This pastoral approach stresses the primacy of the comfort of the gospel, and fears that our own private suffering may compete with the sufferings of Christ on our behalf. Through a grieving process of de-privatizing our own sufferings, our personal story is connected to the larger meta-story of the faith community.

The value of the competence model is that it provides an external reference point for a closed system of suffering and a boundary for the caregiver who is at risk of being incorporated and traumatized in the cycle of woundedness. The model's hazards, however, signal caution to most counsellors. The role of the pastoral caregiver in the competence model is primarily one of the expert with the task of managing the wounded person's pain or saving the person's soul. The focus of the model is on the competence of a care-giver in complementary relationship with the helplessness of a care-receiver. Its toxic potential is dramatized in a rigid rescuer-victim scenario organized by power differences which collapse only when therapy fails, often when therapist and client connect in both feeling victimized by the other.

The Differentiation Model

The two models, the one informed by compassion and the other by competence, are often experienced and presented as diametrically opposed and mutually exclusive styles of healing in pastoral care and counselling. In the compassion model the therapist is the one who does not know and needs to listen to the client. In the competence model the client is the one who does not know and needs to listen to the therapist.

In clinical pastoral education supervisors often experience these differences in students. One student enters a pastoral education program primarily on account of feelings of professional inadequacy, in search of good theory and techniques that work. In supervision this student asks, with an urgency directly proportionate to the degree of difficulty in the case presented, what to know and what to do. Another student appears far more confident, to the point of arrogance, secure in the ability of developing close relationships with clients and claiming inside knowledge of what is going on with the client. While the one student looks primarily for the clinical expert, if not the miracle worker, in the supervisor, the other student is more interested in a supervisory relationship that can support, parallel and deepen the relational dynamics of the ministry experience presented for supervision.

In the third model, I propose a working alliance between the two students mentioned above: an alliance based on differentiation between compassion and competence. By temperament and clinical experience pastoral caregivers can approximate either a type A or a type B student, according to a continuum going from the compassion model to the competence model, as their primary stance in ministry. Type C characterizes a pastoral caregiver not restricted to a fixed point on the continuum but able to differentiate and balance the two ends on the continuum, attuned to the exigencies of the healing situation and process.

The differentiation principle is well expressed in current social constructivist and hermeneutic theories that emphasize the necessity of a "not-knowing" stance for therapists (cf. Freedman & Combs, 1996). In order to learn from the wounded person the therapist becomes the curious listener who does not yet know, but eagerly wants to. True understanding is not something to be acquired apart from the listening process and to be imported into the counselling session. The therapist's pre-understandings are not only irrelevant but will obstruct the healing encounter and thus need to be checked at the door.

This "not knowing" emphasis, however, cannot be simply identified with the empathic presence of the compassion model. The therapeutic "not knowing" stance does not mean that the therapist is totally dependent on the client for knowing anything at all. Rather, the therapist's not-knowing is the stance which teases out unique bits of new and relevant knowledge and dares therapeutic competence to evolve in the counselling dialogue itself. Healing is happening in encounters that mutually enlighten client and therapist, opening up new windows of understanding and hope, going beyond the restrictive and oppressive walls of blind suffering. Active listening for the therapist is responding both to the wounded person and to oneself in meaning-making conversation. Creative listening is being poised for surprises, ready to pick up on what is novel and redemptive, what White and Epston (1990) have referred to as "unique outcomes" and "news of difference" in stories otherwise saturated with doom and dominated by failure. It is the listening ear teamed with the playful pen of the reporter who can punctuate, organize, format the materials, and suggest a headline and, possibly, a cartoon to go with the story.

The third model differentiates between the two knowledges, the inner and the outer, and in so doing separates the wounded from their wound (Table 1). This differentiation creates space for what has been called in pastoral ministry "pastoral conversation" and "theological reflection." In the psychoanalytic tradition this is the space where "soul-making" takes place. In his discussion of the omnipotent demands of trauma, Mogenson quotes James Hillman on the meaning of "soul" and on the need for differentiation for the soul to do its work:

Table 1:

The Differentiation Principle Applied to the Two Models of Care

PERSPECTIVES	COMPASSION MODEL	COMPETENCE MODEL
pastoral paradigm	relational pastoral	classical pastoral
"wounded healer" metaphor	the woundedness in the healer	the healer in the woundedness
therapy mode	"being with"	"doing for"
power distribution	horizontal	vertical
therapist role	companion	coach
gravitation pull	into the suffering	into the helping
therapy direction	towards client	towards therapist
therapy resources	inner	outer
therapy style	facilitative	directive
use of therapist	personal empathy	clinical expertise
way of knowing	phenomenological	theoretical

> By *soul* I mean... a perspective rather than a substance, a viewpoint toward things rather than a thing itself. This perspective is reflective; it mediates events and makes differences between ourselves and everything that happens. Between us and events, between the doer and the deed, there is a reflective moment — and soul-making means differentiating this middle ground (Mogenson, 1989, p. 6).

In diagram form (Figure 3), the differentiation model joins the two triangles representing the compassion and the competence model. The two triangles in interaction become a diamond which can contract and expand as it balances each triangle in shifting therapeutic alliances between the two ways of knowing and doing.

The differentiation between the two knowledges in therapy has been described as a process of *externalizing* the problem or

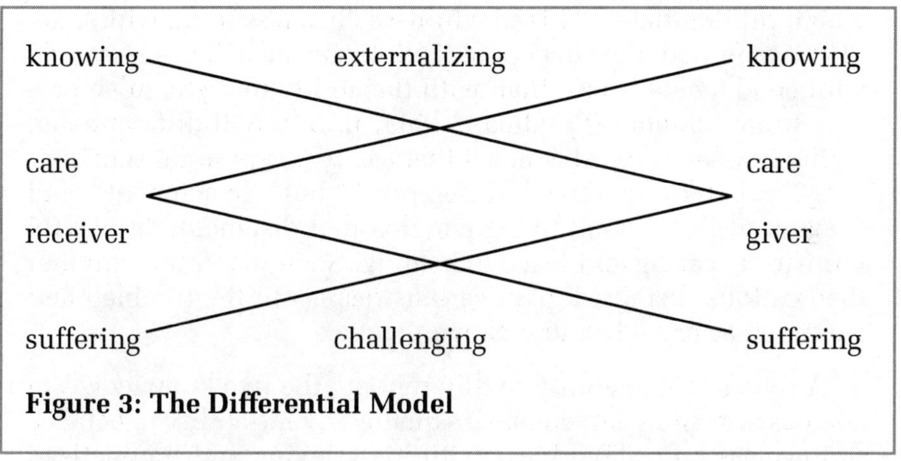

Figure 3: The Differential Model

the pain an externalization intended not for defensive but for reflective purposes (White & Epston, 1990). This differentiation in knowing is paralleled with a differentiation in doing. Rabbi Edwin Friedman (1985), in applying the natural systems concept of self-differentiation to pastoral care, focuses on the pastoral interaction. In an "emotional system" organized by pain the pastor is easily drawn into a triangle consisting of the parishioner, his or her woundedness or problem, and the pastoral role in attempting to support (the compassion model) or rescue (the competence model) the person. Friedman proposes a differentiated style of caring called *"challenging":* "it requires one to nonanxiously tolerate pain, and even to stimulate pain, thus forcing the other to increase his or her threshold" (Friedman, 1985, p. 49). Friedman presents challenge as a radical shift in healing, appealing to practices in modern healing of injecting germs and viruses directly into an organism so as to stimulate its own immune system. In the context of pastoral care through challenge, the compassion model and the competence model share the same parent of chronic anxiety. Empathy for those in pain readily dissolves into emotional fusion, and the seriousness which is anxious to offer competent help is easily "characterized by lack of flexibility in response, a narrow repertoire of approaches, persistent efforts to try harder, an inability to change direction, and a loss of perspective and concentrated focus" (Friedman, 1985, p. 50). This seriousness is contrasted with a therapeutic culture of playfulness which differentiates. This playfulness “has less to do with ‘one-liners’ than with the concept of flexible distance; it has less to do with good ‘come-backs’ than with the ability to distinguish process from content” (Friedman, 1985, p. 51). Self-differentiated caring is a paradoxical concept that easily jars pastoral sensitivities. Terms like “creative indifference,” “holy detachment,” and “benign neglect” point to the paradox that distancing in playful ministry is caring and leads to healing. Such playfulness, rather than callous disregard, pays serious respect to the troubled and wounded as capable and creative people.

Yalom’s (1989) ability to differentiate the two knowledges of compassion and competence is equalled by his ability to balance seriousness and playfulness with his grieving and traumatized patient. When she is sobbing in the pain of ultimate isolation he points to her purse - “that same ripped-off, much-abused purse” — and says:

> “Bad luck is one thing, but aren’t you asking for it carrying around something that large?” Taking the bait she hoists her purse on the table, emptying its contents to prove that she needs everything in it. They banter about everything: the roll of fifty dimes, three bags of candy, a plastic bag of old orange peels, three pairs of sunglasses, a small stapler .... When the great bag had finally yielded all, Elva and I stared in wonderment at the contents set out in rows on my table ... I followed her into her every nook and crevice, awed that one old woman’s purse could serve as a vehicle for both isolation and intimacy ... In that one hour, Elva moved from a position of forsakenness to one of trust. She came alive and was persuaded, once more, of her capacity for intimacy (Yalom, 1989, p. 151).

Today’s sensitivity to human stress and suffering, with a corresponding focus on healing in the psychotherapies, challenges the cure-of-souls pastoral tradition to affirm its roots in healing and to expand its articulation through the contributions from current theories and practices of care. In this chapter the principle of differentiation is the lens that focuses on the interplay between “what to know” and “what to do” in pastoral care for the wounded.

The proposed process of co-authoring in narrative therapy offers a unique contribution to pastoral ministry in counselling the distressed. A joint, cognitive project towards developing a healing theory fits a pastoral style of collaboration and defines "good news" as a message of liberation which creates the open space necessary for reflecting, visioning, and doing. The concept of self-differentiation in ministry further defines the pastoral role of "what to do" by moving beyond the "what to know" to a singular focus on "what to be." The premise that it is primarily the relationship that heals, resonates with the metaphor "pastoral" which is located in the person of the pastor. In the context of the differentiation model, pastoral care practices the paradox that by learning from the other, the other can know, and that by caring for self others can heal.

References

American Psychiatric Association (1994). *Diagnostic and statistical manual of mental disorders.* Washington, D.C.: Author.

Bowen, M. (1978). *Family therapy in clinical practice.* New York: Aronson.

Freedman, J. & Combs, G. (1996). *Narrative therapy — The social construction of preferred realities.* New York: Norton & Company.

Friedman, E.H. (1985). *Generation to generation — Family process in church and synagogue.* New York: The Guilford Press.

Mogenson, G. (1989). *God is a trauma.* Dallas, Texas: Spring Publications.

Mosak, H.H. (1989). Adlerian psychotherapy. In R.J. Corsini & D. Wedding (Eds.), *Current psychotherapies.* Itasca, Illinois: F.E. Peacock Publishers, p. 65-116.

Volz, C.A. (1990). *Pastoral life and practice in the early church.* Minneapolis: Augsburg Fortress.

White, M. & Epston, D. (1990). *Narrative means to therapeutic ends.* New York: Norton & Company.

Yalom, I.D. (1989). *Love's executioner.* New York: Basic Books.

Chapter 6

Fundamental Values and Systems Approach*

Marie-Line Morin, Ph.D.

The family systems approach is a prominent family counselling model. When adding a pastoral dimension to family counselling, clinicians use an integrative approach to account for the theological, religious and spiritual dimensions of a family's life together. The present chapter presents the hypothesis that Fundamental Values constitute, at an unconscious level, a mechanism of homeostasis for family interactions (Braithwaite & Scott, 1991). This hypothesis attempts to blend the results from empirical research on Fundamental Values (Morin, 1999) with the results from theoretical research on the foundational concepts of the systems approach (Morin, 1993). The first part of this chapter presents a definition of value from a psycho-philosophical perspective, a definition of Fundamental Values, and an identification of the Fundamental Values of five research participants. The second part presents the conceptual foundation of the family systems approach, reviews studies that support the stated hypothesis and its rationale, and presents a case study to illustrate how Fundamental Values regulate family systems.

---

*Revision of a paper presented at the 5th Annual Conference of the Society for Pastoral Counselling Research, Waterloo Lutheran Seminary, Waterloo, Ontario, May 16, 1998

Fundamental Values

Definitions of Values

Originating within philosophical literature, but also associated with studies in the fields of anthropology, sociology, and psychology, is the notion of values. Values are "presumed to encapsulate the aspirations of individuals and societies: they pertain to what is desirable and to standards which determine and justify choices of action" (Braithwaite and Scott, 1991, p. 661). Although easily associated with the socialization process, values have also been understood as "having an individual function shaped by the biological and psychological needs of each person" (Braithwaite & Scott, 1991, p. 661).

Efforts to define values for empirical purposes have taken different directions. Values were first associated with behaviour, goal-orientation, and behavioural preferences (Meissner, 1970). They were then related to needs, motivation, and cognition. Kluckhohn's (1951) definition offered grounds for a unifying concept of values: "a value is a conception, explicit or implicit, distinctive of an individual or characteristic of a group, of the desirable which influences the selection from available modes, means, and ends of action" (p. 395).

Rokeach's (1973) Value Survey (RVS) offered the most reliable operational definition of value for empirical research. In the elaboration of his popular instrument, Rokeach (1973) defined values as "an enduring belief that a specific mode of conduct or end-states of existence is personally and socially preferable to alternative modes of conduct or end-states of existence" (p. 5). From the several hundred value descriptors, Rokeach selected and retained 36 values that were representative of most individual values.

Rokeach's value survey scale restricts the possibility of identifying an individual's idiosyncratic and specific values. The restricted number of values measured by this instrument does not adequately assess for individual differences on values (Gibbins & Walker, 1993). The limitation of Rokeach's instrument

(Braithwaite, 1982; Gibbins & Walker, 1993) led to suggestions that a more dynamic system of true values be considered to account for "people's evaluation of the world ... based on more fundamental values" (Gibbins & Walker, 1993, p.797). There was a need, therefore, to broaden the conceptualization of individual values, especially for measurement purposes.

Values as Central to Self

From a humanistic psychology perspective, values have been considered to be a central component of human beings. Maslow (1968) stipulated that human beings possess a hierarchical value structure. Self-realization is most likely to be ensured when persons meet the needs corresponding to values relative to ultimate needs. According to May (1969) "the process of becoming a person relates to the capacity to experience the self as a valuing source" (May, 1969, in Decarvalho, 1992, p. 11). From a psychodynamic perspective, Treurniet (1988) considers valuing as the core of the ego. This conception is drawn from Rangell's psychoanalytic perspective which identifies values as a "central function of the ego" and from Winnicott's idea that values are "ego related" (cited by Treurniet, 1988, p. 1). According to Treurniet (1988), values are "connected with the ego and its interest" (p. 1). The connection between ego and values is supported by Gorsuch (1984) who, discussing Cattell's inclusion of morals and values, hypothesized that the Freudian "Id, Ego, and Superego are lodged within ... various motivational aspects of human personality" (Gorsuch, 1984, p. 212). According to Purzner (1988),

> ... that part of the dynamics can be conjugated with certain elements of the psychic structure... the parts of the psychic structure to which strong dynamic cathexis are attached, are called value structures. The value structure is responsible for the alignment of a person within its environment and leads to a discharge of drive energy into action (p. 144).

In this context, value structures appear to be the most fundamental aspect of an individual's personality.

A Value as Fundamental, Individual and Unique

The centrality of values can be summed up in one, unique, core value, which expresses an individual's self and deepest identity. Saint-Arnaud's (1988) clinical and phenomenological observations led him to state that individuals yearn for an Ultimate Good above all goods. This is what he called a person's Fundamental Value constituting the focal point where all other values and aspects of the psyche converge within the person. The Fundamental Value is considered to be basic, universal and transpersonal in nature. It is a dominant good that integrates, as a core value, all other goods and best expresses the person's psychospiritual identity. A Fundamental Value is said to be fundamental because it is foundational in regard to the structure of personality, it has a unifying effect on all aspects of one's personality, and it has a transpersonal or universal quality.

The concept of Fundamental Values also has a basis in hermeneutic philosophy. Taylor (1989) talks about the concept of "hypergood" which stands for "higher-order goods which are [ranked by individuals as] incomparably more important than others [and] providing the standpoint from which these must be weighed, judged, decided about" (Taylor, 1989, p. 63). According to Taylor, hypergoods give a "sense of wholeness, of fullness of being as a person or self, that nothing else can" (Taylor, 1989, p. 63). In the formation of the concept "hypergood," Taylor was influenced by Aristotle's notion of "supreme goods." Goods of a higher degree than others are ranked according to their relative degree of importance and called supreme goods or hypergoods.

Fundamental Value and Self as Centre of Personality

The concept of Fundamental Value can also be understood in the light of a specific approach in transpersonal psychology, that is, the theory of psychosynthesis. Assagioli (1965), the author of psychosynthesis, clearly asserts the existence of a transpersonal dimension in the human psyche based on the recognition that the self has two levels: the conscious "I" and the Transpersonal Self. The "I" is a "point of pure self-awareness" (Assagioli, 1965, p. 18). It is understood as the essence of one's identity, that which makes one completely different from others. The Transpersonal Self, on the other hand, gives us the full understanding of the conscious "I." It is believed to be the source or the essence of the self: the essence of our essence, that which thirsts for higher realities, for universal and ultimate goods (Assagioli, 1965).

Saint-Arnaud (1988) recognized that the Self, which yearns for ultimate goods, selects one value among others as being most important. That value is called the Fundamental Value. Thus, the Fundamental Value is considered to be the expression par excellence of the Transpersonal Self. Centering on the Transpersonal Self allows the recognition of one's Fundamental Value which, in turn, has the potential to unify the personality that tends to be divided into subpersonalities. From a pastoral perspective one could say that the Fundamental Value can only be fulfilled through one's relationship with the Ultimate Being: God (as God is understood in the different religions). It can, therefore, be viewed as a yearning for a quality or aspect of that Being, a "piece of God." When yearning for trust, it is the Trust "piece of God" that is ultimately desired. When yearning for love, it is the Love "piece of God" that is ultimately desired, and so forth with every possible ultimate value.

The tendency of the personality to divide itself into subpersonalities can be explained by the fact that values address two levels of the personality: the personal and the transpersonal levels. Values at the level of "I" tend to be oriented toward personal and limited goods, and values at the level of the Transpersonal Self are transpersonal and ultimate. Throughout life's development, people struggle to find a balance between these two levels of valuing by remaining fixed to their subpersonalities. In that process, the "I" tends to find compensating ways to find a balance between the "I" and the Transpersonal Self by identifying with the aspects of the personality called subpersonalities. This represents an illusory fulfillment of their aspiration for ultimate goods and prevents them from recognizing the absolute nature of the desires and values coming from the Transpersonal Self. When doing so, the "I" orients and keeps these yearnings for ultimate goods within the range of limited realities. This tendency leaves the personality divided between its yearnings for ultimate values and limited goods. The dilemma or conflict is resolved when one realizes his or her tendency to think of certain aspects of one's personality as absolutes, and then slowly starts to reorient the values and desires for the absolute goods toward their source: the transpersonal and ultimate world and realities. The identification of the Fundamental Value, which is the best expression of the Transpersonal Self, then becomes crucial for resolving that conflict. At that point, the values at the levels of the "I" and of the Transpersonal Self are synthesized into one and allow the integration of the opposite subpersonalities and the unification of the whole personality around its centre: the Transpersonal Self.

Phenomenological Research Results

The application of Giorgi's (1985) phenomenological research method allowed the researcher to identify a Fundamental Value for each of five clients. Through this method, clients' fundamental yearnings were inferred from their discourse in counselling sessions, and from this inference, sets of values were drawn up. Such a fundamental yearning gave grounds for the identification of the following clients' Fundamental Values: Security about her Dignity, Power over Pain, Freedom to be Autonomous, Security about her Personal Identity, Security about the Worth of his Identity. Readers who are interested to know more about the research and the extraction of Fundamental Values and their implication for pastoral counselling can refer to the book by Morin (2001).

Systems Approach

The systems approach emerged out of a new epistemology that appeared in the 1950s and differed from traditional schools of thought in psychology. Unlike other theories, the systems approach considers mental illnesses as symptoms in a relational context rather than as intra-psychic deficiencies. The systems approach emerged at the confluence of many disciplines: (a) systems theory, (b) cybernetics, and (c) information theory and communication. Von Glasersfeld (1988) explained that its philosophical foundation was in line with Kant's and Vico's constructivism, which is opposed to conventional empiricism that supposes the existence of absolute metaphysical realism. In constructivism, knowledge of reality occurs through construction, that is, through experimentation or adaptation from which each individual discovers that which is convenient or reliable for him or her, and that which makes sense in interactions with others (Von Glasersfeld, 1988). Rather than being taken as reliable truth, knowledge is considered to be viable, pertinent and useful because it allows for the explanation, prediction and control of the world around.

Definition of Systems

The systems approach has evolved within four schools of thought: structural, strategic, paradoxical, and new cybernetic (Morin, 1993). Strategic and paradoxical schools focus on intervention strategies. The structural school, the earliest of the four, introduced some of the basic concepts in systems theory. Under the principle of homeostasis, it stipulated that systems tend to move toward equilibrium (emotional stability). On the basis of this tendency, systems have been called *open systems* or systems open to equilibrium (Von Bertalanffy, 1980). The most recent school of thought, cybernetics, considers that systems tend to be move away from equilibrium or stability and towards evolution and change. Thus, systems are seen as *closed systems* or systems open to moving away from equilibrium (Prigogine and Stengers, 1984). In this perspective, systems are thought to have their own autonomy. Rather than tending towards equilibrium, systems tend towards adaptation and change, and they establish a new equilibrium when faced with changes and fluctuations stemming from external sources or occurring within the systems themselves. As a result, members of systems strive for new ways of interacting in order to find a new state of balance.

The originality of the systems approach is indisputably the focus that it places on interaction between members of a system rather than on intrapsychic phenomenon. As stated by Von Bertalanffy (1980), the initiator of this approach, a system is a "complex of elements *in interaction,* these interactions being of an ordered (non- random) nature ... It is not limited to material systems but applies to any 'whole' consisting of *interacting components*" (p. 111).

This definition is supported by authors such as Elkaïm, von Foerster, and Varola (in Van Caloen, 1993), who, from a biological cybernetic's point of view, give examples that make the systems approach accessible. These authors believe that (a) every system has within itself the elements which influence and act upon the system to make it evolve in a non-predictable direction (autonomy and self-regulation of organism), and (b) the systems' evolution is determined by their internal structure and individual characteristics.

The interaction process in human systems is seen as analogous to those in biological systems. The discovery of similar rules in economical, mechanical and biological systems reinforced the belief that human systems operate by these same rules.

The Principle of Homeostasis

One of the basic principles of a systems' approach is that of homeostasis. This principle explains a system's tendency to find equilibrium (to go back to initial state of balance or to find a new state of balance) and to "maintain an internal environment constant" (Ausloos, 1985, p. 4).

In early structural theory, homeostatic tendency was conceptualized within the context of an *open system*, which means that systems are open to equilibrium. This principle stipulated that after information arrives or events occur in a system, instability or crisis is experienced. To avoid a state of imbalance, the system tends to return to its initial state of being balanced. According to cybernetic theory, homeostatic tendency is conceptualized within the context of *closed systems* (understood as moving away from equilibrium). This means that when facing instability or crisis after new information arrives, the system's homeostatic reaction is to look for a new state of balance (Elkaim, 1989).

Norms, Rules, and Boundaries

Homeostasis is a complex process that maintains itself in different ways. A simple way of explaining it is to say that homeostasis is maintained through implicit and explicit norms and rules that organize the interactions between sub-systems and that fix the boundaries or limits between these same sub-systems. In other words, systems include sub-systems such as the couple, children, etc., that form a system. The couple, when having a child, becomes the sub-system called parents. Then, as other children arrive, other sub-systems are formed such as children and siblings. In the case of larger families, the sub-systems may be the oldest children, youngest children, girls, boys, etc.

Homeostasis is maintained on the basis of implicit and explicit norms and rules that organize the interactions between the various sub-systems. The organization resulting from these norms and rules are called boundaries or limits between sub-systems and between individuals. The strength or fragility of those boundaries reflect the cohesion between members of the system and sub-systems and the system's adaptability to new situations.

The system's ability to maintain its homeostasis depends on the qualities of cohesion and adaptability. The strength and weakness of a system is related to the quality of its cohesiveness and adaptability. According to Olson, Russell, and Sprenkle (1983), the cohesion ranges from distant to fused interactions and the adaptability to new situations ranges from chaotic to rigid boundaries. When facing destabilizing events or information, dysfunctional systems maintain cohesion through distant or fused connectedness and adapt to the new situation through rigid or chaotic mechanisms of adaptation. In similar situations, functional systems maintain separated boundaries while remaining related, and they adapt with flexibility while respecting structure.

Family Myth and the Symptom

Homeostasis is not only maintained by rules and norms. It is also enforced by "family myth." Family myth refers to a certain image that a family has about itself and wants to project to the external world. The myth or image enforces homeostasis because the myth is rooted in the internal functioning of the system which, in turn, is a result of the rules of interaction and the roles that members have in the system (Ferreira, 1981). The family myth is generally a positive image. Beliefs about this image are shared by all members of the system in regard to roles, norms and rules that regulate their relationship. Examples of family myths include the following: "We are a united family," "We share everything," and "We cannot communicate" (Van Caloen, 1993).

To maintain the idea that the family myth is real, the identity of individuals is sacrificed in service of the myth. The discrepancy between the family myth and the personal identity of its members creates a paradoxical situation in which the individual must choose between two opposite and apparent responses: a false identity, which allows it to be in tune with the myth, and a real identity, which he/she asserts through behaviours that confront the system and its myth. The consequence of this paradoxical situation is that the members feel obligated to adopt dysfunctional behaviours to secure for themselves an acceptable position in the family.

Such dysfunctional behaviours, from a family systems perspective, are interpreted with reference to the interactive organization. Thus, the dysfunctional behaviour of an individual is considered to be the symptom of a dysfunctional family or of a dysfunctional pattern of interaction. In other words, one or more members of a family that is dysfunctional in its cohesive and adaptive patterns will develop pathological behaviour. The person's problematic behaviour will receive the attention of other members of the family who, as well, offer a solution for this member's pathology. This pathological behaviour has the effect to keep the family distracted from the real problem and thus allow the system to maintain itself. When perceived this way, the member having the pathological behaviour is said to reflect the family's difficulty and needs to be diagnosed and treated as such.

Family Systems Approach and Fundamental Values

Values in Systems Approach

In systems approach, values are often paralleled to norms and rules because of the resemblance of their impact on models of interaction. The difference between norms and values is outlined in the following three sets of distinctions derived from Jackson's (1977) conceptualization: (a) values exist *a priori* (initially) and lead to certain models of interaction, whereas norms are inferred from interactive behaviour, (b) values are manifest and identifiable while norms are hidden and implicit and (c) values are impersonal, relative to content and form, individual, and describe something one values, whereas norms are interpersonal in that they describe interpersonal relationships.

In a systems approach, values are not considered as an entity in themselves but in terms of their use for the system's homeostasis. Jackson (1977) postulates that although values ordinarily originate in the culture and in ethnic or social groups, idiosyncratic values originate from individuals and not from interactions in a system.

> One person may find that a certain thing is valuable, has some value, many people [taken individually] may agree that this certain thing is valuable, but a family considered as a whole [in its totality], may not. Although all members of a family may agree on a certain value, the result is the sum of individuals — so [in that regard] we remain in the domain of individual theory. (translated from Jackson, 1977, p. 39)

According to Jackson, values are not the result of the system's organization but belong to members of a system. However, values have an interpersonal implication. They can be used as a means of "demanding, imposing or justifying a certain type of behaviour in a relationship" (Jackson, 1977, p. 39). For example, let us use a commonly accepted value of democracy in situations where the family norm prohibits all disagreement: whenever arguing takes place between two people, one member will only have to say "Every one speaks in turn" and the implicit rule of "no-arguments" will be respected. In that sense, values constitute a sort of homeostasis mechanism. In this way, Jackson (1977) says that values, in systems theory, are used as "interpersonal tactical means of sustaining or imposing a norm" (p. 39).

Values in Studies on Family Systems

Using a family case study, Füredi, Magda, Gyula and Novak (1993) demonstrated that values have an influence on a system's homeostasis. A brief presentation of that case illustrates that while values change in society, traditional models of family therapy need to adapt to these changes to enhance family systems' adaptability to new socio-political structures.

Jack, 20 years old, restless, aggressive and depressed, drove his car all day long. His parents were worried about the illness and misbehaviour of their child. Jack's mother and father married each other for differing and conflicting values: the husband married into the woman's financial and moral security and the wife married into the man's power and influential position. At the time of marriage, there was a covert power struggle that focused on which set of traditions and values the son would take up.

The family's situation changed when the mother inherited money from her family and when political changes took place in the country that increasingly depreciated the values represented by the father (his job as party secretary was in jeopardy). Prior to this, there was no requirement for the son to reconcile the family's conflict. When the time arrived for him to choose a career (at the time of the mother's inheritance), Jack found himself in a position where choosing a career meant having to choose between the parents' values associated with their respective careers. His choice was thus considered a value judgment about the parents' careers and included the underlying task of restoring the family's unity. He achieved this task by becoming ill, thus manifesting the symptom of the family's system.

Family therapy helped to resolve the problem by identifying Jack's bind. Identification of his own values and career orientation became possible after his parents took responsibility for their own value conflicts and their corresponding career conflicts.

Northey, Primer and Christensen (1997) present an Ecosystemic Natural Wrap-around model in which the focus of therapy is on a variety of interventions reaching different levels of the family structure and contexts. In this model, clinicians are urged to avoid potential forms of social control in the context of therapy on the basis of the belief that "each system's organization results from the unique interpretation and combination of several factors" (Cimmarusti, 1992, in Northey et al., 1997, p. 8). In order that therapists respect the constructivism perspective, the system's unique form of being a system should not be subject to external control. It should, instead, be attended to according to its own unique values. Trying to impose values coming from the dominant culture proves to be counter-productive. The reverse is recommended: while accounting for "the plethora of influences that maintain problematic interactions [...] it is vital to keep in mind the importance of respecting the family values and meaning attributed to their behaviour" (Northey et al. 1997, p. 19). This is developed in the following premises of the Wrap-around model that has been used mostly in working with offenders:

1. Values embraced by a family at the beginning of therapy need not be changed or replaced by values deemed necessary by the therapist (e.g., middle class standards).
2. Long-standing values, beliefs, patterns of interaction, and patterns of attachment in a family and extended family provide a comprehensive assessment of the individual's environment. These, however, must be considered along with individual's intrapsychic experience.
3. Values associated with ethnicity, religion and socio-economic status may conflict with overriding values of the larger culture in which the family is embedded. Asking a family to do something that is against their beliefs or values is counterproductive.
4. Integration of the intrapsychic, family systems, and ecosystemic perspectives will more likely decrease the disso-

nance between the multiple players involved with the delinquent. Accounting for the culture, including differing values of the helping and social control systems along with those of the offender and the family, is essential in providing a truly effective intervention. These recommendations support the idea that family values play an important role in maintaining homeostasis.

Burr (1991) presented a typology identifying three levels of abstraction in family processes. These levels are used to clarify differences in issues identified in family structures. They also correspond to degrees of change (first-order, second-order or reorientation) occurring in families in therapy. The higher levels of abstraction correspond to lower levels of change and are associated with family values, paradigms, and worldview:

1. The first level processes are the least abstract: they are fairly specific, observable, and concrete as patterns of behaviour occurring in temporal, spatial, developmental, and ecosystemic contexts. They are also called transformation processes because they transform, change, exchange, and allocate such things as time, energy, space, concern, money, frustration, creativity, distance and closeness, boredom, love, care, anger, affection, control, power, emotions, and attention in ways that are designed to help the family attain their goal (this level corresponds to first-order change).

2. The intermediate level processes are more abstract than Level-I processes and less abstract than Level-III. This level refers to the structure of the system, the meta-communication and meta-rules, metaphors, the social, political and legal decision-making, the organizational change, the ability to change. This level corresponds to second-order change.

> As long as the parents are thinking about which method of discipline to use ... they are using Level-I transformation. However, if they ... were to back off and think at the more abstract level, (meta-level or Level-II) they might wonder whether they could accomplish their goal better by doing something other than disciplining the child. (Burr, 1991, pp. 442-443)

3. Family values are considered to comprise the highest or most abstract level, along with family paradigms, worldview, etc. (This level corresponds to reorientation or conversion).

Values associated with the third level refer to highly abstract beliefs within families, that is, they refer to individual basic values and value orientations that are part of shared, fundamental, and assumptive beliefs of families. Paradigms refer to enduring, fundamental, and shared assumptions that families create about the nature and meaning of life, of what is important, and how to cope with the world in which they live; they are rarely explicit or conscious.

Burr (1991) suggests that the lowest probability for family problems to occur is when there is a moderately high amount of Level-I change in family systems and that the lowest probability for family problems to occur is when there is relatively little Level-II change. This relationship is proposed because *no* change in Level-II processes would be disabling. Also, since Level-II changes deal with relatively fundamental and enduring aspects of family systems, a *large* amount of these changes would be more disruptive than a large amount of Level-I changes. With regard to the amount of change in Level-III processes, Burr thinks that some changes in these abstract process would be helpful, but it would be very disabling for families to experience much change in these fundamental aspects of their systems.

According to Burr (1991), developmental phenomena need to be viewed as important contingencies. "When families encounter major developmental transitions," Burr states, "it may be that larger amounts of Level-II and Level-III change are enabling" (Burr, 1991, p. 446). Burr explains that the ability to create change in family paradigms may be helpful during courtship, during the initial stages of living together, and for a period of time after marriage. However, during other stages of family development, change could become more disruptive. Yet, when families encounter severe stress, it is helpful to have more Level-III change.

Values in Systems Theory and Fundamental Values

The understanding of values in systems theory shares a certain number of characteristics with Fundamental Values as observed in the research by Morin (1999). The following comprises a list of characteristics pertaining to values from a systems approach. In systems approach, values

1. Exist *a priori* (initially) and lead to certain models of interaction.
2. Are manifest and identifiable.
3. Are impersonal, relative to content and individual, relative to form.
4. Do not come from families considered as a whole but from individuals in a family system.
5. Are unique to a person but can be shared by others.
6. Can have interpersonal implications.
7. Can be put forward as a means of demanding, imposing or justifying certain interpersonal behaviours in a relationship.
8. Constitute a sort of homeostasis mechanism.
9. Are considered to pertain to the highest level of abstraction along with family paradigms and world-view.

As stated in the first section of this paper, Fundamental Values are considered to be basic or core values that unify all other values or yearnings in an individual's life or identity. They are thought of as the expression of one's aspiration for transpersonal and ultimate goods in each member of a system. Fundamental Values can only find complete fulfillment in an individual's relationship to God. Limited goods will never do more then partly fulfill such yearnings or values. Comparison between the definition of Fundamental Values and the notion of values in systems approach makes us identify distinctions between the two: Fundamental Values are not usually manifest or impersonal. They are rarely explicit because people tend to be unaware of them and of their influence on their lives. Yet Fundamental Values identified in clients' discourse (presented earlier) correspond to many of the characteristics and roles played by and found in values from a systems theory perspective. The following characteristics related to values in a systems approach can also correspond to the Fundamental Values definition and role in an individual's personality

1. These values exist *a priori* (initially).
2. These values are identifiable and individual.
3. The can be put forward as a means of demanding, imposing or justifying certain interpersonal behaviours in a relationship (the organization of relationships is based on an attempt to fulfill one's Fundamental Value).
4. These values constitute a sort of homeostasis mechanism for all other values in the personality because they are organized around this one Fundamental Value.
5. Along with family paradigms and worldview, these values belong to the highest level of abstraction because they pertain to an individual's deepest identity and influence the choice of things considered valuable by each member of the system.

The characteristics stated above (numbers 1 to 5) correspond to the characteristics of paradigms that are the enduring, fundamental, and shared assumptions families create about the nature and meaning of life, what is important, and how to cope with the world in which they live. This rapprochement allows us to consider Fundamental Values as being part of the category of the highest level of abstraction. This is also supported by the fact that Fundamental Values are neither manifest nor impersonal, because they tend to be unconscious. Although some differences are found between Fundamental Values and numbers 2 and 3 from the systems approach, this correspondence between Fundamental Values and paradigms appears obvious. The characteristics presented in the first set at numbers 1, 2, 3, 6, 7, and 8 correspond to characteristics applicable to Fundamental Values, presented at numbers 1 to 5 in the second set.

Because they are fundamental to an individual's identity, Fundamental Values play a fundamental role in influencing a system's basic organization. Since paradigms refer to enduring, fundamental and shared assumptions created by families — their assumptions about the meaning of life and world-view — it seems accurate to recognize that Fundamental Values constitute the basis of systems' paradigm and, therefore, influence the establishment of the interaction model that maintain the system's homeostasis.

Fundamental Values and Homeostasis

The hypothesis presented at the beginning of this paper can be justified on the basis of the comparisons made above. From these comparisons we may infer that Fundamental Values play an important role in the establishment of the system's interaction model and that they constitute a core element in the homeostasis mechanism. This can be illustrated by the following scenario.

When two persons meet to form a relationship, each person brings with them their Fundamental Value that plays an implicit but important role in the formation of the system's interaction model. The process of falling in love, which is characterized by a sense of having found the "perfect" person to suit one's fundamental aspiration, can easily be understood as resulting from a strong impression of having found the partner that can fulfill one's Fundamental Value. Since Fundamental Values refer to transpersonal yearning that can only be completely fulfilled in relationship to God, there will be a strong tendency on part of the couple to live out the illusion that the partner will completely fulfill his/her Fundamental Value. To accommodate the couple's mutual yearnings, both work towards the establishment of a system's interaction model.

When children arrive, the interaction model established on the basis of the couple's Fundamental Values prevails and is imposed on the children with the hope that they, too, will correspond to the parents' yearning. The couple's interaction model will also influence the children's development in the sense that the parents will demand, impose or justify certain interpersonal behaviours. However, the children's demands that are addressed on the basis of their own unique personality or under the influence of environmental events, invite the interaction model to adapt to new circumstances. When this occurs, parents tend to experience such demands as a threat to the fulfillment of their Fundamental Value and to the homeostasis that maintains the interaction model.

Trying to maintain equilibrium or to adapt to the new demands can be interpreted as a homeostasis mechanism based on the individuals' yearning to fulfill their Fundamental Values. When a system's interaction model is invited to change, clinicians may interpret that the family members will need to find new and better ways of allowing each individual's Fundamental Value to be fulfilled. This process implies recognizing that members of the family can never be the sole providers of such fulfillment. They need to be considered as being a reflection of what God, as the ultimate provider of ultimate goods, offers. The members of the system can then assume the ultimate fulfillment of their Fundamental Values individually through their relationship with God — through prayer or other religious or spiritual rituals and with the help of others, including family members. In doing so, demands will be diminished on family members to respond to each other's fundamental yearnings. Consequently, the dysfunctional interaction model will also be reduced.

On the basis of this reflection, we feel confident to say that Fundamental Values constitute a core element in the way homeostasis is found and maintained. This is how we can clearly present the influence of Fundamental Values in the organization of systems.

This hypothesis is illustrated by the following clinical case study using a couple's Fundamental Values (presented above): Security about her Identity (the wife's) and Security about the Worth of his Identity (the husband's) — the logic presented in this case illustration is tied to systems approach and thus, can be applied to family systems as well as couples. From a systemic theory perspective, the subject's relationship was described from the following sequence punctuation (series of uninterrupted exchanges): the wife accuses her husband, through outbursts of anger, of being irresponsible; the husband justifies his distance through logical explanation; the husband's reaction makes the wife even more angry and the wife's anger makes the husband distance himself more and react more logically, and so forth. This type of interaction results in endless pathological escalation and this corresponds to the model of interaction established by this couple.

A couple's type of interaction usually reveals important underlying issues. The wife's angry outbursts prevent her from feeling the pain of loneliness and the husband's logical explanations prevent him from feeling the guilt of being irresponsible. The wife, as a child, was adopted by a woman of a different race and she had very little contact with her adoptive father. She knew of her biological family but was unable to identify with them. She married her husband because of his patience, understanding and laid-back attitude, the opposite of what she inherited from her family of origin. The husband's father expected a lot of him because he was the oldest, but he never complimented him. His father was often violent towards him. The husband married his wife because of her strong will, independence, and sense of organization, the opposite of what he received from his family. Their model of interaction is an effort to maintain these advantages, although it may not produce the expected results.

The results from our research indicate the wife's Fundamental Value was Security about her Identity and the husband's Fundamental Value was Security about the Worth of his Identity. The similarity in the couples' Fundamental Values can be explained by the fact that partners attract one another because of the resemblance in their Fundamental Values. The wife interpreted the husband's qualities of patience, understanding and being laid-back as his unconditionally accepting her the way she was. This gave her a sense of security about her identity. Each time that the husband did not live up to these qualities, the wife would be in pain because her Fundamental Value was unfulfilled. The husband appreciated the wife's qualities of strong will, independence and sense of organization because it took away the guilt he felt in situations where he felt to be a failure or irresponsible. This strengthened and preserved his sense of self-worth. Whenever his wife screamed at him for being irresponsible, the husband became logical in order to prevent himself from feeling the intolerable impression of not being worthy in both her and his estimation.

From this point of view, Fundamental Values constitute a core element in the mechanism of homeostasis in the couple's system. However, values serve this purpose in a way that differs from Jackson's understanding of the role of values in systems. Fundamental Values operate at an implicit level, that is, they allow for the imposition or justification of certain interpersonal behaviours in the relationship. In this sense, Fundamental Values are intrinsically part of the implicit rules that determine the interaction model in the relationship.

Fundamental Values, Myths and Symptoms

The understanding of myths can be refined given the clarification of the role and place of Fundamental Values in systems. The positive image that a couple or a family has about itself can be influenced by the sense of duty that members should fulfill their Fundamental Values. This is possible because a myth is based on the way interactions are structured and on the rules that govern the organization of such interactions.

In the case of the couple described above, the myth was "We are perfect for each other." Whenever they were faced with an argument, both the wife and the husband wondered how such a thing could happen since both felt so perfectly matched. Whenever a member of the system believes that he/she must fulfill another member's Fundamental Value, he/she cannot be loved and accepted for himself or herself. This member is loved and accepted only under a specific condition: that of responding to the other's Fundamental Value. No matter how perfect each partner may be, he or she can never fulfill the other partner's Fundamental Value. For a relationship to be fulfilling, each has to renounce his or her unrealistic expectation of the other. To do this, the members of a couple have to admit they are not perfectly matched. To contradict the family myth, however, is generally painful because this is viewed as being disloyal to the system.

It often occurs that family members adhere to the family myth through the interaction between parent sub-systems and children sub-systems. Because of their position of authority, parents are able to impose a mode of interaction based on their Fundamental Value. Whenever the interaction model prevents individual members from exercising their own personality, the children's individual identity is neglected in favour of the myth. Therefore, the discrepancy between the family myth and the family member's personal identity creates a paradoxical situation in which the individual must choose between a false identity in order to be in tune with the family myth or to assert his or her real identity through behaviours that confront the system and its myth. In this context, personal Fundamental Values may be sacrificed to the benefit of the family myth. Parents who are the first agents in the establishment of the family systems tend to impose their values on the children, whose values, in turn, are sacrificed to the benefit of the parents' values. The family member with the problematic behaviour (the symptom) is identified as the one most threatening to the illusion of the family myth. This person's Fundamental Value may differ the most from the values of the other members of the system.

The purpose of the myth, therefore, is to ensure that each member believes that his/her Fundamental Value is fulfilled in the interaction model adopted by the system. In doing so, it maintains homeostasis. To allow the real fulfillment of Fundamental Values to occur, the myth must be changed. Family systems must face the real image of the system, an image that is incomplete, imperfect, and most of all, one that needs to be open to God and to find homeostasis through spiritual or religious values.

Conclusion

The hypothesis that Fundamental Values constitute a core element in the mechanism of a system's homeostasis offers an interesting opening for pastoral counsellors to include the religious and spiritual dimension in their work with couples and families. In addition to constructivism, a religious and spiritual perspective also can explain a system's tendency to maintain equilibrium, that is, homeostasis. In this way, religious and spiritual values and openness to God are added means available to fulfill one's Fundamental Values. Realizing that God alone can completely fulfill one's Fundamental Value has the advantage of reducing the intensity of expectations and demands that family members may have on one another. When facing limitations in a partner and in children, spiritual or religious people will rely on prayer and worship and on their relationship with God to fulfill their Fundamental Value. Whatever cannot be fulfilled by other members of the family can be fulfilled by God, who is the Ultimate answer to our quest, the Ultimate quench of our thirst, and the Ultimate source in the fulfillment of our Fundamental Values. Thus differences in individuals' Fundamental Values and limitations in their capacity to fulfill each other's Fundamental Value will not be so threatening to the system's homeostasis. The real homeostasis, thus, will ultimately be found in the opening up to and relying upon God.

References

Assagioli, R. (1965). *Psychosynthesis: A manual of principles and techniques.* New York: The Viking Press.

Ausloos, G., (1985). Vers un fonctionnement systémique de l'institution. *Thérapie familiale, 6*(3), 235-242.

Braithwaite, V., (1982). The structure of social values: Validation of Rokeach's two-value model. *British Journal of Social Psychology, 21*, 203-211.

Braithwaite, V. & Scott, W. (1991). *Values.* San Diego, Academic Press.

Burr, W. R. (1991). Rethinking levels of abstraction in family systems theories. *Family Process, 30*, 435-452.

Decarvalho, R.J. (1992).The humanistic ethics of Rollo May. *Journal of Humanistic Psychology, 32*(1), 7-18.

Elkaim, M. (1989). *Si tu m'aimes ne m'aime pas: Approche systemique et psychotherapie.* Paris, Edition du Seuil.

Ferreira, A. (1981) Les mythes familiaux, In P.Watzlawick et J.Weakland, *Sur l'interaction, Palo Alto, 1965-1974, Une nouvelle approche thérapeutique*, Paris: Seuil.

Füredi, J. Magda, B. Gyula, K. & Novak, J., (1993). Family therapy in a transitional society. *Psychiatry, 56*, 328-336.

Gibbins, K. & Walker, I. (1993). Multiple Interpretations of the Rokeach Value Survey. *The Journal of Social Psychology, 133*, 797-805.

Giorgi, A., (1985). Sketch of a psychological phenomenological method. In A. Giorgi, *Phenomenology and psychological research*, Dusquesne: Dusquesne University Press.

Gorsuch, R.L., (1984). R. B. Cattell: An integration of psychology and ethics. *Multivariate*

Behavioural Research, 19, 209-220.

Hagues, H, W. J. (1993). Toward a Systemic Explanation of Valuing. *Counseling and Values, 38*(1), 29-41.

Jackson, D. D. (1977). L'étude de la famille. In P. Watzlawick & J. Weakland, *Sur l'interaction, Palo Alto, 1965-1974, Une nouvelle approche thérapeutique*. Paris: Seuil.

Kluckhohn, C. K. M. (1951). Values and value-orientations in the theory of action: An

exploration in definition and classification. In T. Parson & E. Skils (Eds.), *Toward a General Theory of Action*, 388-433. Cambridge, MA.: Harvard University Press.

Maslow, A. (1968). *Toward a psychology of being*. Princeton, NJ: Van Nostrand.

May, R. (1969). *Love and will*. New York: Norton.

Meissner, W. W. (1970). Values as psychological. *Journal of Religion and Health, 9*, 233-249.

Morin, M. L. (1993). *L'approche systémique: apercu general et applications en toxicomanie*. Unpublished Master's Research. University of Sherbrooke, Social Work Department, Sherbrooke, Québec.

Morin, M. L., (1999). Counselling pastoral et valeur fondamentale individuelle. *Sciences Pastorales, 18*, 25-47.

Morin, M. L., (2001). *Pour une écoute en profondeur: la valeur fondamentale.* Montréal: Médiaspaul.

Northey, W. F., Primer, V., & Christensen, L., (1997). Promoting justice in the delivery of services to juvenile delinquents: The ecosystemic natural wrap-around model. *Child and Adolescent Social Work Journal, 14*(1), 5-22

Olson, D. H., Russell, C. S., & Sprenkle, D. H., (1983), Circumplex model of marital and family systems: VI. Theoretical update. *Family Process, 22*, 69-83.

Prigogine, I., & Stengers, I., (1984). *Nouvelle Alliance* (Order out of chaos: man's new dialogue with nature). Boulder, CO: Random House.

Purzner, K. (1988). Psychoanalysis and therapeutic crisis induction: Affect and emotions as a prerequisite of radical change. *Psychopathology, 22*, 143-148.

Rokeach, M. (1973). *The nature of human values.* New York: The Free Press.

Saint-Arnaud, Y. (1988). (Director of research) Masters Thesis Seminars on Psychosynthesis. *Institute of Pastoral Counselling.* Ottawa: St. Paul University.

Taylor, C., (1989). *Sources of the self, the making of the modern identity*, Cambridge: Harvard University Press.

Treurniet, N., (1988). On having and giving value. *Sigmund Freud House Bulletin. 13*(1), 1-14.

Van Caloen, B., (1993). Travail avec les familles et les réseaux sociaux. *Systems Approach Class Manual.* University of Sherbrooke, Social Work Department, Sherbrooke, Québec.

Von Bertalanffy, L. (1980). *General system theory: Foundations, development, applications.* New York: George Braziller.

Von Glasersfeld, E. (1988). Introduction à un constructivisme radical. In P.

Watzlawick, *L'invention de la réalité.* Paris: Seuil.

Chapter 7

Le désir, marque structurante de l'être humain: Systématisation de la théorie du désir chez Denis Vasse*

Claude Mailloux

La société contemporaine propose le bonheur par la satisfaction de tous les désirs. Que ce soit maintenant ou au moment de la retraite, nous sommes promis(es) au rassasiement tant et si bien que la question du bonheur ne devrait même plus se poser. Pourtant, le fait qu'il y ait autant de gens déprimés, désabusés de la vie ou en crise existentielle est une réalité difficile à cacher. Leurs existences posent le problème d'un désir qui ne semble pouvoir être comblé par les possessions matérielles.

La préoccupation de ce chapitre trouve son point de départ dans la constatation d'un mal de vivre très présent à l'époque contemporaine. Ce mal de vivre soulève la question de ce qui fait réellement vivre l'être humain. Le paradigme contemporain, qui vise à atteindre le bonheur par la satisfaction de tous les désirs, semble vicié à la racine parce qu'il ne produit pas les fruits

---

*Révision d'une présentation faite dans le cadre de la troisième conférence annuelle de la Société de Recherches en Counselling Pastoral, Université Saint-Paul, Ottawa, 11 mai 1996.

attendus. Denis Vasse (1969, 1991) propose dans son œuvre l'inversion de ce paradigme. Il prétend que la satisfaction des désirs pluriels ne fait pas vivre mais que l'être humain est plutôt convié à se mettre en route vers le désir singulier qui l'anime.

Ce renversement de perspective qualifie le mal de vivre en tant que dérèglement de la vie du désir. Vue sous cet angle, la thérapie du mal de vivre devient une thérapie du désir qui fait passer de l'éclatement fantasmatique du désir à la redécouverte de celui-ci, singulier, comme mouvement vital de la personne. Vasse intègre de ce fait les données du vécu psychologique et de l'expérience religieuse. La vie du désir se situe à l'articulation de la psychologie et de la théologie. Plus encore, la vie du désir s'incarne d'une manière unique dans la vie réelle d'un individu inséré dans un contexte social particulier.

Afin de comprendre ce modèle anthropologique, il faut ramasser, sous la forme d'un système théorique, les enseignements de Vasse sur le désir. La première section de ce chapitre relate la construction d'une grille de forme utilisée pour la cueillette des donnés. La cueillette des triplets de sens nécessite un processus continu de réélaboration des définitions conceptuelles au fur et à mesure que les données s'accumulent en élargissant la compréhension des concepts. Cela demande plusieurs exercices de cueillette. La seconde section élabore la mise en modèle de la théorie vassienne à partir d'une clé interprétative découverte dans le corpus à l'étude. La troisième section aborde la question du désir et de la structuration humaine à partir de la mise en modèle obtenue à l'étape précédente. La conclusion du chapitre ouvre sur l'éclairage possible que cette théorie du désir propose au problème du mal de vivre. Dans la perspective en question, le mal de vivre indique un repliement de la dimension aspirative de la personne sur sa vie psychique et son enfermement dans un imaginaire réfractaire à la question du sens à la vie.

Cueillette et analyse sommaire des données

Il faut définir une méthode de cueillette et d'analyse des données qui permette d'étudier à fond et fidèlement la partie des écrits de Vasse retenus pour le traitement de la question. Pour ce faire, il convient de

> découper l'information en unités informationnelles, classer ces unités en thèmes ou en catégories, [...] dénombrer, corréler, comparer ces unités par toutes sortes de traitement, *etc.*, voilà des opérations « classiques de l'analyse » de contenu (Mayer *et al*, 1991, p. 480).

L'analyse de contenu permet de s'attaquer au contenu manifeste des écrits de Vasse et de répondre aux besoins de la recherche. La grille retenue pour la cueillette des données s'intéresse à la relation de signifiance qui unit un premier terme à un second.

Cette forme est assimilable à un triplet relationnel. Le premier élément du triplet correspond à une première catégorie, un terme détecté dans le texte et lié de près ou de loin au désir. Le deuxième élément relève d'une seconde catégorie définie elle aussi par le même procédé. Enfin, le troisième et dernier élément cerne la relation qui existe entre les deux premiers éléments (Voir la Figure 1). C'est cette forme particulière qui est appelée triplet relationnel, ou triplet de sens, dans la suite du texte. En fait, ces triplets devraient être appelés quintuplés en raison des deux éléments supplémentaires qu'ils comportent: l'identification de

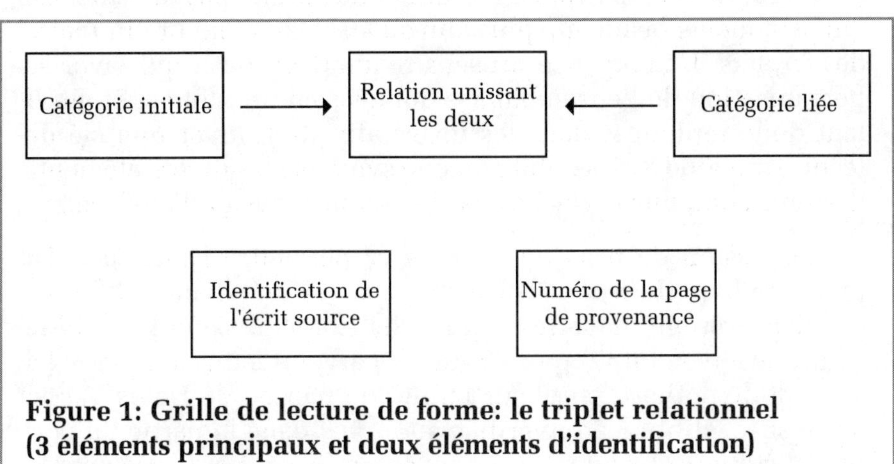

Figure 1: Grille de lecture de forme: le triplet relationnel (3 éléments principaux et deux éléments d'identification)

la source et le numéro de page spécifique d'où le triplet est tiré. Ces éléments étant d'importance relative moindre dans la recherche du sens, le terme de triplet relationnel est conservé.

La seule lecture au moyen d'une grille de forme est insuffisante au point de vue méthodologique. Il faut adjoindre la confection d'un lexique des termes vassiens afin de définir les catégories utilisées. Cette étape d'analyse apparaît préalable à une bonne cueillette et à un bon traitement des données. Comment est-il possible d'analyser adéquatement par une grille de forme de concepts non définis et par trop flottants? Et, en même temps, comment définir *a priori* des concepts sans d'abord les comprendre à l'aide de la méthode choisie? En pratique, le lexique est établi de manière intuitive à partir d'une première lecture. Et il a est ensuite corrigé par un processus de va-et-vient continu entre les deux temps de la méthode. Il y a, en fin de compte, re-vérification continue de chacun des mouvements de la méthode.

La cueillette des données génère un peu plus de mille cinq cents triplets relationnels qui peuvent être regroupés sous trente-six catégories principales. La Table 1 présente les trente-six catégories de classement obtenues à partir de l'ensemble des données.

Mise en modèle de la théorie vassienne du désir

En lui-même, le triplet relationnel ne permet pas une analyse qui peut mener beaucoup plus loin qu'au classement préliminaire des triplets. L'émergence du sens requiert un outil qui favorise l'organisation de l'ensemble des données en un tout cohérent. Il faut donc replonger dans les textes afin de trouver une clé de lecture qui aide à rassembler en une synthèse les divers éléments des sens contenus et révélés par le premier niveau d'analyse.

L'émission de trois hypothèses va permettre l'avancée. La première hypothèse consiste à supposer qu'une théorie du désir est bien présente dans les écrits sous examen. Cette hypothèse s'infirme advenant l'impossibilité de parvenir à une synthèse. La seconde hypothèse porte sur l'unité de pensée de Denis Vasse, unité susceptible d'être vérifiée au moins dans la partie du corpus à l'étude. Cette hypothèse peut être infirmée par la découverte

Table 1

Regroupement des données par mot clef et fréquence d'apparition

Mot-clef (catégorie principale)	Sous catégorie 1	Sous catégorie 2	Sous catégorie 3	Fréquence d'apparition
père	paternel	vide		25
manque	absence			38
inconscient	conscient			45
mort	mourir			48
présent	présence			48
prière	demande			49
foi	peur			49
volonté	vouloir			50
lieu				55
mensonge	orgueil			57
ouverture	faille			58
Acte	action	service		60
travail	œuvre			60
objet				66
témoi(gne-gner et n)	révéler	signe	révélation	74
origine	originaire			75
Réel	impossible			76
amour	aimer			82
connaissance	connaître	compréhension	comprendre	82
besoin	besogne			83
renoncement	renoncer	détachement	détacher	90
sujet				92
don	pardon			95
vérité	vrai	humilité		106
image	imaginaire	possible		109
esprit	âme	spirituel		109
rencontre	rapport	référence	relation	112
être	exister			123
Dieu	Christ			128
Vie	vivant			129
loi	limite	interdit		132
même	soi	moi	fusion + fondre	212
parole	parle			314
A(a)utre	A(a)ltérité	différence		445
désir	attente			513
homme	humain	corps	chair	633

de contradictions importantes dans les données recueillies. Enfin, la dernière hypothèse porte sur la valeur des données recueillies. Elle suppose une égale importance des triplets de sens qui constituent l'ensemble des données recueillies. En d'autres termes, il faut émettre que le résultat de l'analyse arrive au même point indépendamment de la position de départ retenu. Une fois de plus, la découverte de contradictions importantes dans les résultats à partir de points de départ différents infirme, après coup, l'hypothèse de la valeur égale des éléments des données.

Une fois ces hypothèses en place, il devient possible de s'attaquer au travail de formulation d'une synthèse à l'aide d'une clé interprétative fournie dans le texte de Vasse. Cette précieuse clé se découvre dans sa compréhension du corps humain. Il place l'unité du corps de l'humain au point d'intersection de trois axes différentiels. Sa définition d'un axe différentiel correspond à un axe caractérisé par deux pôles, ou vecteurs, opposés maintenus écartés l'un de l'autre à l'origine. Ces axes sont différentiels dans le sens que la différence est maintenue sans réduire l'un des termes à l'autre, ni rejeter l'un ou l'autre des termes ou bien les deux à la fois. À l'origine, ces axes ont pour particularité que leur "différence est l'unité" (Vasse 1991, p. 228) entre eux-mêmes.

La nature différentielle des axes correspond, à peu de choses près, à la définition vassienne du désir qui tient ensemble les différences sans les réduire ni les exclure. Donc, ces axes différentiels sont des axes de désir. Celui-ci cherche les différences et s'exprime dans l'union féconde des deux termes dans la rencontre intersubjective. L'union se produit à l'origine et de celle-ci jaillit l'altérité qui donne à chacun son identité profonde. L'altérité caractérise en propre chaque partenaire de la rencontre au niveau de son identité profonde qui est son identité dans la vie et pas seulement son "moi" ou sa personne sociale. L'altérité de chacun lui échappe ainsi qu'à tous les autres dans le mouvement même qui rend chacun inaliénable à toute prise. L'altérité échappe en se laissant chercher. L'Autre caractérise ainsi cette échappée propre à l'altérité.

À l'instar de Vasse, notre modèle synthétique propose un système de trois axes différentiels au croisement desquels se situe l'unité de l'être humain dans son corps. Ce point de croisement, l'origine, est représenté par l'Autre sous trois aspects particuliers. Le premier aspect est celui d'Origine; il s'agit ici du père symbolique cher à la psychanalyse et de la figure du Dieu chrétien vu comme Père. Le second aspect de l'Autre est celui de la Parole; il s'agit ici du langage étudié par la psychanalyse lacanienne et du Verbe, Fils du Père, engendré par le Père. Le troisième aspect de l'Autre est celui de l'Esprit; il s'agit ici de l'esprit de l'homme dont parle Lacan (1966) et de l'Esprit de Dieu qui procède du Père et du Fils.

L'Autre se situe à l'origine d'un système d'axes différentiels (Voir la Figure 2) tridimensionnel. Une première dimension est celle de la différence sexuelle. On y trouve la Femme et de l'Homme unis par l'Autre dans son aspect de Père originaire qui suscite et maintient les différences individuelles. La seconde dimension se caractérise par la Vérité et le Mensonge. L'Autre sous son aspect de Parole assure l'unité entre ces deux opposés en autorisant l'humain à vivre à partir d'une vérité humaine limitée par les apories de sa connaissance. Finalement le dernier axe est celui de la Vie et de la Mort retenus ensemble par l'Esprit qui anime la chair.

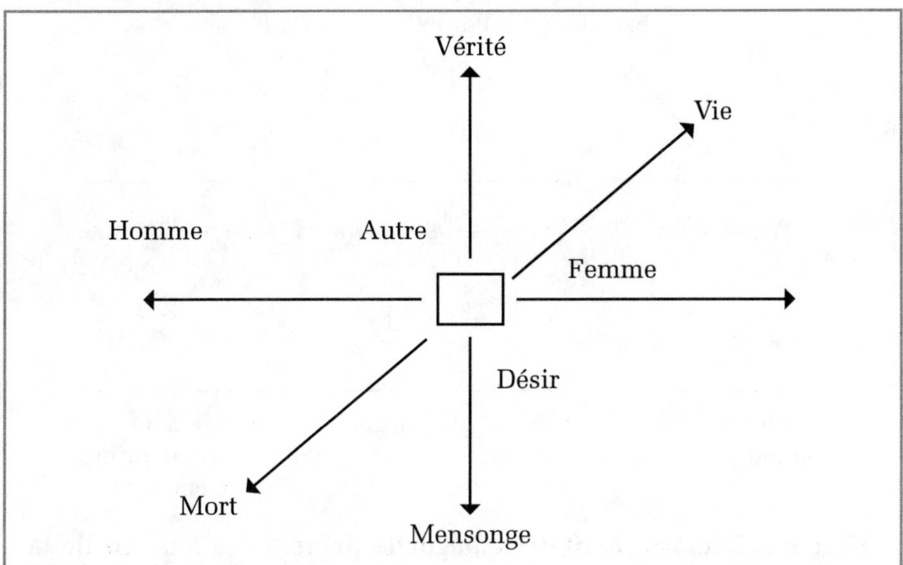

Figure 2: Modèle interprétatif de la théorie vassienne du désir

Dans la théorie de Vasse, l'être humain vit de ce que, en lui, des opposés qui peuvent s'exclure de manière radicale, s'unissent dans un mouvement qui ne rejette ni ne réduit aucun des termes en aucune manière. Ce mouvement d'union des différences est le désir qui fait vivre (Voir la Figure 3). La désunion de la différence se produit lorsque la tension n'est plus maintenue entre les différences au moment ou l'un des termes de la relation tente de consommer l'autre à son profit ou de le supprimer. Au désir qui fait vivre s'oppose la dislocation qui cherche à réduire l'autre à soi afin de se préserver dans la vie.

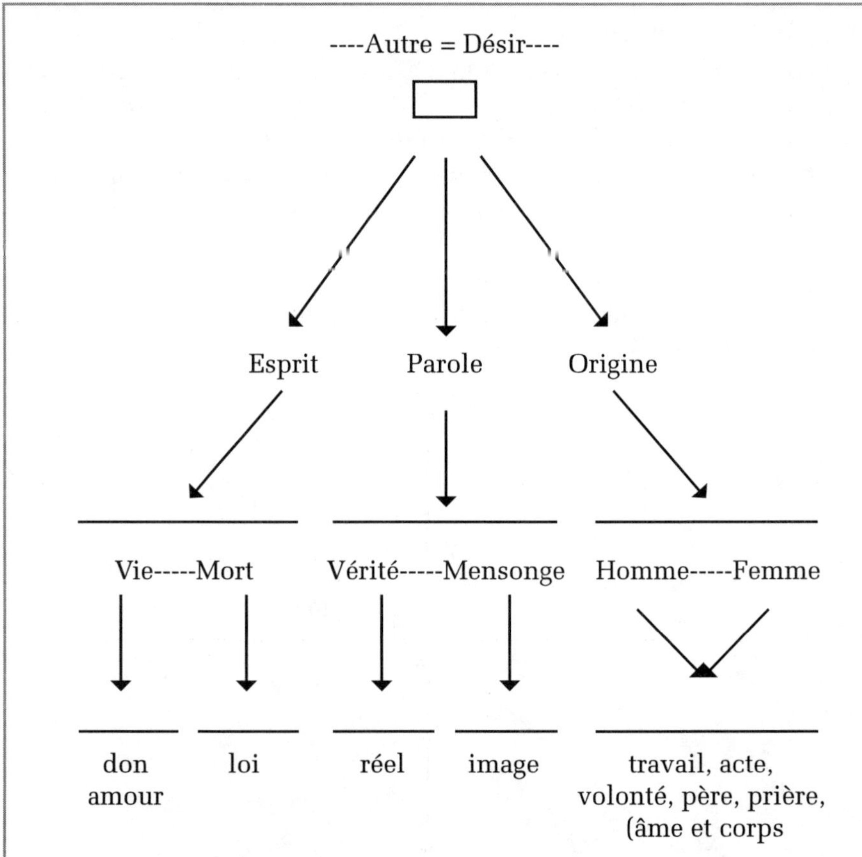

Figure 3: Reclassement des catégories principales à partir de la mise en modèle

Désir et structuration humaine

Le titre de ce chapitre présente le désir en tant que marque structurante de l'être humain. Qu'est-ce-que ceci signifie? Pour répondre, il convient de se situer dans une perspective développementale en remontant au commencement de la vie. Au moment de sa naissance, le poupon dépend radicalement des soins d'une personne. Dans le sens de sa dépendance radicale, le poupon fait ainsi l'expérience d'une Personne qui représente Tout pour lui ou pour elle. Il semble alors que cette personne puisse être en mesure de le combler ou de le frustrer totalement étant donné son pouvoir de vie ou de mort sur le bébé. "Freud émet comme étant vraisemblable l'hypothèse que le nouveau-né est dans une impression d'unité" (Gauthier 1989, p. 27).

Cette impression d'unité vient de ce qu'à ce stade, l'autre n'a d'existence propre que comme produit à consommer pour la satisfaction d'un besoin. Mais entre cette impression d'unité et l'unité réelle d'un être humain, il y a un énorme pas. L'écart, ou le chemin à parcourir, est constitué par le travail de structuration qui s'effectue sous la poussée du désir. Il convient de le rappeler, le désir vise l'intégration harmonieuse des opposés sans réduire ni rejeter.

Ainsi l'expérience de la "Personne-Tout" permet au nourrisson de passer graduellement du désir de la mère, aplati au besoin de celle-ci, à l'ouverture graduelle vers un véritable désir de présence alors même que le nourrisson a toujours besoin de sa mère. La phrase qui précède énonce une mouvance qui perdure tout au long de la vie humaine et qui, en même temps, court toujours le risque de l'aplatissement sur une pulsion qu'il suffit de satisfaire pour vivre en humain. Le désir de la présence d'un autre, des autres et de l'Autre est ce qui, plus profondément que l'objet à consommer, fait vivre l'être humain.

Le processus de différenciation des autres et de l'Autre se réalise par le renoncement à tout être ou à tout avoir qui est inhérent à la rencontre des autres. Il s'agit pour un humain d'apprendre à renoncer à consommer son semblable pour lui accorder le même degré d'existence qu'à soi-même. L'instrument médiatisant, le renoncement, est la loi de celui ou de celle qui cherche à vivre par amour et non dans le seul refuge du besoin lié à la vie biologique.

Tout l'effet de structuration apparaît dans la résolution d'un conflit assez simple à énoncer. "Si je consomme mon semblable, il n'existe plus comme autre. En conséquent je me retrouve seul." "Si je n'accorde pas aux autres le même statut de sujet inaliénable que je m'accorde en propre, je me réduis moi-même, comme semblable, à un objet à consommer en vue de rassasier un besoin." L'effet structurant se produit dans une tension impossible à résoudre: l'humain est habité de deux dynamiques opposées. D'une part, le besoin réclame sans cesse de nouvelles satisfactions. Son argument est de taille puisque la négligence à répondre à ses ordres peut conduire à la mort du corps physique. D'autre part, le désir ne vit que de chercher la présence de l'Autre, de la différence en laquelle il trouve sa source subjective. Son argument est également convaincant. En lui se joue la naissance d'un sujet désirant, d'un humain pouvant aussi vivre par amour. Dans son corps, l'être humain n'est ni seul besoin ni pur désir; il est union du besoin et du désir. Il est naissance d'un être de désir porté dans un corps de besoin.

La théorie de Vasse mène donc à voir la vie d'une personne humaine comme l'histoire de sa recherche d'une unité besoin/désir qui n'est possible que sous les auspices de l'Altérité. L'unité se présente sous la forme de la transcendance des limites et non dans leur négation ni leur rejet pur et simple. En fin de compte, c'est d'avoir à transcender les limites en les accueillant et en demeurant ouvert à l'Autre qui est structurant pour un être humain. Mais, parce que structurant, le désir maintient également la possibilité du refus. Le refus dans le consentement au désir engendre des paradoxes qui deviennent sans issue autre que la leur propre : l'enfermement en soi-même.

Au regard de l'altérité, trois métaphores symbolisent les impasses propres à la vie humaine. La première métaphore trouve sa place dans le paradoxe de l'accueil de l'Autre et des autres sans se perdre. Il s'agit alors de l'impasse de la fermeture qui se fait passer pour ouverture. Cela se vérifie dans la négation de l'Autre et des autres. Il n'y a que le moi. La volonté de s'ouvrir nie le travail du désir. Selon Vasse, ce n'est pas la volonté qui provoque l'ouverture, mais la souffrance qui, comme traversée, se manifeste sous la mouvance du désir. Le totalitarisme du moi peut également être remplacé par son absence tout aussi délétère. La seconde métaphore porte sur la pensée de l'être humain. Il y a impasse lorsque la pensée s'affirme comme la seule rationalité possible. Elle prétend alors qu'il n'y a rien d'autre qui existe que ce qu'elle arrive à imaginer ou percevoir. La personne s'enferme ainsi dans ses propres productions intellectuelles ou fantasmatiques. Finalement le troisième paradoxe porte sur la transcendance. Il rejoint la difficulté d'accueil de la transcendance du sein de la limite même. Comment un être humain peut-il faire pour accueillir l'illimité, qui lui apparaît comme la négation de sa limite, sans disparaître ni se fermer complètement? Ou bien une personne peut se refuser à suivre son désir en raison de ses limites, ou bien elle se prétend elle-même sans limite. Dans les deux cas, elle se perd dans une fusion avec un idéal interne ou externe.

Conclusion

La fonction structurante du désir, nous venons de le voir, atteint autant la quête de transcendance que celle des idéaux vécus sous le mode des absolus fusionnels. Ces deux opposés forment une structure qui perdure de la naissance à la mort de la personne. Elle se trouve, sa vie durant, immergée dans une situation paradoxale.

Au point de vue psychique, le désir d'altérité va dans le sens de la dé-fusion d'avec les autres, d'avec soi-même et d'avec les absolus de l'enfance. Un minimum de cinq étapes est repérable dans ce processus à jamais en devenir. La première étape consiste dans la prise de conscience de la différence. La seconde étape se présente au moment où la personne commence à tolérer la différence. La troisième émerge avec l'acceptation conditionnelle des différences. L'acceptation inconditionnelle des différences devient possible à la quatrième étape. Finalement, une union pleine peut prendre corps dans une cinquième étape.

Au point de vue de l'expérience religieuse, le même genre de scénario se répète. Seul le niveau change pour rejoindre la question de la transcendance. Le même processus en cinq étapes se reproduit : identification de la différence, tolérance de la différence, acceptation conditionnelle, acceptation inconditionnelle et, finalement, union pleine et libre.

Ce tableau sommaire et prospectif cherche à traduire la direction psychique qui émerge de la théorie vassienne du désir. Cependant, la principale fusion, qui n'a jamais finit d'achever sa course impossible, est la fusion avec l'imaginaire de la vie. Dans l'état actuel de l'esquisse que nous traçons, nous pouvons déjà percevoir que la théorie du désir chez Vasse présente une compréhension où l'on découvre l'être humain divisé en lui-même en même temps qu'il cherche son unité psychique et religieuse.

Nous croyons que cette théorie porte en elle-même des germes de guérison des structures profondes et premières de l'être humain, c'est-à-dire au niveau de la quête de sens à la vie de chaque personne. Du fond d'un camp de concentration nazi, Viktor Frankl témoigne de la profondeur de l'expérience religieuse personnelle. “Quant à l'intérêt religieux, dès qu'il peut germer dans l'âme du déporté, il est d'une nature très profonde et la plus intime qui soit” (Frankl, 1967, p. 68). Frankl (1967) et ses compagnons ont dû puiser à cette source du sens à la vie pour trouver l'énergie de vivre et de mourir.

> Il s'agissait, pour nous, du sens à la vie conçue comme un tout dans lequel la mort est également comprise; et ainsi ne recouvre-t-il pas seulement le sens de « vivre », mais aussi celui de souffrir et de mourir: et c'est pour ce sens-là que nous avons lutté! [...] La souffrance nous était également devenue une tâche, et nous ne voulions pas nous fermer à sa signification. À nous la souffrance a révélé son caractère d'accomplissement (p. 133).

L'expérience de Frankl illustre véritablement la transcendance que lui et ses compagnons ont pu vivre même dans des conditions innommables. Ces personnes ne sont-elles pas parvenues à vivre une expérience réelle de transcendance tout en survivant à des conditions comportant des limites cruelles et arbitraires?

Même si Vasse ne cite pas Frankl parmi ses sources, il est clair que la vie du désir ne peut se soustraire à l'expérience de la souffrance et de la mort. Ces deux expériences nous ramènent directement à la quête de transcendance. Le témoignage de Frankl met en lumière un autre paradoxe de la société contemporaine. Comment pouvons-nous arriver à expliquer que des humains en situation de dénuement extrême ont pu trouver à survivre et à vivre alors que dans notre société d'abondance, des gens de plus en plus nombreux songent à mourir. Le suicide "ne cesse de croître au fil des années, ne pouvant plus être relégué au rang d'événement 'isolé'" (Volant, *et al*, 1990, p. 15). Il est difficile de comprendre ce paradoxe sans référer à la présence ou l'absence de ce désir qui fait vivre: le désir de l'Autre. L'absence correspond à l'aplatissement de la dimension désirante de la personne à la seule dynamique du besoin.

Références

Frankl, V. (1967). *Un psychiatre déporté témoigne*, Paris: Chalet.

Gauthier, J. (1989). *La théopoésie de Patrice de la Tour du Pin*, Montréal/Paris: Bellarmin/Cerf.

Lacan, J. (1966). *Écrits*, Paris: Seuil.

Mailloux, C. (1996). *Le désir de l'Autre chez Denis Vasse.* Ottawa: Université Saint-Paul. Mémoire de maîtrise inédit.

Mayer, R. et Ouellet, F. (1991). *Méthodologie de la recherche pour les intervenants sociaux.* Boucherville: Gaëtan Morin.

St-Arnaud, Y. (1985). *Le counseling pastoral.* Bruxelles: IFOR.

Vasse, D. (1969). *Le temps du désir: Essai sur le corps et la parole.* Paris: Seuil.

Vasse, D. (1989). Une demande d'amour: Que ta volonté soit faite. *CHRISTUS, 144,* 402-413.

Vasse, D. (1991). *L'Autre du désir et le Dieu de la foi. Lire aujourd'hui Thérèse d'Avila.* Paris: Seuil.

Vasse, D. (1992). La plus grande violence. *Laennec*, 24-28.

Volant, E., Douville, M., Boulet M., et Pierre J., (1990). *Adieu la vie. Étude des derniers messages laissés par des suicidés*. Montréal: Bellarmin.

Part Three

Healing in Practice

Chapter 8

A Mother's Healing from a Son's Tragic Burn

Loretta Wiseman

The form that lay on the narrow hospital bed did not move. White and blue gauze bandages covered every part of the body except for the eyes, nose, mouth and fingertips. A collar neck-support held the head motionless. From the doorway I could not tell if this patient was alive. I was about to enter the isolated, sterile room of a burn clinic unit for the first time. And the patient was my son.

We see the images of trauma on the front pages of our daily newspapers and on television; we hear experts recommend prevention and treatment. Yet first-hand experience of a traumatic event provides a hard-earned knowledge of suffering and healing — the extents and limits of one's own internal resources and the range of family, community and professional resources available for support. No amount of reading or research can equal such lessons. In this chapter, I offer my experience of my son Colin's injury and recovery, the most traumatic experience of my life, as an illustration of the process of healing that this book addresses in a more scholarly fashion. Perhaps my account will make more vivid the important topics that the companion chapters explore.

August 9, 1994 began as another pleasant summer day; it ended as a nightmare. The most traumatic experience of my life began in the later part of the evening when two police officers visited our house. Their presence as I opened the door shocked and frightened me. They had come to inform me that our son had been in an accident. In response to my question about the seriousness of the accident, they gave me a hospital name and a number to call. Their manner was calm and sympathetic. My subsequent conversation with the nurse was brief. She told me that Colin had been badly burned and I should come as soon as possible. The full extent of his injuries, including injury to his eye, had not yet been determined. After I phoned my husband Bill at work, the police officers left. Upon Bill's arrival, we made immediate plans for me to go to the hospital which was some distance away.

I arrived in Edmonton around three o'clock in the morning and went directly to the Burn Unit of the University of Alberta Hospital. During the journey to the hospital, I tried to prepare myself. I recalled the information that I had been given. I prayed to God and I bargained with Him. If He would let Colin have his eyesight, then I would accept any other kind of injuries; I could handle anything except his being blind. I imagined Colin with a few bandages on and a machine or two nearby. As I was being led through the door of the Burn Unit into a small isolated room, I realized the futility of my attempts to prepare myself.

The sight of Colin, eyes closed, lying motionless and wrapped in bandages was overwhelming. I was alone in the room except for Bill's sister and her husband who had driven me to the hospital. I sensed their calmness as they approached the bed with me. Colin slowly opened one eye as I held the tips of his fingers. I had a frightening thought that he might be blind and only later did I realize that he had his sight in at least one eye.

After my initial shock I slowly began to learn the facts that Colin could recall. The accident happened at the unloading facilities at Wells Construction Asphalt Plant near Fort Saskatchewan. Hot oil exploded from his truck trailer when a valve released, covering him with hot tar from head to toe. After being thrown some fifteen feet, he crawled to a small water puddle to splash water on his burned arms. He then called for an ambulance.

Up to this point in my life, I had had numerous hospital experiences. I witnessed the illness and eventual death of several close family members. Yet I had never seen such an array of hospital technology. The sight of so many machines, lines and monitors terrified me. I assumed they were symbolic of the gravity of the situation.

From the hospital staff I would learn of the necessity of the tubes and lines that were connected to pumps, machines, and monitors surrounding Colin's bed as he lay flat on his back. A ventilator, cardiac monitor, tube feeding infusion pump, endrotracheal tube, urinary catheter and a patient-controlled analgesia infusion pump (PCA) filled his room. The PCA allowed him to administer his own analgesic under controlled limits. During the next three weeks, at varying times, these machines would be an essential part of his life.

Even visiting Colin was a complicated matter. Before entering the intensive care unit to see him, visitors and staff used an intercom system. In addition, we had to wash our hands and wear a gown each time we entered his room.

Of similar complexity were Colin's injuries; they were major, multiple and extensive. He was suffering from first, second and third degree burns. His back, upper extremities, face and both flanks extending down to his hip regions were involved. We were told that he would require several weeks in the hospital.

Surgery was scheduled four days after the accident. At that time debridement and grafting would be done. Damage to the skin and nerve endings from the burn made it impossible for some of the burned area to heal. Skin would have to be taken from the healthy part of the body and placed on a burn wound area.

Following surgery, another dimension was added to Colin's recovery program. He would spend part of each day with a physiotherapist as he began a healing and strengthening exercise program. Raising his arms high enough to feed himself and walking his first two steps were major accomplishments.

Among the tests and procedures that needed to be carried out daily, there was the precise and detailed measurement procedure for the fitting of a Jobst garment which he would need to wear. For the skin to become as normal as possible, it was necessary for Colin to wear a tight fitting pressure garment called a Jobst garment. It covered his arms, chest and back. He wore it constantly day and night for over a year. He removed it only for showering or laundering purposes.

On August 30, Colin was discharged from the hospital into our care. He would remain living with us until he was able to perform the activities of daily living independently. I had mixed feelings about his return home. I was relieved that he was discharged. I was also anxious to return home and get back into my routine. But I was a bit apprehensive while Colin was still hospitalized. I had made a decision to become his primary caregiver after his discharge. Now I began to have flickerings of doubt as to my capability as caregiver, especially without the assistance of the professional staff. I had been asked by one of the doctors whether I felt confident in changing Colin's bandages and applying dressings after his hospital discharge. I practiced the procedure a few times with a nurse. Colin had large areas of burned and grafted skin. My biggest fear was that I would cause him more pain when touching these tender, unhealed areas. Another thought that was causing me to doubt my capability was the fact that since childhood I could not stand the sight of blood or an open wound without feeling sick. In spite of any doubts or fears, the decision was mine to make, and I chose to be Colin's caregiver. I felt that if Colin could tolerate all that he had been through, I could somehow handle this.

Once we arrived at home, more issues surfaced. Up to this point, our main focus had been on Colin's physical pain and recovery. Now, in addition to these, Colin had to deal with his temporary loss of independence. I knew that he missed his own home, his friends and activities, and his life style before the accident. Colin's caseworker from the Workman's Compensation Board offered to arrange counselling for both Colin and me. We agreed, so were given the name and address of a psychologist. We drove several hours only to find an empty office building. I felt disappointed and rejected. Later we received a phone call from this same professional. She apologized and offered to drive to our home. In talking to her I experienced a certain sense of freedom. I could openly express my anger to her without upsetting anyone. I expressed my feelings about the accident, especially the anger. I was angry that it had happened, that it had upset our lives, and that recovery took so long.

Almost immediately there were medical appointments, trips for garment fittings, sessions with occupational therapists and regular weekly sessions with physiotherapists. All of these involved a lot of traveling, some trips taking many hours, making overnight traveling necessary. One of the family tried to accompany Colin, especially at first when he found it difficult to set for any length of time.

Insomnia became another problem for Colin. He could not remain comfortable in one position for any length of time due to the tightness and tenderness of both burned and grafted skin areas. One treatment that would bring relief was that of frequent back massages and the application of lotions and creams. Since Colin could not manage his own back treatments, I became his night nurse. Getting up several times a night, and then going to work the next day left me exhausted. It was still my decision to continue in doing whatever I could to help in his recovery. In comparison to the pain and suffering that Colin had been through, my problem of fatigue seemed trivial.

The recovery process was sometimes stressful and frustrating because it felt like it moved very slowly. Colin's father and brothers, Brad and Steven, offered their support by accompanying him on some of his numerous trips. They tried to plan activities that they could all do together. Family support got us through some of the rough spots.

During the following year, Colin began yet another challenge as he attempted to return to work. Several times he returned to work only to have to quit a few days later. The back pain that he was experiencing created many difficulties.

Throughout the entire traumatic experience of the accident, the critical hospitalization, the rehabilitation and the long recovery, I experienced many emotions. The first were shock and disbelief when I heard the news; later I felt a certain amount of gratitude when I learned that Colin's eyesight would not be affected by the burn. Fear and pain, frustration and depression were often a part of my day.

Yet throughout those long days, there were scatterings every so often of some feelings that were quite opposite in nature. These were bright and striking, the kind that made me feel proud and grateful. They were comparable to bright twinkling stars that shine amidst the dark skies at night. Colin's positive attitude, brave example and sense of humour were like those bright, twinkling stars which, in turn, became a driving force in my own healing.

Colin's sense of humour impressed everyone who worked with him. There were stories of humorous comments he made to the Emergency Medical Technicians (EMT) on the ambulance trip to the hospital. One story pertained to Colin's suggestion that maybe now he could be a celebrity and appear on the TV show *Rescue 911* to which the EMT responded, "I think you're going to be okay." Colin's bravery and positive attitude were also witnessed by others. "I will never forget how calm you were in the emergency room," and "the most enduring, strong and positive patient to work with" along with the humorous note "fun to bug!" were all comments by hospital staff who got to know him during this three-week stay.

I was grateful for my close and highly supportive nuclear as well as extended family system. They all had a marked influence and important role in aiding the healing of my own grief and pain. During the three weeks that I stayed in the motel room near the hospital, one of the family accompanied me much of the time, either physically, in a telephone conversation, or through correspondence. Through them I had many opportunities to vent my feelings.

Indeed, the care and concern of friends — their calls, visits and cards — helped to brighten a lot of days. The small community in which we lived also offered support. A local service club contributed financial help. A neighbour who was a former burn victim kept in close contact, sharing her own experiences and providing support and encouragement.

Besides family and friends, another group of caring individuals helped in the healing process. Experienced and skilled doctors, nurses, social workers and therapists offered professional explanations and support. They gave us much of their time answering questions and encouraging us. Spending as much time as I did in the hospital gave me the opportunity to observe some commendable nursing care. I took comfort in knowing that Colin was being so well looked after.

My having an active, direct involvement in Colin's care and recovery, whether it was brushing his teeth when he could not raise his arms, changing his dressings and bandages, or giving back massages, was helpful not only to him, but for me also. My work with him also assured me that he was getting care; it was valuable therapy to be active and involved. Although he benefited from my caregiving, my involvement in turn helped my own healing.

After the initial shock passed, I experienced a need to search for information on burns, types, healing, effects on the body and any other associated information. In response to my first questions, I was given a booklet entitled *Introduction to the Burn Unit* by the hospital staff (University of Alberta Hospitals, 1992). It was written by members of the Burn Team that is comprised of doctors, nurses, dietitians, occupational, physical and respiratory therapists as well as social workers. All were involved in Colin's treatment. Four days following the accident, Colin underwent surgery for skin debridement and grafting. Then another search for information began. I needed to know what was involved in the surgery and what we could expect. Once again the nursing staff came to my rescue. They gave me information along with some graphic photos that answered some of my questions. Another valuable resource was the University Hospital Library where I scanned shelves on several occasions looking for relevant available information (e.g., Bernstein, Breslau & Graham, 1988; Bernstein & Robson, 1983; Richard & Stanley, 1994). Having enough information allowed me to become aware of the facts and try to understand what was happening with Colin's injury and treatment. Only then could I begin my healing.

My faith was a source of inspiration and strength in my healing process. In the quietness of the hospital chapel, I looked for strength. Sometimes I experienced an element of peace. I said many prayers in the hospital room as I sat near Colin's bed week after week. It was not only my prayers that gave me comfort; I found strength and hope through the many prayers that others were sending as well. Having the belief that there is a God who is powerful and loving, and having faith that He would give us the strength to face each day, were major sources of healing.

Throughout the entire experience, relationships within our own family unit, which had previously been strong, became further strengthened. In our larger extended family, as well, we had security in the knowledge that we could rely on family members to be present for us whenever we needed their support. My journey towards healing reaffirmed this fact many times.

As I reflect on my healing, I can see links between my experience and the five stages that people go through when faced with tragic news that Kübler-Ross (1969) writes about in her book, *On Death and Dying*. These stages are denial and isolation, anger, bargaining, depression, and acceptance (pp. 38-137).

Shortly after being notified of Colin's accident, I bargained with God (Kübler-Ross, 1969, pp. 82-84). If He would allow Colin to have his eyesight, then I would accept whatever else had happened to him no matter how bad it might be. I begged Him not to take away Colin's eyesight. Later, when I realized that Colin could see with both eyes, I was certainly grateful. Yet I could not completely accept my part of the bargain; I still felt a lot of pain and anger.

Once I reached Colin's hospital room, the reality of the tragedy lay there on the bed facing me. Even though confronted so plainly, I still wanted to think that the doctors were being extra cautious, so maybe it wasn't really as bad as I thought. I was sure that in a day or two some of the wrappings from his body and the machine from his room would be gone; then he would look more himself (Kübler-Ross, 1969, pp. 38-49).

While I never considered myself to be an angry person, I experienced anger more than I wanted to. It angered me that the accident happened, that Colin had to suffer extreme pain, and that new limitations and obstacles changed his life and ours to a certain degree (Kübler-Ross, 1969, pp. 50-81). I was also angered by an unfortunate incident which happened. One night Colin's call button had been moved out of his reach, meaning that he was unable to call for any assistance. The knowledge that he had been left with no way to communicate his needs during the entire night greatly upset and angered me.

I found it easier to remain in a positive state of mind when Colin was still in the hospital and we were surrounded by professional staff who offered support and looked after Colin's needs. In addition, the support of family and friends during that time was very strong. It was more difficult to remain positive once we left the hospital to return to our home. I felt like we were on our own. I missed the close contact of others (Kübler-Ross, 1969, pp. 85-111)

In the fifth stage of her model, Kübler-Ross (1969) writes about a stage of acceptance, "a stage during which he is neither depressed nor angry about his fate" (p. 112). Eventually, after what seemed like a very long time, the realization gradually came to me that I was neither angry nor depressed any more. Recalling Colin's accident on August 9, 1994 and what it entailed, is not a pleasant experience but I am at peace with it. I can accept the fact that it did happen and we lived through it.

Colin's accident on August 9, 1994 was the first major traumatic experience for our family. From the moment I first saw Colin following the accident until his partial recovery much later, I witnessed the manner in which Colin handled tragedy. I saw the inner strength and courage that he possessed in his attempts to overcome many limitations and new obstacles in his daily life. It was a valuable learning experience for me in the sense that it offered me the assurance and the confidence that Colin could handle tough situations in life. As a mother, I found this precious knowledge most reassuring.

References

Bernstein, N.R., Breslau, A.J., & Graham, J.A. (Eds.) (1988). *Coping strategies for burn survivors and their families.* New York: Praeger.

Bernstein, N.R., & Robson, M.C. (Eds.) (1983). *Comprehensive approaches to the burned person.* New York Hyde Park, New York: Medical Examination Publishers.

Kübler-Ross, E. (1969). *On death and dying: What the dying have to teach doctors, nurses, clergy and their own families.* New York: Macmillan Publishers.

Richard, R.R., & Stanley, M.J. (1994). *Burn care and rehabilitation: Principles and practice.* Philadelphia: FA Davis.

University of Alberta Hospitals (1992). *Introduction to the burn unit.* Alberta: University of Alberta Hospitals.

Chapter 9

Bereaved Counsellor Counselling a Bereaved Client: A Journey of Healing

Bernell Anstey*

Resuming my work as a counsellor one week following the unexpected and sudden death of my father, I found myself approaching my work in a vastly different light than before my loss. As a grieving counsellor, I became very concerned about how I might cope with my sorrow while maintaining my professional role in addressing the needs of my client. I feared that my emotions and thoughts arising from my own loss would overcome me despite my best efforts to suppress all affects. I worried about how I would respond if I became overwhelmed by my grief during a session. Since this tragedy in my family, I have observed how, as a counsellor, I have embarked on an emotional journey in search of healing.

Throughout the working lives as counsellors, it is inevitable that we will suffer the loss of a loved one and be confronted by various clinical dilemmas that arise from the loss. Conducting grief therapy as a bereaved counsellor may present complex chal-

---

*I would like to thank Dr. Fred Reekie and Dr. Sam Robinson, College of Education, University of Saskatchewan, Saskatoon, Saskatchewan, for their academic expertise in co-supervising this study.

lenges in therapy including managing countertransference reactions and simply coping with one's own sorrow and increased sense of vulnerability. In my view and experience, grieving the loss of a loved one inevitably affects the work that we as counsellors do.

This research elicited many challenges for myself within my role as the bereaved counsellor. It became evident that supporting my grieving client while searching for my own healing was indeed a challenging endeavor. Not only was it necessary to thoughtfully consider the needs of my client, but also it was necessary to consider my own emotional needs as I grieved the death of my father. As I underwent the challenges of managing countertransference reactions with my client, I experienced the intensity of my own grief. In effectively attending to both the needs of my client and myself, it was imperative that I addressed my own difficulties that arose from my loss including confronting the challenges of mourning and forgiveness.

A review of the literature will be presented including a description of the concept of countertransference, an overview of loss and grief, and a description of the process of forgiveness. The methodology of this study follows the literature review providing details regarding the research method and procedures. The final sections provide a synthesis of the findings and reflections on my journey as a bereaved counsellor conducting grief therapy.

Review of the Literature

Countertransference

Over the past century, the definition of the psychoanalytic concept of countertransference and the effects of countertransference in therapy has been hotly debated. The conceptualization of countertransference has undergone intense examination since Freud first introduced this term to describe inappropriate unconscious and defensive reactions on the part of the therapist toward the patient (Hayes, McCracken, McClanahan, Hill, Harp, & Carozzoni, 1998; Robbins & Jolkovski, 1987). Freud's assertion that countertransference creates strictly adverse effects on the therapeutic process and his subsequent caution to therapists to avoid these reactions with their patients have been widely negated by therapists (Hansen, 1997). This "classical" representation of countertransference was subsequently broadened to consider "all of the counselor's thoughts, feelings, and behaviours to be countertransference manifestations" (Watkins, 1985, p. 356). Unlike the classical definition that considered countertransference reactions to be strictly unconscious defensive reactions, this alternate approach asserted that the reactions could arise from either the conscious or the unconscious. An additional differentiating feature of this approach was the recognition that countertransference could provide a valuable contribution to the therapeutic process when therapists address their own responses to the client by engaging in self-analysis to develop deeper personal insight into their own cognitive, emotional, and behavioural presentations (Peabody & Gelso, 1982). Despite acknowledging the positive value of countertransference within this "totalistic" or more inclusive approach, this definition was inevitably contested for being unduly amorphous and meaningless, as all counsellor's actions or experiences could be defined as countertransference manifestations (Hayes et al., 1998, p. 468). Current understandings of countertransference incorporate aspects from both the classical and totalistic conceptualizations, recognizing that countertransference may arise from the unconscious or conscious and may prove to be either a destructive or constructive facet of therapy (Watkins, 1985). This unnamed approach, which is attentive to the therapist's internal reactions, feelings, and attitudes, is currently favoured and widely accepted by therapists professing that it provides a more realistic view than the classical and totalistic vantages. The principle that countertransference may function as a positive or negative force in counselling is endorsed in this study.

According to Hayes et al. (1998), therapy events that touch on or elicit the therapist's unresolved issues may trigger countertransference reactions. The origin of a therapist's unresolved issue might be provoked by a wide array of events, or triggers, that arise within the counselling situation. In a study conducted by Hayes et al., it was found that events that most frequently triggered countertransference fall within either the domain of the clients' presenting problem (e.g., death, marriage difficulties) or the clients' presenting styles (e.g., hostile, seductive). When a reaction is triggered, the therapist may experience countertransference internally through thoughts and feelings, including anxiety or antipathy for the client, or externally through behaviours, including withdrawing or becoming overinvolved with the client (Robbins & Jolkovski, 1987).

Watkins (1985) contends that countertransference reactions may ensue from the counsellor's ability to identify and share with clients in his or her experiences. When optimal identification occurs, the counsellor is able to relate to and understand the client while maintaining appropriate distance. When this distance is lost, overidentification occurs whereby the therapist becomes enmeshed in the client's material and is unable to remain adequately separated from it. Kantrowitz (1996) argues that overidentification poses a potential detriment to therapy as there exists the possible danger of the therapist failing to explore the client's experience adequately; the therapist assumes he or she already knows and understands the client's thoughts and emotions because of the similarity to his or her own experience. Conversely, when this distance becomes too great, disidentification occurs; the therapist fails to identify with the client effectively, thereby resulting in a lack of empathy for the client.

When optimal identification with the client is not achieved, Watkins (1985) asserts, the therapeutic relationship and process may be thwarted by countertransference behaviours that may be characterized as overprotective, benign, rejecting, or hostile. Overprotective and benign behaviours illustrate overidentification, whereas rejecting and hostile behaviours represent disidentification with the client. Overprotective countertransference may be presented through the counsellor's oversolicitous attitude toward his or her client, regarding the client as needing care and protection from hurt, anxiety, or guilt. Counsellors actualize overprotective behaviours by talking in a more quiet voice than usual, reducing the rate of speech, speaking in a balmy tone of voice, patting the client on the back or hugging the client (Watkins, 1985).

Overidentification with the client may also be manifested through benign countertransference in which the counsellor seeks to be liked and approved of by the client. Rather than maintaining the professional role, the counsellor encourages a friendly, cheerful, peer-to-peer relationship with the client and becomes both overly disclosing and gratifying. In an attempt to maintain this milieu, the counsellor strives to perpetuate an equality and sameness with the client. Watkins (1985) asserts that the counsellor's exploration of the client's concerns consequently lacks any real depth of incisiveness as the relationship between the client and counsellor degenerates to become merely a friendly exchange between peers.

Disidentification with the client may result in rejecting or hostile countertransference. Rejecting countertransference occurs when the counsellor views the client as being dependent and needy, and so responds in a rather punitive manner in order to establish a sense of considerable distance and separateness from the client. Watkins (1985) describes such counsellors as being minimally involved in the therapeutic process and as remaining continually on the periphery, thereby resulting in a unilateral quality of the counsellor-client relationship. Frequently, the counsellor attempts arduously to remain distant either out of fear of the potential demands imposed by the client or fear of being responsible for the welfare of the client. This pattern of countertransference may be exemplified by the counsellor delivering interpretations in a sharp, direct, and hurtful manner or neglecting to provide intervention when necessary. Hostile countertransference evolves from the counsellor's disapproval of the client's attitude or behaviour, or from the counsellor's own fear of being infected by the client's disturbing behaviour or pathology (Watkins, 1985). The counsellor's hostile behaviours often manifest through being short, curt, or blunt when communicating with the client and may result in a mutually abusive relationship in which the counsellor and client persistently castigate each other.

Loss and Grief

Grieving the death of a loved one, a marriage, one's health, or a job are all very personal experiences. Much research has been conducted on the experiences of the bereaved in relation to how they cope with their loss. One of the first pioneers, and certainly one of the most influential researchers in the field of death and dying, Kübler-Ross (1969), proposed a five-stage model of the dying process, a model that was founded on the responses offered by 200 patients who endured facing the reality of their own death. Despite the development of these stages to reflect the process of an individual facing his or her own death, Kübler-Ross's findings have also commonly been applied to those grieving the death of a loved one (Cook & Dworkin, 1992). The five components, as they relate to bereavement, are (a) denial, (b) anger, (c) bargaining, (d) depression, and (e) acceptance.

Based upon the work of Kübler-Ross, Worden (1991) proposed a model that conceptualizes the process of mourning into four tasks consisting of (a) accepting the reality of the loss, (b) working through the pain of grief, (c) adjusting to the environment in which the deceased is missing, and (d) emotionally relocating the deceased and moving on with life. According to Worden, the bereaved individual must actively engage in these tasks, which are accomplished in a fluid manner, in order to heal and proceed with life.

Notable research documented by Klass, Silverman, and Nickman (1996) expands our understanding of the bereavement process by suggesting that a continuing bond exists between the bereaved and the deceased. Klass et al. affirm that survivors hold the deceased in loving memory for long periods, often forever, while maintaining an inner representation of the deceased. While this bond with the deceased may shift over time, the connection remains. Unlike modernist grief theories which claim that grief is resolved by mastering a set of tasks associated with mourning, Rosenblatt (as cited in Klass et al., 1996) proposes that individuals "grieving major losses will not ever reach a time when they completely stop grieving" (p. 45).

Following from Worden's (1991) research and Klass et al.'s (1996) model of grief, Neimeyer (2000) espouses that mourners must address tasks of grief; however, mourning is not completed upon accomplishing these tasks. According to Neimeyer (2000), tasks are never completed in any final sense as the bereaved grieve and relearn the lessons of loss upon many events in life's journey. Accordingly, grief work is an ongoing process in life.

Despite their similarity to Worden's task model, the tasks of mourning that Neimeyer (2000) has proposed are neither accomplished in a particular order nor completed in a final sense.

As in Worden's model, Neimeyer's (2000) first task comprises acknowledging the reality of the loss, which requires the bereaved individual to confront his or her loss and the limitations thereby posed. In expanding on Worden's task, Neimeyer further asserts the need to respond to the loss within the system of the family by responding to the emotional needs of each family member.

Neimeyer (2000) characterizes the second challenge of mourning as opening yourself to the pain. While acknowledging that most individuals who learn about a death will attempt to distance themselves from the pain in the immediate aftermath, Neimeyer recognizes the potential harm that this may pose in either delaying or perpetuating the grieving process. In contrast, focusing relentlessly on the pain of loss can also be harmful. Opening oneself to the pain of the sorrow requires periodic work allowing active grieving interspersed with respite from the anguish.

Neimeyer (2000) defines the third challenge as revising one's assumptive world. this requires the bereaved individual to alter his or her beliefs and assumptions about life that have been invalidated upon his or her loss. Revising philosophies of life, renewing priorities, gaining a clearer sense of what is important, and what is not worthy of concern frequently evolve from the challenge of this task.

The fourth challenge of mourning consists of reconstructing one's relationship to that which has been lost (Neimeyer, 2000). Older grief theories postulated the significance of withdrawing emotional energy from the relationship with the deceased to allow for the bereaved individual's reinvestment in future relationships. While Worden (1991) acknowledges the need for the bereaved individual to emotionally relocate the deceased, Neimeyer agrees with Klass et al.'s (1996) model which affirms that the bereaved individual needs to transform his or her relationship with the deceased in order to continue the bond. Neimeyer asserts that, rather than ending the relationship through distancing oneself from the memories of the loved one, one needs to embrace the memories and develop a symbolic connection with the deceased. Cherishing a "linking object" (Klass et al., 1996, p. 66; Neimeyer, 2000, p. 46), such as an item that was favoured by the deceased — a piece of clothing, or a dear memory of the deceased — is a means to continuing the relationship with the lost loved one.

The final challenge of mourning as identified by Neimeyer (2000) includes reinventing oneself. "In a very real sense, a part of us dies each time we lose someone we love" (Neimeyer, 2000, p. 46). Inevitably, major losses evoke significant identity changes in those individuals who are affected by the loss. As a result, bereaved individuals are faced with the challenge of redefining who they are. The outcome of this challenging task may indeed be powerfully transforming and renewing as it may cultivate skills that were dormant, interests that were neglected, and relationships that were unexplored. This study will be framed within these challenges of mourning.

Forgiveness

Forgiveness is a process to mend ruptured relationships and restore peace between individuals. Forgiveness is a mechanism for righting wrongs, a way for people in intimate relationships to let each other off the hook for acts of ruthlessness and unkindness, a process that allows the wounded person to reopen his or her heart and to reaccept his or her offender (Flanigan, 1992). Forgiveness does not take the hurt and pain away, but rather sets the path for healing and restoration of oneself.

Injuries between individuals vary in intensity as depending upon factors such as the relationship of those involved, the nature of the event, and the extent to which moral rules have been violated. Flanigan (1992) and Klassen (2000) identified the following characteristics of injuries: intimate family or friends initiate injuries which begin with a singular betraying event; the betraying event violates moral rules and belief systems, inflicting deep wounds, and shattering personal belief systems; the assault is deeply personal and uniquely individual. Through forgiveness, a rebirth of hope, reorganization of thought, renewal of dreams, reconstruction of moral rules, and new interpretation of life can evolve.

The journey of forgiveness is a liberating process of changing hearts and minds; upon culmination peace between the injurer and the injured is restored. Flanigan (1992) proposes a five-phase model leading to liberation granted through forgiveness. Accordingly, the first phase involves naming the injury to facilitate in the interpretation of the meaning and underlying beliefs about the injury, while acknowledging that the injury has created a permanent change within. The second phase consists of owning the injury and claiming, "This is my injury — no one else's. Other people may have been hurt, too. But I can't do anything about that. I just forgive this injury because this is the one that harmed me" (p. 93). The third phase consists of blaming the injurer and making the injurer accountable for the harm. Phase four includes balancing the scales: the injured reflects upon and identifies his or her strengths and assets in an attempt to equalize the balance to that of the injurer. For the injured to regain strength to rebalance the scales, he or she may consider the injury over and done with if it was decided that there exists mutual responsibility for the damage between the injured and the injurer. The final phase consists of choosing to forgive: the injured no longer expects that the injurer owes anything to him or her in repayment for the wound and no longer reflects upon why the injury happened. In successfully being able to forgive, the injured is able to emerge with a sense of empowerment, renewed dreams and expectations, and to find and create new answers that, in a way, make him or her a new person.

According to Safer (1999), this process of forgiveness is a living experience that accompanies the wounded person throughout life, proceeding in tiny increments with starts and retrenchments and revelations and reversals. Successfully choosing to forgive can mark a significant turning point in the life of the wounded individual; the injured person is liberated from the pain and sorrow and is invited to move forward in life with a new sense of meaning and purpose. Safer (1999) has identified two indicators that authenticate the granting of genuine and successful forgiveness. Accordingly, forgiveness is verifiable when the injured has engaged in mourning, insight, and personal transformation. In addition, Safer (1999) indicates that forgiveness with a deceased injurer is deemed to be successful when a posthumous relationship is better than the relationship was when the inured was alive

Method

Research Question

This research was conducted to answer the fundamental research question, namely; what is my experience as a bereaved counsellor counselling a bereaved client? Specifically, this study examined how my capacity as a bereaved counsellor was facilitated or impeded by countertransferential interactions between the client and myself.

Autoethnography

To study the above questions, autoethnography was utilized to allow for reflection upon my experience as a bereaved counsellor. Autoethnography, as a method of allowing another person's world of experience to inspire critical reflection on one's own, entails exploring one's personal life and world while observing and identifying emotional and bodily feelings in addition to cognition (Ellis and Bochner, 1996). The use of autoethnography and narrative involves persons who individually and communally tell stories in order to better understand the ways humans experience the world and characterize the phenomena of human experience (Connelly & Clandinin, 1990). Because this is an autoethnographic study and evocative representation of my journey as a bereaved counsellor, we may not assume that this investigation will generalize to work with bereaved clients r to counsellors working through issues similar to those of their clients. Rather, my story, which exemplifies particular experiences of my life, may have commonalties for some individuals and vast differences for others.

Procedures

Within this autoethnographic study, my unique role of examining both my interactions with a client and my ability to cope with my loss characterizes myself as both participant and researcher. To reflect on my capacity to counsel a bereaved client while coping with my own loss, I selected a client through word of mouth. Specifically, I sought a volunteer who had the following characteristics: (a) a male who had experienced the death of a parent within the previous six months, and (b) someone who was willing to partake in grief counselling.

Assurances of confidentiality and safety from harm were implemented throughout the study. For instance, to preserve the identity of the client, it was ensured that she was not visible on the video recordings of the counselling sessions. In addition, due to the unique nature of my role as a bereaved counsellor, it was acknowledged that there was a possibility that my own grief might interfere with my ability to conduct grief counselling. In the event that my own needs would have disrupted the therapeutic process, I had identified an alternate counselling service for my client.

To gather data regarding the counselling sessions, all sessions were videotaped with pertinent segments being transcribed as needed. Following each session, I remained in the interview room for approximately one hour to videotape my reflections and thoughts about the interview. These reflections and thoughts were transcribed. In addition, I reviewed video recordings of each session to reflect upon my emotions and reactions and specifically observe both my verbal and nonverbal responses to my client.

Throughout my study, I documented my thoughts and reflections in my reflexive journal and fieldnotes. Emotional recall, a term coined by Ellis (1995) to describe a process whereby an individual enters a past scene, both emotionally and physically, to facilitate the recalling of specific details of an emotionally-charged event, was also utilized throughout this study.

As an autoethnographic study, the purpose of my evocative narrative was neither to explain nor to generalize to bereaved clients or counsellors, but rather to display the complexities, struggles, and triumphs of my journey. As such, formal analysis was not conducted, but, rather, transcripts, fieldnotes, and journal entries were synthesized to convey how my father's death influenced me as a counsellor and how my mourning shaped my capacity to conduct grief counselling.

Results

This research examined my experience of conducting grief counselling as a bereaved counsellor. The intent of this chapter is not to comprehensively illustrate the many struggles I encountered as a counsellor coping with my own grief, but to highlight several challenges and achievements that I encountered on my journey of healing.

Conducting Grief Counselling as a Bereaved Counsellor

Two months following the death of my father, I began conducting grief counselling with my client, Lisa. She was also grieving the death of her father who had passed away four months prior, at the age of 56, following a three-week battle with cancer. Even though two months had passed since my father's sudden and unexpected death at the age of 60, I still felt intense sorrow and sadness. Given my heightened emotional disposition, I experienced great trepidation and anxiety; as a bereaved counsellor I had fears and concerns to face. How would I cope with my grief during the session? What would happen if I became overwhelmed with my own grief? Would I be able to fulfill my role as counsellor? Such fears greatly influenced my counselling capacity as I frequently responded to my client with reservation and caution that were evidenced when I adopted a less directional approach and engaged in receptive silence.

My ability to conduct grief counselling was also greatly influenced by the commonalties between Lisa's experience and relationship with her father and that of my own. From childhood to adulthood, Lisa experienced a conflicted, demeaning and turbulent relationship with her alcoholic father. Rather than expressing love, affection, tenderness and support, which she greatly yearned for, her father responded to her with criticism and disapproval. Lisa presented with significant emotional pain as she shared on many occasions the anger she felt toward him in his neglect to tell her that he was proud of her or that he loved her. As she recounted in detail many of her distressing memories, I found that her experiences often triggered my reflection upon my own relationship with my dad, a relationship that had many resemblances to that of Lisa and her father. Although I knew that my dad loved me, he was neither expressive of his love nor affectionate toward me. One of the few emotions that he displayed was anger and he would communicate his disappointment and irritation through both words and actions. Consequently, I considered my relationship with him as being injurious, oppressive, and tumultuous. As a result of my own unresolved issues with my dad, I frequently was unable to fully attend to Lisa's story since I was often subjugated to my own painful memories. Despite attempting to repress my own memories, I was frequently inundated and distracted by distressing recollections of injurious events that I had experienced as a child. Nevertheless, reflecting upon my memories did not appear to detract from the therapeutic process, as I maintained a respectful presence of receptive silence in which I offered Lisa the freedom to tell her story without interruption while I listened with respect, compassion, and detached silence (Popov, Popov, & Kavelin, 1997).

My ability to relate to and understand Lisa's experience did certainly facilitate the development of our therapeutic relationship; however, due to the many similarities between our experiences, I believe that my effectiveness as a counsellor was impeded as the therapeutic distance between Lisa and myself gradually diminished due to my overidentification with her. Countertransference reactions were evident throughout the counselling sessions. Overprotective countertransference behaviours were demonstrated by my overly gentle disposition toward Lisa as I attempted to protect her from feeling emotional discomfort. Benign countertransference behaviours were apparent on such occasions as when I neglected to encourage Lisa to further examine some emotionally distressing memories of which she spoke. Not only did I seek to protect her from the emotions that would arise from further investigation, but also, and perhaps more significantly, I attempted to protect myself from the unearthing of my own thoughts and feelings that might have been triggered from her recounting such events. Such an occurrence was evident when Lisa described the intensity of the physical pain her dad experienced prior to his death. Despite recognizing the potential usefulness of having her articulate her thoughts and feelings regarding these memories, I chose not to examine these further, as I feared that I would be confronted by images relating to the pain that my dad may have encountered upon his death, an image that I was not emotionally prepared to consider. At other times, I neglected to facilitate further exploration, simply assuming that I understood Lisa's experience given the similarities between our stories.

Grief and forgiveness

Coping with my own grief inevitably presented many challenges as I conducted grief therapy. In addition to the internal struggle of maintaining emotional composure, I also constantly struggled to repress thoughts and memories that were frequently triggered from the experiences about which Lisa spoke. Despite these challenges, this study helped me confront many unresolved issues that ensued from Dad's death. Although Lisa's material often provoked the unearthing of my own sadness, desolation, anxiety, hurt, and anger from my past relationship with my dad, confronting these emotions was necessary in recognizing and addressing my own grief.

By examining my thoughts and emotions, I actively engaged in healing my pain through addressing the challenges of mourning as delineated by Neimeyer (2000). Adopting the role of the bereaved counsellor facilitated my ability to acknowledge the reality of my loss and open myself up to the pain as I was perpetually emerged in my grief throughout the counselling sessions. Conversing with family, friends, and colleagues about Dad's death also was effective in realizing the sorrow of my loss. Engaging in active self-reflection has been instrumental in the process of revising my assumptive world. Re-evaluating my priorities and philosophy of life in light of Dad's death assisted me in renewing my perspective and value for family and friends and in seeking joy and fulfillment in life. Undoubtedly, this study has assisted me in reconstructing my relationship with my dad. In addressing and working through the anger, hurt, and disappointment I experienced in my relationship with him, I have come to a greater understanding of our interactions and the reasons for our behaviours. This process of self-reflection has resulted in my decision to forgive Dad. As a result, my relationship with him has been transformed to one defined by peace, understanding, love, and trust. Reinventing myself has directly evolved from addressing my emotional fears and traumas, re-evaluating my priorities, and developing a loving and caring relationship with Dad. Addressing Neimeyer's challenges of mourning have resulted in my significant growth and healing.

In my journey, the process of mourning has been inextricably woven together with the process of forgiveness, as they both have imparted healing, reconstructed relationships, and renewed strength and hope. My journey of forgiveness has been ongoing, formally beginning nine years ago when I initially identified and began exploring the injuries I experienced growing up. Although I named and claimed the injury and blamed the injurer nine years ago, the process of forgiveness ceased at that time upon Dad's absence of contrition when I confronted him about the injuries. However, through identifying and examining the many wounds and assaults that were painfully unearthed during this research, I have once again been able to embark on the journey of forgiveness. Despite Dad's physical absence, I have gained more insight into his behaviours, as well as my own, and have come to consider the injuries over and done with. I have chosen to forgive him. Though the memories and accompanying hurt, sadness, and anger remain, I feel greatly liberated and empowered by the reconstructed intimate and loving relationship with my dad that has evolved. I feel transformed and gratified for the renewed and enriched relationship with him. Having developed this newfound relationship, I have been able to move on with Dad's spiritual presence accompanying me.

Reflections

Through this examination of my capacity to conduct grief counselling as a bereaved counsellor, I have certainly faced many challenges, including coping with my own grief as a bereaved counsellor and addressing countertransference reactions. Likewise, I have also experienced many accomplishments, addressing the challenges of mourning and developing a renewed relationship with my dad. This journey of healing has indeed been therapeutic and healing.

There are various tasks that I undertook in the search for emotional healing. Becoming vulnerable and exposing myself to the pain of my grief was at times a very onerous task. When the acuteness of my grief exceeded my capacity to address it at that time, I provided myself the permission to retreat from the sorrow and anger in order to heal and restore my energies. As affirmed by Neimeyer (2000), "focussing relentlessly on the pain of loss can be a bit like staring unblinking at the sun — it may actually be damaging if our gaze is sustained too long" (p. 42).

Engaging in active self-reflection has been an instrumental agent of healing and growth for myself. Despite being an emotionally exhausting endeavour, reflecting on my countertransference reactions and the many emotions and thoughts that were evoked while conducting grief counselling was an essential task that resulted in great insight into the many unresolved issues with which I struggled. Documenting my reflections and consulting with others about these insights were paramount in working through these challenges and developing greater understanding of my experiences.

Choosing to forgive my dad has inevitably resulted in significant inner healing and peace. As affirmed by Hargrave (1994), forgiveness not only has the potential to ease our pain, but to also offer healing from the past. The work of forgiveness has been a tumultuous process as I examined many of the wounds that I encountered from my previous relationship with my dad. On several occasions I retreated from this process due to the exacting nature of this task; however, through self-reflection and reliance upon my faith, I have been able to resume this therapeutic journey and have attained the blessings of a loving and peaceful relationship with my dad.

In summary, this chapter presents my experience as a bereaved counsellor counselling a bereaved client. Countertransferential reactions were evident throughout the counselling sessions and did pose implications for my capacity to conduct grief counselling as a bereaved counsellor. Despite this, the insight gained from confronting my grief and addressing my unresolved issues was therapeutic and facilitative in my journey of healing.

References

Connelly, F. M., & Clandinin, D. J. (1990). Stories of experience and narrative inquiry. *Educational Researcher, 19*(5), 2-14.

Cook, A. S., & Dworkin, D. S. (1992). *Helping the bereaved: Therapeutic interventions for children, adolescents, and adults.* New York: Basic Books.

Ellis, C. (1995). *Final negotiations: A story of love, loss, and chronic illness.* Philadelphia: Temple University Press.

Ellis, C., & Bochner, A. P. (1996). *Composing ethnography: Alternative forms of qualitative writing.* London: AltaMira Press.

Flanigan, B. (1992). *Forgiving the unforgivable.* New York: Macmillan.

Hansen, J. T. (1997). The counseling process and the management of countertransference anxiety with disturbed clients. *Journal of Mental Health Counseling, 19*(4), 364-372.

Hargrave, T. D. (1994). *Families and forgiveness: Healing wounds in the intergenerational family.* New York: Brunner/Mazel.

Hayes, J.A., McCracken, J. E., McClanahan, M. K., Hill, C. E., Harp, J. S., & Carozzoni, P. (1998). Therapist perspectives on countertransference: Qualitative data in search of a theory. *Journal of Counseling Psychology, 45*(4), 468-4.

Kantrowitz, J. L. (1996). *The patient's impact on the analyst.* London: Analytic Press.

Klass, D., Silverman, P. R., & Nickman, S. L. (Eds.) (1996).*Continuing bonds: New understandings of grief.* Washington, DC: Taylor & Francis.

Klassen, D. (2000). *The forgiveness workbook.* Unpublished manuscript. Thunder Bay, Ontario: The Listening Centre.

Kübler-Ross, E. (1969). *On death and dying.* New York: Simon & Schuster.

Neimeyer, R. A. (2000). *Lessons of Loss: A guide to coping.* Memphis, TN: Center for the Study of Loss and Transition.

Peabody, S. A., & Geslo, C. J. (1982). Countertransference and empathy: The complex relationship between two divergent concepts in counseling. *Journal of Counseling Psychology, 29*(3), 240-245.

Popov, L. K., Popov, D., & Kavelin, J. (1997). *The family virtues guide: Simple ways to bring out the best in our children and ourselves.* New York: Penguin Books.

Robbins, S. B., & Jolkovski, M. P. (1987). Managing countertransference feelings: An interactional model using awareness of feeling and theoretical framework. *Journal of Counseling Psychology, 34*(3), 276-282.

Safer, J. (1999). *Forgiving and not forgiving: Why sometimes it's better not to forgive.* New York: Quill.

Watkins, C. E., Jr. (1985). Countertransference: Its impact on the counseling situation. *Journal of Counseling and Development, 63*, 356-359.

Worden, J. W. (1991). *Grief counseling and grief therapy: A handbook for the mental health practitioner.* New York: Springer.

Chapter 10

Death in the Family: A Family Process Approach to Pastoral Care*

Peter L. VanKatwyk

In 1993 I wrote a case study on family bereavement based on my own family's grief experience at the sudden and accidental death of our 18 year old daughter in 1985. The essay was printed in *The Journal of Pastoral Care* (VanKatwyk, 1993). Rather than focusing on the individual grief process, this chapter will explore grief in a systemic and developmental context. From this perspective, grief marks a crisis event in the life of the family in which the loss of one of its members triggers disruption both in family stability and personal identity and provides a powerful impetus for the family to develop its resourcefulness and enhance its growth.

In keeping with the majority of clinical research studies on bereavement, the pastoral care and counselling literature on grief has focused on the dynamics of the individual experience of loss and attending potential perils in the readjustment process. However, alternative grief theories are emerging which seek to balance individual with relational dynamics, pathological with normative developmental processes, loss with growth.

---

*Revision of a paper presented at the 2nd Annual Conference of the Society for Pastoral Counselling Research, Saint Paul University, Ottawa, Ontario, May 13, 1995

In a recent edited volume of significant contributions from the intergenerational school of family therapists, in which Murray Bowen figures highly, the grief experience is primarily located in the family life cycle which guides the developmental process within the family system over many generations. Significantly, the book is entitled *Living Beyond Loss — Death in the Family* (Walsh & McGoldrick, 1991).

In a more recent book, *Grief as a Family Process,* Shapiro (1994) presents a stunning multidimensional, contextual perspective on the grief experience, integrating psychoanalytic with interpersonal and family systems concepts. This grand theoretical synthesis of a "systemic developmental model of family bereavement" is intended not so much to gain converts for a new theoretical model as to provide clinicians with a more comprehensive and encouraging working model:

> A family developmental view model allows us to formulate our interventions as grief counsellors and therapists with children, adults, and families so as to expand the family's emotional encounter with their loss while at the same time supporting their growth-enhancing strategies for stability. With a developmental approach that considers the family as a unit of distinct yet inextricably interconnected members, we can help families survive and grow while bearing the burden of death and loss. (Shapiro, 1994, p.18)

In my original article (VanKatwyk, 1993) on a family system's perspective on grief, I distinguished between three levels of family organization. The first level I called the *biophysical*, the second the *psychosocial*, and the third the *spiritual-vocational.* These three levels of family organization can be placed on a continuum of differentiation between the family and its individual members.

Dimensions of Family Organization

Biophysical Dimension

I remember how our initial grief reactions were overwhelmingly physical. There was a sense of broken hearts, a hurting womb from which a life had been ripped, screams of protest when we first heard the news, followed by seemingly incessant crying. Grief was manifested at the very bodily foundation of our being.

Erich Lindemann's (1944) research with survivors of the Coconut Grove nightclub fire in Boston emphasized somatic distress in grief, and what seems like the body's protest to the loss of the deceased family member through sensory distortions, including auditory and visual hallucinations. In my 1993 article I wrote,

> The most basic level of the family context is found in the concrete, biophysical expressions of family life. Developmentally this is the way each person is initiated into life. At birth the infant appears to be sensitive only to bodily functions and bodily contacts, to the physical comfort and/or deprivation experiences between the infant and the caretaking parental presence. The home environment is unique in retaining, also in later developmental stages, this grounding in the body and in providing a sense of basic security.
>
> Families occupy physical space which becomes one. The home might be viewed as the family-body. It provides for the physical needs and biological functions of family members' items such as food, shelter, and hygiene. The home creates a one-flesh union between family members. In the home we are surrounded by a multitude of sensory stimuli — seeing, hearing, touching, smelling, tasting — in which we were initially baptized into the body, and which in later experiences continue to gather family members into one "body." Significant places in the home where "sacraments of communion" are administered are the kitchen/dining-room, the bathroom, and the parental bedroom where, according to Freudian theory, even the children share the conjugal bed.
>
> In theological terms the family home is the sacramental context of our incarnation. Pastors value their traditional access to the "family-body" through home-visits with parishioners. Family therapists often ask their family-clients about their home situation, including its physical outlay, whether doors are left open or closed, what hap-

> pens in the morning when the family gets up, and what the routines are around the use of the bathroom and breakfast in the kitchen. All of this forms a sensual texture which organizes and punctuates a person's life space and self-experience.
>
> When somebody dies in one's family this physical texture that holds our life is torn apart. Grief includes this sense of physical dislocation and lostness. There is the empty chair, the sudden silence. Peter, in our case illustration, is aware that he cannot touch his daughter any more and he can actually feel an aching sense of sensory deprivation. Myra is aware that as she hears the school bus stop, out there is no follow-up response of the backdoor. The sound of voice and feet coming down the staircase does not mark any more the beginning of a new day (VanKatwyk, 1993, p. 143)

The family as a mystical union is symbolized by the one "home" which through its various "sacraments" and ritual activities punctuate the family experience and gather its members into the one-flesh union of the family body. Murray Bowen's (1976) concept of the "differentiation of self from the family of origin" (Kerr & Bowen, 1988, pp, 95-97) states that families organize themselves along a scale of levels in self-differentiation within the family. Families with little self-differentiation are "fused" and are described as an "undifferentiated ego-mass" (Bowen, 1976). These families identify themselves by high levels of anxiety and emotional reactivity when their shared identity and common experience as a family are being threatened.

I find it helpful to understand Bowen's concept of self-differentiation as a flexible and developmental continuum, rather than a rigid point on a scale. In times of stress and crisis, like those as encountered in the real or anticipated loss of a family member, family members may regress on the scale of self-differentiation and experience extreme anxieties, such as overwhelming feelings of helplessness in the face of impending disintegration and extinction. These feelings are part of the acute grief reactions and most directly manifest themselves through the body.

Psychosocial Dimension

In my experience of grief in the family, I became aware that the initial emotional shock which registered somatically was followed by more complex interpersonal reactions. The psychosocial context for grief is found in the family as a covenantal community where individual family members reciprocally define the family as a unique entity and as the context for each member's individual identity. While family members are differentiated through their special position in the family, individual social roles and psychological functions serve primarily the needs of the family in maintaining its corporate identity through a collaborative family process. This is the family socialization process that is central in infancy and early adolescence. Daniel Stern (1985), in his research study on the interpersonal world of the infant, states that at the age of two to three months "the infant's first order of business, in creating an interpersonal world, is to form the sense of a core self and core others" (p. 70).

In my earlier article (VanKatwyk, 1993) I wrote,

> The family as an interpersonal system consists of persons who perform interdependent social roles and psychological functions which provide each member, and the family as a whole, with an identity. Families also tend to have special vocations to which family members are called. Families often have identified patients, clowns, chaplains, stars. Often family roles follow complementary patterns, such as leaders and followers, peace-disturbers and peacemakers, saints and sinners. Once recruited into these functions, each person stabilizes the family homeostasis which, in close interdependence, confirms the individual roles and identities of each family member. In theological terms the biblical concept of the covenant conveys this contractual structure of relational roles and relationship rules which define each person's identity in reciprocal, interpersonal terms" (VanKatwyk, 1993, pp. 143-144)

Bowen (1976) discusses that a death in the family is largely defined by the family's level of differentiation and by the significant function of the deceased individual in the family system. The death of the main care giver in a family of young children, or the death of a child who carries the pain or the hope of the family, is likely to be followed by major family disruption and an "emotional shock wave" (Bowen, 1988, p. 82-86).

Spiritual-vocational dimension

A third dimension in the family constellation is the acknowledged place and uniqueness of the individual in the family. At this point, Bowen's (1976) concept of self-individuation becomes critical. Developmentally this focus on individual autonomy gains prominence in adolescence, when the task of individual identity needs to be balanced with family loyalties and interpersonal connectedness.

The family's main task in this regard is to be the confirming voice recognizing the separate individual vocations of its members. The family's spirituality is expressed through transcending its own corporate concerns and celebrating the uniqueness of each of its members.

> This further family developmental task often is highlighted in psychology theories as the supreme goal for the actualization of human wholeness. It is the movement from an identity primarily constituted by the performance of certain social roles and psychological functions for others in the family to a sense of self clearly differentiated from others. It is the moral capacity of the family to see its members both as family members and as distinct from the configuration of family expectations and needs. The covenantal structure of the family now transcends its own interests and survival . The covenant of contractual obligations becomes secondary to a covenant of grace. Identity is now found primarily in the personal experience of acceptance and confirmation. Intimacy is now experienced in the interpersonal interaction of knowing and being known. (VanKatwyk, 1993, p. 144)

I think that it is at this point that Carl Rogers' self-theory (Raskin & Rogers, 1989) fits in with family systems theory. From the perspective of family systems theory, Rogerian concepts are often understood as pertaining mainly to individuals as opposed to social systems. However, developmentally the family is in a precarious and continual process of balancing its own family identity with the emerging individual identities of its members. It is the vocation of the family to accentuate the uniqueness and worth of each family member in the context of the shared family context.

Family Grief Process

The family grief process can be mapped along the continuum of self-differentiation. Pastoral care for bereaved families is described as a multidimensional process.

The various dimensions of family systems, the biophysical, the psycho-social, and the spiritual-vocational, are arranged and integrated in a developmental hierarchy, and in this complex configuration define the grief experience in the family. In the initial, acute phase of bereavement, the family will often experience the loss in physical ways, with overwhelming sensations of abandonment, panic and confusion. In the second phase, bereavement is also a deeply felt deprivation experience, but now it is felt primarily in the loss of one's place with others and in the question of one's identity and place in life.

Much of grief ministry in the acute stages of bereavement appears to be the ministry of *replacement*, the Rogerian support of empathic identification, the ministry of presence for those who feel lost and lonely (VanKatwyk, 1993, p. 146). However, beyond the need for surviving the initial catastrophic blow of traumatic loss, families face the larger question of the spiritual and vocational identity of the family. Charles Figley (1989) in his book, *Helping Traumatized Families*, presents a structured helping model for families in stress. He states that the final process of recovery from trauma is helping the family develop a "healing theory." In constructing a family healing theory, "family members enable each other to propose a perspective of the trauma and its wake that fits for the family" (VanKatwyk, 1993, p. 146).

Most of the grief literature, following the psychoanalytic bereavement model, has emphasized that successful grieving requires relinquishing one's attachment to the deceased person and re-investing this energy into somebody or something else. This classical Freudian theory seems to be in line with the classical Christian paradigm (cf. John Patton, 1994) of grief ministry, which directs the bereaved person to focus on God or Christ as the heavenly replacement figure (cf. Martin Luther in Volz, 1990: to continue the suffering of grief is to deny the suffering of Christ).

Current relational bereavement models provide a more humane view those that would claim we shift human beings as interchangeable objects of need gratification. As summarized by Ester Shapiro (1994),

> A systemic developmental perspective on adult bereavement suggests that the end point of successful grief work is not relinquishment of the lost relationship but the creation of a new bond, one that acknowledges the enduring psychological and spiritual reality of someone we have loved and made a part of ourselves. In this culture we have a difficult time granting even to children the need to retain an enduring bond with the dead, so determined are we to promote the reality oriented "letting go" process. Yet both children and adults require the security and safety provided by the spiritual and emotional presence of their important formative attachment figures. Grief, from a systemic developmental perspective, is seen as a family life cycle transition that requires the transformation of enduring relational bonds. Grief does not require the relinquishment of the lost love but the re-establishment of a new relationship, still vital and enduring but now internalized.(p. 41-42)

The concept of relocation (VanKatwyk, 1993, p. 146) in some of the grief literature is perhaps the best way to describe this concept of family grief healing. This term acknowledges the sense of defiance in refusing to give up the dead person for dead. The dynamics of *replacement* emphasizes finding one's own place again in order to go on in life. Relocation, as opposed to replacement, finds a place for the dead person, without letting the person get into the way of ongoing life. This approach emphasizes the paradox of the ongoing life of the dead person in the family, while acknowledging the reality of the person's death. Grief healing is found in the search to locate the meaning of the person who has died, to grasp and be grasped by the living memories of the dead, and to incorporate, within one's own life and family circle, the essence of the other.

This grief work, developmentally, is part of the spiritual vocation of the family. Its success is in direct correlation with the level of self-differentiation in the family. The deceased family member needs to be confirmed in his or her uniqueness and to be remembered in ways which encourage ongoing life.

A story from the Hebrew *scriptures* that stood out for me in this regard is the Joseph story. Father Jacob did not want to accept his son Joseph's death and refused to be comforted. Later he found his son relocated in Egypt, in line with his son's unique vocation, feeding the family of Israel in a time of famine. When Joseph died as an old man, he insisted that his bones be carried along by the Israelites on their ongoing journey to the promised land. This is a story of relocation: the dead participate in the ongoing journey of the living without becoming a stumbling block. And the Joseph story continues in the Jesus story: the life that cannot be left behind but is carried forward into the next generation, from generation to generation.

Without reducing the *Christian scriptures* to a monumental enterprise in grief work, the New Testament is a testimony to the power of the early Christian community's living memories of the Christ which couch His ongoing presence with his people. The relocation theme of transformation, central in the Joseph story, comes to a transcendent expression in the story of Christ's ascension. As interpreted by John Calvin (1559/1960) in his Institutes,

> When he ascended into heaven he led a captivity captive, and despoiling His enemies, He enriched His own people, and daily lavishes spiritual riches upon them. He therefore sits on high, transfusing us with his power, that He

> may quicken us to spiritual life, sanctify us with His Spirit, adorn his church with diverse gifts of His grace, keeps it safe from all harm by His protection... . (II, 16, p.504)

Translation into Family Systems

How will our deceased daughter Martina accompany us as we continue our journey? One story that has guided us right from the beginning is the story of the wounded dove. Martina had found a dove hurt in an accident. She had nursed the bird back to health and released it to freedom by the river only days before her own accident.

> At first we identified with the woundedness: Martina's accident in which we also were mortally wounded. And the story tells us that Martina is committed to life and is a healer. She wants us also to heal and fly again. It is the experience of how her living memories can transform within us into healing memories. The story also goes beyond its private meanings and connects with the larger healing narratives of universal meaning: the dove as the messenger of peace and the presence of the Spirit who will incorporate that which has been lost into the living and preserve its ongoing meaning and presence. (VanKatwyk, 1993, p. 147)

Journal Notes

More and more of our energy is going into building living memories. We begin to sift through a pile of old pictures, letters, mementos, babybook collections — trying to piece together a life, creating a canvass of images, a collage of impressions of one never to be forgotten.

Peter starts rebuilding Martina's unfinished room into a study, using thick, solid golden pine for book shelves, incorporating her many sport trophies, soccer boots and ski caps, posters and pictures. His wife, Myra, commissions an artist to create a huge steel garden sculpture of three geese, symbolizing the three girls who died in the accident, as they spread their wings heading for the river. Another artist, Myra's sister, makes a bronze head depicting Martina, to be placed just outside our large window overlooking the flood lands.

Prior roles in our couple relationship may well have prepared us for this partnership in grief work. An important family role for Myra is to be the ritual coordinator: she organizes frequent get-togethers and special events, punctuating our family experience with significant remembrances and celebrations. Each year in July, on the weekend that the three girls had the accident, we go early in the morning into the fields, picking wild flowers to take to the grave sites. Together, as family members of the girls, we then enjoy a generous luncheon together.

Three years after the accident (we keep calling it "the accident" — something that never should have happened), we invite all those who have been close to us in our loss to a memorial event. The sculpture of the three geese had been completed and placed in the garden. Relatives come from The Netherlands and gather with friends and co-workers. We share with them that our lives no longer are dominated by grief. We thank them for their support, and mark this day as a day of life. We have come together to remember and celebrate.

This violent and destructive event — of a car with three young girls hitting a truck, that was parked without lights at the side of the highway — tells also the story of us as a couple and a family. Unexpectedly we, at full speed, ran into something unforgiving and unforeseen. It should have killed us. What saved us?

Conclusion

This chapter draws from a systemic and developmental model which incorporates a variety of perspectives on the experience of bereavement and family grief counselling. While supporting the grieving family, pastoral care will also attend to the task of facilitating the emergence of a healing theory and practice, and a transforming relocation of the dead person which fits the family's own experience.

References

Bowen, M. (1976). Theory in the practice of psychotherapy. In P. Guerin (Ed.), *Family therapy*, New York: Gardner Press, 42-89.

Bowen, M. (1988). Family emotional equilibrium and the emotional shock wave. In F. Walsh, & M. McGoldrick, *Living beyond loss — Death in the family.* New York: Norton, 82-86.

Calvin, J. (1960). *Institutes of the Christian religion* (J.T. McNeill, Ed.; F.L. Battles, Trans.), Philadelphia: The Westminster Press. (Original work published 1559)

Lindemann, E. (1944). Symptomatology and management of acute grief.

American Journal of Personality and Social Psychology, 51, 797-802.

Figley, C. (1989). *Helping traumatized families.* San Francisco: Jossey-Bass.

Kerr, M., & Bowen, M. (1988). *Family evaluation: An approach based on Bowen theory.* New York: Norton.

Patton, J. (1994). *Pastoral care in context: An introduction to pastoral care.* Louisville, KY: Westminster Press.

Raskin, N.J. & Rogers, C.R. (1989). Person-centered therapy. In R.J. Corsini & D. Wedding (Eds.), *Current psychotherapies*, Itasca, Illinois: Peacock Publisher, 155-194.

Shapiro, E. (1994). *Grief as a family process: A developmental approach to clinical practice.* New York: Guilford Press.

Stern, D. (1985). *The interpersonal world of the infant.* New York: Basic Books.

VanKatwyk, P. L. (1993). A family observed: Theological and family systems perspectives on the grief experience. *The Journal of Pastoral Care, 47*(2), 141-147.

Volz, C. (1990). *Pastoral life and practice in the early church.* Minneapolis: Aaugsberg Fortress.

Walsh, F, & McGoldrick, M. (1991). *Living beyond loss — Death in the family.* New York: Norton.

Chapter 11

Pastoral Counselling in a Secular Setting*

Lucille Smeltzer-Legault

This chapter represents preliminary reflections based on my experience in pastoral counselling following the completion of my degree at Saint Paul University in 1991. My association with the university began before the birth of my first child; a friend referred me there for counselling with Father St-Arnaud, who helped me deal with some issues around becoming a mother. The compassion and insight that I experienced in these sessions, as well as in growth groups led by Jacques Cloutier and by Julien Mercure, created in me the desire to help others in the same way. I began my studies at Saint Paul University on a part-time basis in 1973, and, after taking time out to raise a family of three children, completed the program in 1989. I was finally ready to make my dream of working as a pastoral counsellor, a dream begun so many years before, become a reality!

I had several reasons for choosing the pastoral counselling program at Saint Paul rather than the Masters in Social Work at nearby Carleton University. Because I had been helped by integrating experiences of God into my psychological growth, and

---

*Revision of a paper presented at the First Annual Conference of the Society for Pastoral Counselling Research, Saint Paul University, Ottawa, Ontario, May 6, 1994

because my models of counselling were pastoral, I believed that the program offered at Saint Paul was the best fit personally and professionally. Upon graduation, I hoped to use these counselling skills in an explicitly pastoral setting.

This part of my dream was not realized. As it turned out, I opened an office for private practice and through it I contracted with the Department of Health and Welfare to deliver EAP (Employee Assistance Program) services for them. At the time, I saw this as using only the counselling elements of my training and began to ask myself why I had not taken my degree from Carleton instead of Saint Paul's since I wasn't using my pastoral training. At least, I thought, my degree would be more acceptable to social service agencies. Though I tried to find other settings where I could use the pastoral elements of my training, this did not work out, and, reluctantly, I settled for employing my counselling skills in a secular setting.

It wasn't until a brief conversation at a family gathering that I began to see things differently. I was talking with a cousin who is a deacon in the Episcopal Church; I asked her if she was working full-time as a deacon or if she was continuing her first career as an elementary school teacher. She responded that teaching and helping young children grow were connected to God and therefore an important part of her ministry.

This led me to reflect about what, in fact, denotes ministry and what specifically defines one's involvement as pastoral. I thought of possible definitions of pastoral counselling and realized that they seemed to depend for their legitimacy on two possibilities: either that the service is offered by an ordained person in or out of a church role, or that a specifically pastoral setting lends legitimacy to a non-ordained person acting in a pastoral role. I had concluded that my work could not be pastoral according to these definitions since I was neither ordained nor working in a pastoral setting.

However, on further reflection, another possible definition presented itself, a definition that depended neither on the necessity of ordination nor on a pastoral location, but on the content of the interaction. This led me to another way of viewing my own possible pastoral experience. I began to look at the people I had helped through the Employee Assistance Program and to understand that, in our work together, they had often grown in both self-acceptance and in the love of God. The kinds of questions they asked and the kind of presence I maintained with my clients had more to do with effecting such outcomes than did any official title. Reflecting on some of my clients' personal growth, I began to realize that "pastoral counselling" is not necessarily doing "counselling in a pastoral setting," but working with the pastoral elements in the material clients present, often through questions that invite or challenge them to stretch their limits. I began to be aware that my counselling of Federal Government employees, often in Federal Government offices, was indeed "pastoral."

In her book *The Art of Spiritual Guidance*, Carolyn Gratton (1992) cites a Sufi mystic's story which reflects my inner experience. In this story a group of fish share their anxieties, worries and confusion as they frantically swim in circles searching for water. Upon meeting a wise fish, they ask him, "Where is the Sea?" He replies, "If you would stop swimming so busily and struggling so anxiously, you would discover that you are already in the sea. You need look no further than you already are" (p. 5).

Until I began to recognize my work as pastoral, I was very much like those fish looking for the Pastoral Sea. I now understand that I was in that sea all along. In the discussion that follows, I will attempt to provide some indications that support my understanding. First I will define pastoral counselling as it is used in this chapter. Next I examine my caseload of EAP clients from a four-year time span, and finally, I will share some intuitions about counsellors as pastoral agents in secular settings.

This discussion will make use of the three ways of knowing cited by Meier in his 1990 paper to the Group for Research in Pastoral Studies: intuition, reason and empiricism (Meier, 1990, p.22). It is to be noted, however, that research supporting the intuitive way of knowing is in its elemental stages. We can look forward to further research, clarifying certain points and demonstrating others, as the subject of future presentations.

Definition

Consulting a number of books and articles about pastoral counselling led me to the conclusion that few agree on a definition (Cavanagh, 1962; O'Brian, 1968; Hamilton, 1972; Vanderpool, 1977; Oates, 1974; Clinebell, 1984). Some authors concentrate more on the pastoral element as an extension of Christ's care, and some focus on improving counselling skills for pastoral agents.

In attempting to define my terms, I turned to a paper by F.C. Power (1990) on "The Distinctiveness of Pastoral Counselling." He argues for a Christian humanistic approach that integrates the sacred and the secular without collapsing them, and suggests that a cognitive developmental framework can make place for both the sacred and the secular because of its focus on the way people process information and the types of questions they ask at different levels of growth. He states that nonreligious counselling furnished by members of the clergy should not automatically be defined as pastoral. This definition should be reserved for a type of counselling which permits clients to confront the limits of their existence and to advance in their journey towards God. That which is really essential in defining whether the counselling is pastoral is the way in which the sacred is developed within its secular shell. Power (1990) states that "the religious dimension of life underlies the secular in such a way that the potential for specifically religious counsel is always at hand" (p.77).

Because of the overlap between the sacred and the secular, because we are neither only material nor only spiritual, it is always possible for persons to experience growth in both dimensions. Thus, teaching little children to read can indeed be a pastoral activity when offered in a way that reveals the caring presence that heals and expands and opens the potential for fully receiving the love of God. Helping people to integrate their pain and resolve their problems in a secular setting can also be pastoral. Power grounds his vision of the specificity of pastoral counselling on the theology of Karl Rahner (1978), who explains the continuity between the religious and the secular by calling the human person the "grammar through which God speaks" (Power,

1990, p.79). This means that for the Christian there is no purely secular sphere of existence. There is a

> continuity, but non-identity between God and humanity. Human beings are creatures who transcend their finite nature in openness to God. The Christian symbol of the cross is a constant reminder of the reality of death and human limitation. The unrestrained pursuit of self-fulfillment and self-actualization represents an avoidance of this reality. The Christian humanist accepts the ambiguity of all finite forms of self-realization and achievement. Fulfillment is ultimately to be found only in relationship with God. Yet this relationship which transcends the human, does not entail a denial of the worth of the self and of human development. (Power, 1990, p.80)

It is through helping others come to terms with both their finite nature and their ultimate call to God that the pastoral counsellor participates in the continuing work of redemption, since, as Power explains, the continuity is founded on the assertion that redemption does not contradict but completes the work of creation; the counsellor, through participating in redemptive work, is facilitating the client's (and his/her own) continuity with God.

The pastoral counsellor, who has an awareness of this final destination in God, can help clients move ahead on their journey while they struggle to find meaning in whatever brought them to counselling. Power (1990) points to faith as the largely tacit trust that reality can sustain the human quest for meaning and worth (p. 83). It is often when people's trust in this certitude has broken down, when they have reached the limits of their understanding of life's events and meaning, that they seek professional help. This sometimes happens when a person perceives their experience as being incongruous with their beliefs about a just God, or when their life circumstances change in a significant way. Such individuals need to somehow expand their vision of both themselves and God in order to make sense of new events and to reaffirm life.

To examine more clearly certain experiences conducive to this kind of pastoral counselling and to see how a pastoral approach can develop in a secular setting, I will refer to my caseload of clients within the context of an Employee Assistance Program (EAP) for federal government employees.

Caseload Study

While providing EAP services from September 1991 to March 1994, I saw a total of 529 cases. Of these, 43 were of an administrative nature: coordinators arranging for training sessions or supervisors inquiring about how to refer people to the program. The remaining 486 counselling cases involved a full range of problems and dynamics. They included problems of substance abuse (self or other), marital and family problems ranging from communication gaps or questions about children's education to family violence, adjustment to life's transitions, and work force issues such as job dissatisfaction and different kinds of harassment.

In all of these cases, I helped clients define their problems and get in touch with their inner strengths, and informed them about the community resources available to assist them. Using a brief therapy model, I assisted some to discover the areas of their lives in which they are functioning well and to apply their identified strengths towards developing a solution in the area causing them discomfort. For the vast majority, counselling facilitated my clients' improved human functioning but did not engage them at a deeper, more foundational level. In a way, such a service could have been provided by most trained mental health counsellors. It seemed, at least superficially, that these clients did not necessarily experience any movement towards God or address ultimate questions. Of course, it is possible that more happened than was reported or could be observed. For now I will set these questions aside and concentrate on some cases where the pastoral involvement was more evident.

For a significant minority of 50 cases, about ten percent of my caseload, counselling moved into the areas that redefined human existence and changed their notions about God. They arrived at new conclusions about the meaning of life by focusing on the ultimate questions raised by their crises. This counselling went beyond supporting mental health and explicitly moved the clients ahead in their journey towards God. I do not think it could have been provided by someone who had not been trained to listen for the client's (at first) unvoiced question about the meaning and the destination of life. This type of interaction seems to define the specific domain of pastoral counselling. It is not dependent an a specific locale, nor can it be performed only by ordained persons. It can be effected at any time or in any place by a person who has been trained to listen for and to address questions pertaining to ultimate meaning.

For clients with whom counselling became more obviously pastoral, their presenting questions often arose in relation to some type of injustice or loss. As a result, the person was forced to look at reality in a new way in order to come to terms with their own weakness or that of others. The presenting problems did not vary significantly from those of the cases for which the counselling goal was to modify or maintain daily functioning, but their resolution involved a shift in how the clients understood the meaning of life.

It is interesting to note that, after an interval of time, some clients returned to counselling. Sometimes, an issue that might have first been dealt with on a problem-solving basis would move to a much deeper level during these subsequent sessions. It would seem that these clients had reached the limits of what they had learned; they understood that, in order to fully integrate their problem, they must deepen their life experience. Two examples bear this out.

One man who consulted me was referred by his supervisor, who complained that he smelled of alcohol in the afternoons. Despite an evaluation that confirmed the supervisor's concerns, this client left counselling convinced he did not have an alcohol problem. As he explained, given the supervisor's over-sensitive nose, he would avoid trouble in the future by chewing Clorets. Follow-up phone calls indicated that he was satisfied with his progress. Then, three years later, the same client called again. At the Christmas office party, having had too much to drink, he had made advances to a colleague, who then threatened sexual harassment charges. She was ready to drop the charges if he would get treatment, but he was afraid and unable to accept what he had done; it was seriously out of line with his image of himself as a good person. This time counselling went much deeper, allowing him to arrive at a new image of himself as a good person with a weakness. He understood that he was deserving of his own special care because of his special needs. He no longer needed Clorets to mask a weakness he rejected in himself, but was ready to formulate a plan through which he would take care of himself. This reflected a new awareness of the meaning of life for him.

In another instance, a woman came with a long list of her son's problems, which she presented in a detached way. She accepted a referral to a psychologist who directed the son's substance abuse treatment and saw the mother and son together for counselling. In order to keep me informed, which would not have been necessary according to the program's requirements, she would check in from time to time with a progress report and I would confirm her growth. This continued for about a year and a half. Then, beginning a new marriage, she wanted to establish some new priorities. She became aware that she had always been last in line to receive any of her own care and attention. Perhaps this had something to do with what she thought God wanted from her: continuing self-sacrifice to gain redemption. We examined this belief; her awareness that she is already redeemed, and that all God wants is that she recognize this, gradually became stronger.

Her process was a long one and required a good deal of patience on my part. Initially, due to a variety of experiences, this client was not ready to trust me with anything remotely resembling the care of her soul. Such trust was built up slowly because I accepted her where she was. When counselling began, she was not ready to look at herself, but focused on her problems with her son, and I did not force her to do otherwise. Because of this, she was able to see that she was all right as she was; she could begin questioning how it happened that she was so ready to let others decide her fate. Because the program did not require her to pay for my services, her ability to trust was supported. Someone could be there for her who did not in some way profit from her. Thus, relieved of the idea that people could care for her only when they required something of her, she could receive from me.

Though the previous two cases became more explicitly pastoral only after an extended time, others have quickly developed this quality because of the nature of the presenting problem. This happens when clients come to counselling because of a situation that in some way challenges the foundations of their existence. They know from the outset that they are not looking for the solution to a problem, but for the meaning of life that will help them understand their experience.

In this context, I think of a man who had, through no fault of his own, accidentally killed a young person who jumped in front of his car on the expressway. He was well within the speed limit and had the headlights on. The police qualified the accident as a suicide and did not blame the driver. In fact, they judged him to have done everything possible to avoid the tragedy, and commended him on his quick reflexes and on the quality of first aid administered to the victim. The driver, however, could not forgive himself. He relived the scene in nightmares and felt ostracized by colleagues at work. He was able to better integrate the experience through an understanding of the effects of post-traumatic stress. Yet this did not help with his questions about the meaning of life.

The experience had led, without warning, to a complete revision of his personal code of meaning. He had always believed that, because of his excellent training and intellect, he would be able to prevent tragedy, to protect himself and his family from disaster. Unable to prevent this accident and death, he realized that many other things were beyond his control. He no longer felt safe in the world and could no longer be sure of his ability to protect his family from harm.

In order to assist this client, it was necessary to accompany him in a search for meaning. This led to his new awareness that life was not necessarily about proving one's competence. It was about receiving goodness from the universe and marveling in its gift, caring for it to the best of one's abilities, and then giving it back. He began to integrate this understanding into his life and to be open to receiving as well as to giving. Such a change had profound pastoral implications.

Another client came to me as the result of an accident that happened in quite different circumstances. She was trying to come to terms with the death of her child in an automobile accident caused by the negligent driving of her ex-husband. Working with her involved helping her realize that she would never resolve this loss in the sense of finding a meaning for it or finding a time when it would no longer hurt. Exploring her pain and sense of betrayal led to her expression of feeling betrayed by God as well as by her husband. It was important that she be allowed to feel her rage at the unfairness of life in order to eventually find a deepened presence of God dwelling in the midst of her chaos and living her pain with her.

Some of the pastoral interventions can be examined within certain categories of problems. Several clients presented with feelings of rage and betrayal because of incidents of childhood abuse. They often expressed outrage that God, who was supposedly good, should allow this to happen to a defenseless child. I believe that the secular setting was helpful in allowing these clients to vocalize pain that they would not have dared mention in a place where they thought that the counsellor was required to defend God. Because I did not attempt to do this, these clients were better able to give up the notion that God hated them. Freed from that malignant idea, they began a process of healing old wounds.

I provided another type of pastoral presence in helping some clients to forgive themselves for their various "crimes against humanity" and to see themselves as broken persons who need healing rather than as despicable monsters. These issues often come up in relation to past abortions. Certainly, "unconditional positive regard" has been an essential element in helping these clients move. But it has been even more important to listen for the subtle ways in which they bring up their relationship with God, often revealing that they believe God blames them for these sins. Once they have openly articulated this, it has been possible to help them come to terms with God's forgiveness, freely offered to those who ask.

A pastoral presence has also been useful with some clients who felt they were stagnating in jobs they no longer liked. They had initially found great meaning in these occupations, but they no longer experienced such satisfaction, and circumstances made it impossible for them to leave. Many felt trapped because the work in which they had invested so much could not provide a true meaning for their lives. In order to help them discover a purpose in their existence, while fully recognizing the limitations of their jobs, we needed to go well beyond practical suggestions of job search techniques.

I found it important to listen to my clients' unspoken questions about their worth as persons in order to lead them to a deeper awareness of the gifts of their lives. Through this awareness, they were better able see the beauty surrounding them, to attempt to develop other talents, or to develop relationships. It became possible for them to view such things as bringing meaning to life, and to understand their jobs as a means to an end, providing the material resources to live, but not providing ultimate meaning as such.

In most of the cases where I believe I effected a pastoral role, the client's orientation was within a Christian framework. In some cases, however, I was able to intervene on the basis of my knowledge of other religions and to take the lead from the client regarding his/her questions.

For example, I worked with an aboriginal person to find ways to develop an appreciation for her culture in the life of her son, who had never lived on the Reserve and whose father was non-native. A beaded eagle feather decorated my office wall. Giving it to my client, I suggested that it might lead her in finding an answer to her questions. She reported in the next session that she had initiated a sweet-grass ceremony with her son, using the feather to direct smoke on them. He was now investigating what this ceremony meant and had asked her to repeat the ritual so he could participate more actively in it.

These cases provide an overview of situations in which I feel my presence was explicitly "pastoral." I am convinced that a person who had not learned to listen for questions about the fundamental meaning of existence could not have helped these clients in the same way. Though they might possibly have helped the clients through an immediate crisis or assisted them to find new ways of coping with their difficult presenting problems, non-pastoral practitioners might have ignored essential elements in the clients' journey towards God. When one supports clients towards a fuller realization of God in their lives, both client and counsellor are provided with opportunities for growth.

The EAP Counsellor in Pastoral Roles

Possibly due to the lack of adequate avenues for religious expression in our society, there are opportunities for pastoral action within the EAP role in addition to that of pastoral counselling. Because employees have had the opportunity to become comfortable with EAP counsellors in the workplace, they often turn to these counsellors on occasions when they formerly would have sought out a member of the clergy. Though I am less aware of religious practice in other provinces, in my province of Quebec, church attendance has fallen dramatically. One of the initiatives of Quebec bishops has been a project called "Risquer L'Avenir," an attempt to involve people in developing the future of the Church. In the Gatineau-Hull Diocese, the project has apparently revealed that many people simply discount the Church's ability to be meaningfully involved in their lives or to have anything relevant to say to them.

Paradoxically, while people find that the parish church has little to offer, pastoral activity in more secular settings has been growing. Here are some examples of how this is manifested in the EAP context.

In times of bereavement the EAP counsellor is often one of the first persons contacted to provide either counselling to the surviving friends or family or to provide group interventions in the workplace. In the past, a priest or minister might have been the initial contact. Yet many people no longer find meaning in a clergy presence, so they turn to other sources of comfort. I am aware of one counsellor who was recently asked to deliver the eulogy at an employee's funeral. In all likelihood, because employees were accustomed to turning to this counsellor for support in the workplace, they thought of him as being able to provide meaning in the context of the funeral.

On several occasions, when the sudden death of a colleague has upset a group of employees, I have presented sessions on grieving. I have also participated in a such a session for employees who shared the devastation of a colleague, a young mother whose child was hit by a school bus. These sessions provided a forum for people to normalize their reactions, to express their feelings of sadness, and to collectively recognize what the dead person had meant to them.

In another day and age, when meaningful relationships tended to be with one's family and neighbours, local parish members responded well to the needs of the bereaved. At the funeral where the bereaved were joined by fellow parishioners, all listened to the clergy person who attempted to help them understand the meaning of their loss in a shared context that everyone understood. The bereaved could meet with neighbours on the church steps to talk about their loss and could count on some of them to help out where needed.

This world no longer exists for most people. With the advent of telecommunications and rapid transportation and our growing awareness of the world's diversity, we do not necessarily share a common world view even with immediate neighbours. A funeral gathering brings together people of many different religions or of no religion at all. People often travel from great distances to attend a funeral, but will not remain to comfort members of the family. Many of those in attendance will typically be the deceased person's work colleagues who are marking the end of a relationship forged through common activity. Because working together toward a common goal often creates solid bonds, employees experience significant loss when one of their colleagues dies. If that person's death has been sudden, unexpected or violent, the remaining employees often find some kind of a workplace intervention useful in addressing their grief.

Along the same lines, many EAPs offer a variety of sessions to help employees cope with job loss and with those elements of loss present in any transition. Frequently, participants not only gain an understanding of what is happening to them physically and emotionally, but also discover inner resources that enhance their lives. These sessions bring a pastoral presence to the workplace and help fill the vacuum created as people have turned away from churches.

Another type of pastoral presence is demonstrated in the actions of those EAP counsellors who make extraordinary efforts to meet with distressed employees.
I am aware of one who regularly visits people in the hospital to show that they are cared for. I have met with an employee in special need in her own home. Similarly, another counsellor, who had responsibilities at the national level, went out of his way to comfort an ill colleague; while on regional business, he supported his colleague, then in the terminal phase of cancer, by visiting with her and with her family. This presence surpassed the call of duty and was of a type that would formerly have been expected only from clergy persons.

Conclusion

The preceding reflections and examples point to a pastoral presence in the workplace. We will need to develop our understanding of this, and to discover what types of questions and what type of presence lead a person to move ahead in looking at his/her relationship with God.

References

Cavanagh, J.R. (1962). *Fundamental pastoral counseling.* New York: Mercier Press.

Clinebell, H.J. (1984). *Basic types of pastoral counseling.* New York: Abingdon Press.

Frankl, V. E. (1973). *Man's search for meaning: An introduction to logotherapy.* New York: Simon and Schuster.

Gratton, C. (1992). *The Art of spiritual guidance: A contemporary approach to growing in the spirit.* New York: Crossroad.

Hamilton, J.D. (1972). *The ministry of pastoral counseling.* Grand Rapids, Michigan: Baker Book House.

Meier, A. (1990). Future directions in pastoral counselling: I. Constructing theoretical models. *Pastoral Sciences, 9,* 131-152.

Oates, W.E. (1974). *Pastoral counseling.* Philadelphia: Westminister Press.

O'Brien, M.J. (1968). *An introduction to pastoral counseling.* New York: Alba House.

Power, F. C. (1990). *The distinctiveness of pastoral counselling. Counselling and values. 34*(2), 75-88.

Rahner, K. (1978). *Foundation of christian faith: An introduction to the Idea of christianity.* New York: Seabury Press.

Stearns, A. K. (1984). *Living through personal crisis.* New York: Ballantine Books.

Vanderpool, J.A. (1977). *A person to person: A handbook for pastoral counseling.* Garden City, New York: Doubleday.

Chapter 12

L'exploitation sexuelle des enfants: Ouvrir les yeux et tendre la main

*Micheline Boivin**

Que l'on soit parent, ami, voisin, enseignant, pasteur ou intervenant de différentes disciplines oeuvrant dans des milieux variés, l'enfant exploité sexuellement que nous rencontrons souhaite et a besoin que nous ouvrions les yeux, que nous nous rendions compte de sa détresse et que nous sachions décoder les signes d'anxiété qu'il nous donne. II a besoin que nous nous rendions compte que quelque chose ne va pas et que nous le comprenions. Il a également besoin que nous lui tendions la main, c'est-à-dire qu'on le protège, le supporte, le guide et l'aide à traverser ses difficultés bouleversantes. En notre jargon professionnel, nous parlons de prévention, de dépistage, d'évaluation et de traitement dans les cas d'exploitation sexuelle. L'enfant ne pense pas et ne parle pas en ces termes. Il pourrait nous dire très simplement: "Ouvrez-vous les yeux et tendez-moi la main."

L'exploitation sexuelle implique toute activité avec intention sexuelle où l'inégalité entre les deux personnes engendre un contexte de pouvoir, c'est-à-dire où il y a une relation d'autorité, de confiance, ou de dépendance. Il peut s'agir d'une activité où il

---

*Révision d'une présentation faite dans le cadre de la troisième conférence annuelle de la Société de Recherches en Counselling Pastoral, Université Saint-Paul, Ottawa, 10 mai 1996.

y a un contact corporel, direct ou indirect, d'une incitation à des contacts sexuels, directs ou non, avec une partie du corps ou un objet. Il peut s'agir également d'exhibitionnisme. Selon la Loi canadienne (Wells, 1990), les enfants ayant moins de 14 ans n'ont pas la maturité pour consentir de façon éclairée à toutes ces activités sexuelles. Elle considère, par ailleurs, l'âge de moins de 18 ans pour d'autres formes d'exploitation sexuelle, notamment toutes les infractions liées à la prostitution juvénile et à la corruption d'enfants. La Loi prévoit des nuances dans le cas d'activités sexuelles entre adolescents selon la différence d'âge, le consentement des deux parties et l'existence d'une relation d'autorité ou d'une position de dépendance.

Les termes "exploitation sexuelle" et "abus sexuel" sont interchangeables dans ce chapitre, bien que le premier soit préférable, car sa définition est plus vaste en englobant d'autres formes d'exploitation telles les activités pornographiques et la prostitution, et aussi parce que le terme "abus" peut insinuer que seulement le degré excessif du comportement est inacceptable.

La plupart des enfants dont il est question ici ont vécu une expérience d'exploitation sexuelle extra-familiale.

Ce chapitre comporte deux parties intitulées, respectivement, "Ouvrir les yeux" et "Tendre la main." Dans la première partie, je présente concrètement ce sur quoi nos yeux doivent s'ouvrir car un enfant peut manifester à son entourage de nombreux signes de détresse et d'anxiété. Le cas d'une enfant exploitée sexuellement est illustré en rendant compte de l'évolution des signes et de la réaction de son entourage. J'indique ensuite ce sur quoi l'évaluation doit porter en considérant l'ensemble des signes manifestés par l'enfant, son état psychologique, les antécédents de l'enfant et de la famille, les conséquences à court et à long terme de l'expérience d'abus, l'impact sur la famille, dont les parents principalement et finalement, les ressources et les besoins de ces derniers. Dans la partie "Tendre la main," j'aborde le travail thérapeutique avec l'enfant en mettant l'emphase sur la méthode de la thérapie par le jeu.

Ouvrir les yeux

Signes de l'exploitation sexuelle

Dans le cas d'exploitation sexuelle, les signes qu'un enfant manifeste à l'école, à la maison ou à la garderie peuvent être d'ordre comportemental, relationnel, cognitif, émotif et physique. Les signes peuvent être non verbaux, verbaux, directs ou clairs et, indirects ou vagues.

Signes aux plans comportemental et relationnel

Aux plans comportemental et relationnel, nous observons que l'enfant peut être agressif. À l'école, il rudoie ses camarades, il a de la difficulté avec les figures d'autorité tels les enseignants. À la maison, il se montre contrariant, il refuse d'écouter, il fait des crises de colère et il n'est pas "parlable." À la garderie, il tire les cheveux des autres enfants, les bouscule, les mord. L'enfant peut aussi manifester des comportements régressifs. Il devient anxieux dans les situations où il doit se séparer de sa mère et de son père. Il craint maintenant d'aller à l'école. Il appréhende l'absence de son enseignante et ainsi la venue d'une remplaçante. À la garderie, il tend à vérifier si le mari ou l'ami de la gardienne sera là et s'il viendra à la maison. Partout où il va, il exige davantage d'attention et de sécurité. Il s'accroche à sa mère, veut se faire prendre. Il peut recommencer à parler en bébé, à se souiller ou à se mouiller, à se sucer le pouce, à se mettre en boule et à réutiliser un objet de transition qui le réconforte tel une peluche ou une couverture.

De plus, nous constatons un changement soudain d'attitude envers une personne ou un lieu en particulier. Ainsi, bien qu'il acceptait auparavant le gardiennage par son cousin, maintenant il refuse carrément d'être en sa compagnie; ou bien, il manifeste de la réticence à visiter ses grands-parents et il fait une scène lorsqu'on lui en parle. Il peut insister pour changer de parcours pour se rendre à l'école, ou refuser d'aller jouer au parc comme il en avait l'habitude. Il peut refuser d'aller à toutes toilettes situées dans un endroit public ou à l'école parce que c'est l'endroit où il a été attaqué. Il peut, sans explication rationnelle, vouloir soudainement abandonner une activité ou un sport qu'il aimait.

Un changement d'attitude vis-à-vis le toucher peut se manifester également. Par exemple, il résiste fortement à être changé de couche, il ne veut pas que ses parents le lavent ou le baignent; il est particulièrement vigilant à ce qu'on ne lui touche pas les fesses. Un autre est terrifié à l'idée de prendre une douche. Un enfant d'âge scolaire refuse de changer de vêtements pour le cours d'éducation physique. Les jeux qui deviennent agressifs peuvent aussi refléter le désarroi de l'enfant. Tel fut le cas d'une fillette de quatre ans qui maltraitait ses poupées et ses peluches. La reproduction de gestes sexuels très explicites dans les dessins des enfants et dans leurs jeux, soit avec d'autres enfants ou des poupées soit avec des peluches ou des animaux, est un autre indice.

L'enfant peut avoir des comportements sexualisés. À l'école, la fillette s'auto-stimule de façon incontrôlée sur sa chaise. Un garçon moleste un plus jeune dans les toilettes. Les enfants ont des jeux sexuels précoces et/ou inhabituels. À la maison, la petite fille introduit des objets ou son doigt dans son vagin ou celui d'une autre enfant. Plusieurs fois par jour, le bambin se cache derrière les rideaux pour s'auto-stimuler. II baisse ses culottes et se frotte sur les genoux d'un adulte. À la garderie, lors de la sieste, il insiste pour aller toucher les parties intimes des autres enfants qui dorment. À tout âge, dans tous les milieux, l'enfant peut exprimer son affection et/ou son besoin d'attention à l'endroit des adultes de façon inappropriée (caresses intimes, baiser avec langue).

Il arrive que l'enfant s'isole particulièrement de ses pairs. Il évite le contact visuel, a peu d'amis et se replie sur lui-même. Par contre, un autre enfant semble avoir une relation privilégiée avec un voisin de palier qui lui accorde une attention bien particulière. Certains enfants ont des comportements destructeurs soit dirigés vers l'extérieur, soit dirigés contre eux-mêmes en se faisant mal de diverses manières ou en ayant une propension aux accidents.

Un changement dans le rendement et l'apprentissage scolaire est observable. Ses notes baissent, il semble rêveur, il est dans la lune. L'enfant a une pauvre concentration et certains sont agités sans qu'on ait une explication médicale ou réactionnelle à un stress. Dans certains cas où l'enfant a été attouché par un autre élève ou un membre du personnel, il ne voudra plus aller à l'école. Parfois, l'enfant teste le terrain avec les adultes. Il vérifie s'il peut parler du sujet sexuel: "Puis-je tout dire?" ou "Serai-je puni si tu sais que j'ai fait quelque chose de pas beau?"

Signes au plan émotif

Au plan émotif, l'enfant peut éprouver une grande peur ou de l'anxiété vis-à-vis un lieu comme le chemin pour se rendre au parc, ou vis-à-vis des étrangers, des adultes ou des adolescents, en particulier ceux du même sexe que l'abuseur. Il semble terrifié, sursaute à l'occasion et développe des phobies comme dans le cas de cette fillette de trois ans qui ne pouvait tolérer la vue de crucifix, de clowns et du Père Noël. II s'est avéré que la petite pouvait voir le crucifix sur le mur lorsqu'elle était abusée et que l'abuseur s'était déguisé en clown et en Père Noël durant la période où elle était gardée chez lui.

L'enfant peut avoir des cauchemars et des terreurs nocturnes. Il pleure plus souvent, il semble triste, découragé, parfois même déprimé au point d'avoir le goût de mourir. C'est ainsi qu'un garçon de sept ans et une fillette de huit ans disaient vouloir mourir; ils planifiaient, respectivement, de se lancer devant un véhicule et de se pendre. À l'école, on dit d'eux qu'ils sont bébés, braillards, renfermés, anxieux, qu'ils recherchent beaucoup d'attention et qu'ils ont souvent besoin d'être rassurés.

Nous remarquons que les enfants ayant vécu une expérience d'exploitation sexuelle manquent souvent de confiance dans les autres, mais aussi en eux-mêmes, dans la vie et dans le futur. Par exemple, un garçon dit: "Ma vie est finie. Il n'y a plus rien de bon qui va m'arriver." Après avoir vécu l'expérience d'abus multiples (sexuels, physiques et émotifs) un autre enfant avait le sentiment que sa vie était chaotique et que tout se brisait autour de lui. Il avait la nette impression que sa vie n'était qu'une suite de catastrophes. Quant à l'affect de certains enfants, il peut être émoussé et avoir l'air engourdi.

Certains enfants présentent des changements d'humeur importants. Le parent dit de son enfant qu'il est irritable, colérique, soupe au lait, se sentant coupable de tout ou bien qu'il semble triste et distant. On se rend compte que certains enfants sont hostiles ou agressifs à l'endroit des adultes et que d'autres sont complaisants envers eux.

Signes au plan cognitif

Au plan cognitif, nous notons que certains enfants ont des connaissances précoces de la sexualité et qu'ils font preuve d'une curiosité excessive. Leurs questions et le langage utilisé sont sophistiqués pour leur âge. Ils connaissent des gestes sexuels privés, parfois hors de l'ordinaire, et leurs informations sont erronées. Ils ont une faible estime d'eux-mêmes et une pauvre image de soi. Certains ont internalisé qu'ils sont mauvais, qu'ils ne valent rien, qu'ils sont abîmés, qu'ils sont un objet de satisfaction sexuelle pour l'autre, qu'ils sont coupables ou qu'ils seront toujours trahis ou maltraités dans leurs relations avec les autres.

Nous pouvons remarquer qu'ils ont l'air absents, rêveurs. Les parents se plaignent que l'enfant n'a pas l'air à les entendre. À l'école, ils ont du mal à se concentrer et ils se dissocient, c'est à dire qu'ils sont déconnectés ou ont l'air absents. Certains enfants ont des pensées intruses. Par exemple, une mère observe fréquemment la scène suivante alors que sa fillette de quatre ans joue avec sa petite soeur de deux ans. En plein milieu du jeu, sans raison apparente, elle prend sa petite soeur par le cou et lui dit d'un air protecteur: "Personne ne va te faire mal." Il arrive que des enfants aient des reviviscences (souvenirs sensoriels) comme cette fillette, âgée de neuf ans, qui a des problèmes au coucher parce que dès qu'elle sent sa main au bord du lit, elle voit une main qui va l'attraper.

Signes au plan physique

Au plan physique, un enseignant peut constater le changement dans l'apparence de l'enfant ou de l'adolescent: elle est moins soignée ou il s'habille trop et porte des vêtements larges. Un autre enfant peut présenter des troubles somatiques nouveaux (maux de tête et surtout maux de ventre) ou des troubles alimentaires. Les signes les plus évidents sont les blessures anales ou génitales, les douleurs génitales et les démangeaisons. La personne qui prodigue les soins à l'enfant est la mieux placée pour observer ces signes. Une consultation médicale aidera à déterminer s'il y a matière à soupçonner que l'enfant a été abusé sexuellement.

Ces divers signes donnent un aperçu de ce que nous pouvons observer afin de dépister si un enfant est ou a été exploité sexuellement. Toutefois, une mise en garde concernant l'ensemble de ces signes s'impose afin que nous ne voyions pas de l'exploitation sexuelle où il n'y en a pas. Il faut ouvrir les yeux, oui, mais non porter les lunettes de l'abus. La majorité de ces signes peuvent être reliés à une problématique autre que celle de l'exploitation sexuelle ou à une autre difficulté vécue par l'enfant et l'adolescent. Les blessures aux parties intimes et, selon Gil (1993, p.97), les comportements sexuels qui sont excessifs, compulsifs et persistants malgré les limites parentales et qui distraient l'enfant des activités qui seraient appropriées pour son âge sont plus directement associés à la possibilité d'exploitation sexuelle. Le lien est moins direct en ce qui a trait aux autres signes. Il faut donc être prudent et attentif dans nos observations et nos déductions. Dans certains cas, les soupçons naissent et une enquête et/ou une évaluation s'en suivent. Dans d'autres cas, ce n'est qu'après la divulgation que les parents (et parfois les professionnels) font un retour sur le passé et établissent le lien entre les différents signes. Il s'agit donc d'une compréhension en rétrospective.

Illustration d'un cas

Quelques-uns des signes présentés plus haut sont maintenant illustrés par le cas d'une petite fille de deux ans et demi qui a été en garde familiale pour une durée de 10 semaines.

Au cours des deux premières semaines de gardiennage

Réactions de l'enfant: Elle ne veut pas se faire garder et proteste: "Maman, je m'ennuie de toi. Je t'aime trop." Elle pleure, fait une crise jusque dans la nuit et elle demande à sa mère d'arrêter de travailler.

Réactions des adultes: Les parents se disent: "Elle a de la difficulté à se séparer de sa mère." "C'est une première expérience de séparation." "Notre enfant tente de nous manipuler, de contrôler notre vie." "Je (la mère) ne me laisserai pas faire."

La gardienne leur dit: "Tous les enfants réagissent ainsi au début. Dans une ou deux semaines, cela aura passé."

La mère dit à l'enfant: "Ce n'est pas plus facile pour moi de te laisser chez la gardienne. Ne rends pas les choses plus difficiles." "On va t'habituer. Il le faut, car je dois aller travailler."

Une ou plusieurs de ces explications adoptées par le parent le dispose à ne pas entendre la détresse de son enfant.

Après deux ou trois semaines

Réactions de l'enfant: L'enfant arrête de protester et va chez la gardienne sans faire de crise. Elle a peur de la noirceur, s'endort tard, a un sommeil agité et se réveille au cours de la nuit.

Réactions des parents qui se disent: "À bien y penser, la gardienne avait raison. Notre fille s'habitue, elle est plus autonome." "Je (la mère) ne me suis pas laissée manipuler, j'ai bien fait." Ils la bercent lorsqu'elle pleure la nuit.

Les parents interprètent ce changement d'attitude comme une amélioration pensant que leur fille s'est habituée à aller chez la gardienne, qu'elle est plus coopérative et qu'elle s'est finalement adaptée. Ils font malheureusement fausse route. En réalité, après deux ou trois semaines de pleurs et de protestations, incomprise, l'enfant se résigne et va chez la gardienne sans faire de crise.

Divulgation et réactions plus à long terme de l'abus

La fin du travail de la mère marque la fin du gardiennage. Un mois plus tard, l'enfant révèle à sa mère qu'elle a peur de monsieur X (le mari de la gardienne), qu'il l'a touchée aux parties intimes (elle l'imite), qu'il a fait pipi sur son ventre, que la madame l'a lavée et lui a dit qu'elle était une méchante petite fille. Les signes s'accumulent, s'intensifient et se prolongent: elle est plus timide et réservée; elle refuse les baisers et les caresses de ses parents; elle a des jeux sexuels avec sa soeur et son amie; elle s'insère un crayon dans le vagin; son sommeil est encore perturbé;

elle éprouve des émotions intenses de haine et de peur où elle veut protéger sa soeur; et elle crie lorsqu'elle revoit le mari de la gardienne.

C'est à ce point que les parents demandent de l'aide. Lorsque questionnés, ils rapportent les nombreux changements qu'ils ont observés chez leur fille et ils comprennent en rétrospective ce qu'elle a vécu. Ils se sentent manifestement coupables de ne pas avoir protégé leur fille et de n'avoir pas compris plus tôt sa détresse. Ils sont, de plus, en colère envers la gardienne et son mari en qui ils avaient confiance.

Il y a des parents qui sans pouvoir comprendre la cause des réactions de leur enfant répondent avec sensibilité à son besoin d'être sécurisé et ils réagissent à sa détresse avec une disponibilité émotionnelle, du support et de la curiosité. Un parent dira: "Je ne sais pas ce qu'il y a, mais il se passe quelque chose d'anormal." Ces parents tendent à réagir assez rapidement.

Le dépistage constitue le premier volet de "Ouvrir les yeux," ce besoin qu'a l'enfant qu'on se rende compte de ce qu'il vit et qu'on détecte les signes de détresse et d'anxiété qu'il nous donne. Les adultes autour de lui ont parfois du mal à saisir ce qui se passe et un certain temps s'écoule avant que la lumière ne se fasse et que l'enfant ne soit protégé. Il faut noter que l'enfant lui-même a maintes raisons de craindre de dévoiler l'abus. Par exemple, il craint le rejet de ses parents en les peinant, il croit les diverses menaces de l'abuseur ou il a peur d'être puni ou de n'être pas cru. De plus, il est difficile de trouver les mots pour expliquer ce qui est arrivé.

Compréhension

Le deuxième volet de "Ouvrir les yeux" porte sur la compréhension du sens de tous ces indices qui s'accumulent, se combinent, s'intensifient et persistent. En d'autres mots, il s'agit de l'évaluation de l'état psychologique de l'enfant et de ses comportements interpersonnels. Pour ce faire, dans les grandes lignes: (a) nous recueillons les renseignements pertinents concernant son fonctionnement physique, comportemental, relationnel, émotionnel et cognitif d'avant et après l'expérience d'abus; les renseignements en rapport à ses expériences passées et au stress qu'il a vécu; et les données sur les réactions de l'enfant aux expériences stressantes antérieures; (b) nous évaluons sa perception de son expérience d'abus sexuel, sa perception de soi, des autres, du futur et du monde et le stade de développement de l'enfant; (c) pour être complète, l'évaluation doit également porter sur des données concernant les membres de la famille de l'enfant dont principalement les parents.

De façon plus spécifique, l'évaluation s'élabore selon deux axes principaux:

1. Les antécédents de l'enfant et de la famille. L'enfant a-t-il été traumatisé ou stressé auparavant? Les manifestations problématiques présentes sont-elles reliées à des difficultés antérieures à l'expérience d'abus ou à d'autres difficultés actuelles? Quelle est la qualité du lien ou de l'attachement avec ses parents? Quels sont ses ressources et ses aspects vulnérables? Comment était la vie familiale avant l'abus? Quels sont les facteurs qui auraient pu contribuer à l'abus et dont le thérapeute devra tenir compte lors du traitement? Par exemple, si l'enfant est carencé affectivement, et l'on sait que les manques d'attention et d'affection peuvent le rendre vulnérable aux abuseurs sexuels (Conte, Wolf & Smith, 1989), comment le thérapeute va-t-il s'assurer que les parents apprennent à répondre aux besoins affectifs de leur enfant et ce, de manière stable?

2. La gravité de l'expérience de l'abus sexuel et ses conséquences à court et à long terme. Pour évaluer cela, nous tenons compte des circonstances de l'abus, de sa nature, de sa durée, de sa fréquence, de l'âge de l'enfant et de son abuseur, du type de lien avec ce dernier, de la différence de grandeur ou stature, du stade de développement de l'enfant, du type de menace ou de coercition, du chantage ou de la séduction, des circonstances de la divulgation de l'abus, à qui l'enfant s'est ouvert et du laps de temps depuis l'incident, de la réaction des parents et de l'entourage, de la qualité du support parental, des démarches déjà entreprises dans les domaines

judiciaire, légal et de l'aide professionnelle. Au plan familial, nous évaluons l'impact de cet évènement traumatisant sur tous les membres de la famille, en particulier sur les parents. Ce point sera abordé plus loin.

Au plan psychologique, nous évaluons: (a) les dynamiques propres au traumatisme telles la stigmatisation, la trahison, l'impuissance et la sexualisation traumatisante (Finkelhor & Browne, 1985); (b) les effets post-traumatiques (Briere, 1992) tels les symptômes d'intrusion et les cauchemars; (c) les distorsions cognitives résultant de l'hypervigilance, de l'impuissance, de la pauvre estime de soi et des internalisations de soi; (d) l'émotivité altérée comme la dépression et l'anxiété; (e) les symptômes de dissociation; (f) le soi appauvri; (g) les difficultés comportementales et relationnelles.

Les internalisations que l'enfant élabore à partir de cette expérience d'abus nous éclairent sur ses perceptions et ses sentiments par rapport à lui-même, aux autres, au monde et au futur. Avant le monde de l'enfant était sécuritaire et prévisible, à la condition bien sûr, que l'enfant ait été épargné de vivre d'autres formes d'abus. Par conséquent, le monde a changé pour lui et cela est bouleversant ou perturbant, voire même traumatisant. Il peut voir le monde comme imprévisible et dangereux. Pour plusieurs, la relation de confiance qu'ils avaient a été brisée et l'enfant vit un traumatisme relationnel. Il internalise alors qu'il ne peut désormais faire confiance à autrui. Les internalisations nous donnent une idée de l'abus psychologique concomitant à l'abus sexuel chez l'enfant qui se perçoit mauvais, coupable, endommagé, ou comme un objet sexuel. Quel sens y attribue-t-il? Conclut-t-il qu'il méritait d'être abusé? Sur qui l'enfant place-t-il la responsabilité de l'abus? Il arrive qu'il se sente à la fois impuissant et responsable de l'abus. S'il se blâme, il risque de se sentir honteux. Comment réagit-il? En se renfermant ou en étant agressif? Devient-il désorganisé, incohérent?

Le processus d'évaluation porte également sur les parents qui sont évalués à partir de/du: (a) leur état de détresse psychologique, leurs émotions, leurs perceptions et leurs internalisations par rapport à leur enfant et à eux-mêmes; (b) leur habileté à faire face à la révélation de leur enfant ainsi qu'à l'impact du traumatisme sur lui; quelles sont leurs réactions? Soutiennent-ils leur enfant? Sont-ils bouleversés, en état de choc, enragés? Prennent-ils l'histoire de leur enfant au sérieux? (c) leur expérience personnelle, à savoir s'ils ont eux-mêmes vécu une expérience d'abus qui se trouve réveillée par celle de leur enfant et qui affecte leur capacité de le comprendre et leur façon d'être avec lui? (d) leurs ressources et leurs difficultés; (e) leur besoin d'aide individuelle ou de groupe pour traverser cette période de crise?

Il est important de considérer la fratrie de l'enfant qui a vécu un abus et de poser les questions suivantes: Y a-t-il aussi des frères et des soeurs à risque d'avoir été ou d'être victimes d'abus? Que savent-ils de ce qui se passe? De quelle façon réagissent-ils à la crise familiale et à leur frère ou leur soeur en détresse? Quelle est la nature du lien entre eux? Comment les parents réussissent-ils à s'occuper des autres enfants? Y a-t-il un réseau qui les supporte?

Tendre la main

Une fois le dépistage et l'évaluation accomplis (bien que l'évaluation soit continue), nous pouvons tendre la main à l'enfant en le croyant, le protégeant, le supportant, l'encourageant, l'aidant à traverser cette période difficile et en lui offrant une expérience réparatrice et corrective. Plusieurs enfants s'engagent dans un processus thérapeutique.

Philosophie de base

Quelle approche nous permet d'entrer dans le monde intérieur de l'enfant tel qu'il le vit et non pas selon une théorie? C'est l'approche phénoménologique (Briere, 1992). En étant curieux de connaître l'expérience interne de l'enfant, sa façon de percevoir les choses et sa manière de transiger avec elles, nous posons les questions nécessaires et nous faisons des affirmations plus empathiques. Nous entrons dans le monde interne de l'enfant au rythme de celui-ci, sans risquer de le brusquer, d'aller trop vite ou trop lentement. L'expérience de l'enfant nous sert de guide en thérapie. Nous favorisons ainsi une approche où l'enfant se découvre tout en se révélant ou en s'exprimant et où nous le comprenons de son intérieur (Meier et Boivin, 1987).

Relation thérapeutique

La relation thérapeutique naît à travers notre interaction avec l'enfant. Mon image de la relation thérapeutique est celle d'un courant qui passe dans les deux sens; il y a du dynamisme. Elle est comme un pont que l'on construit ensemble, une structure solide sur laquelle l'enfant peut marcher pour aller vers autre chose, vers la découverte de soi, des autres et du monde. Ce pont n'est pas construit sous vide car il est enveloppé, entouré d'un climat de respect, d'empathie, d'authenticité et d'acceptation inconditionnelle.

Lorsque nous intervenons avec l'enfant, nous avons besoin de le mettre en confiance et d'établir une atmosphère où il se sent en sécurité, se sent supporté, respecté, compris, validé dans son expérience et où il se sent libre de s'exprimer. Nous bâtissons une relation thérapeutique empreinte de confiance. L'enfant sent qu'on lui tend l'oreille et la main.

Au début du processus thérapeutique, je laisse toujours à l'enfant la possibilité d'être accompagné de son père ou de sa mère (beaucoup sont de familles monoparentales). Graduellement, son anxiété diminue, il devient plus familier avec moi, l'étrangère, et avec l'environnement de mon bureau et ce qui s'y passe. Un lien de confiance se crée entre nous et l'enfant devient capable de laisser son parent dans la salle d'attente durant notre rencontre. Il est essentiel de prendre l'enfant où il est et d'ouvrir les portes au développement d'un rapport empreint de confiance, de sécurité et d'acceptation. Brusquer ce processus ne serait pas productif.

Comment un jeune peut-il percevoir cette relation thérapeutique? Lors d'une entrevue de relance, une petite fille âgée de six ans regardait les dessins qu'elle avait produits un an plus tôt en thérapie. Elle commente ainsi: "J'ai fait ces dessins quand nous sommes devenues amies." Elle n'avait jamais parlé en ces termes auparavant. Là, elle a exprimé comment elle percevait notre relation comme importante et significative. Entre d'autres mots, elle avait internalisé la thérapeute comme un "bon objet" (Klein, 1948, 1975) ce qui constitue un bonne expérience pour elle. L'objectif de la relation thérapeutique n'est évidemment pas que le thérapeute et l'enfant deviennent amis. L'objectif de la relation thérapeutique est d'offrir à l'enfant les conditions qui encouragent sa croissance et son développement.

Approche multidimensionnelle

Le travail thérapeutique avec un enfant qui a vécu un abus sexuel peut se faire selon une combinaison de modalités. Les modalités de thérapie sont les suivantes: individuelle avec l'enfant, individuelle avec le ou les parents, parentale, dyadique c'est-à-dire mère-enfant ou père-enfant, familiale, thérapie par le jeu avec l'enfant et intervention auprès du personnel enseignant. Une combinaison de base que j'utilise avec les enfants qui ont été exploités sexuellement par un tiers est la thérapie individuelle avec l'enfant, associée à la thérapie par le jeu, l'intervention dyadique (parent enfant) et le travail individuel avec le parent ou le travail parental. Il m'apparaît crucial et efficace de travailler en étroite collaboration avec les parents et de leur offrir le soutien, l'information et l'aide nécessaires. Aider les parents, c'est les aider à tendre la main à leur enfant.

Éléments travaillés lors de la thérapie avec l'enfant

Notre accès à l'expérience intrapersonnelle et interpersonnelle de l'enfant et les objectifs thérapeutiques formulés suite à l'évaluation nous orientent vers le matériel à travailler. Le plus souvent les éléments abordés sont: (a) l'assurance de la protection et de la sécurité de l'enfant dans son milieu; (b) l'attribution du blâme et de la responsabilité du geste sexuel sur la personne vraiment responsable. On se trouve à déresponsabiliser l'enfant et à le déculpabiliser; (c) la normalisation des réactions ou symptômes compte tenu du stress ou du trauma que l'enfant a vécu; (d) la reconnaissance que les gestes étaient inappropriés et inacceptables; (e) la dissipation de la confusion en éduquant sur les touchers OK et non OK; (f) le travail sur ses sentiments ambivalents à l'endroit de l'abuseur ou des gestes sexuels, car l'enfant peut être tiraillé entre ses sentiments positifs comme celui de se sentir bien qu'on lui accorde de l'attention et ses sentiments négatifs comme ceux d'être trahi, trompé, utilisé. Son ambivalence et sa confusion peuvent aussi provenir du fait que l'enfant a éprouvé des sensations agréables durant l'expérience ou qu'il a collaboré afin d'obtenir une faveur de l'abuseur; (g) l'exploration des circonstances avant, pendant et après la divulgation et du vécu associé; (h) l'exploration de l'expérience traumatique ou bouleversante pour l'enfant; (i) l'identification et l'expression de ses souvenirs, ses perceptions, ses sentiments, ses besoins, ses comportements et ses attitudes; (j) le travail sur les conséquences à long terme de l'abus: les réponses psychologiques telles que le stress post-traumatique, les distorsions cognitives, l'émotivité altérée, la dissociation, le soi appauvri, les relations perturbées et les comportements d'évitement (Briere, 1992), les dynamiques d'impuissance, de stigmatisation, de trahison et de sexualisation traumatisante (Finkelhor & Browne, 1985) et les internalisations découlant de son expérience d'abus. Il demeure que parfois l'emphase initiale du travail doit être sa stabilisation dans son milieu familial, scolaire, ou de la famille d'accueil avant que l'enfant ne soit prêt à aborder son expérience d'abus.

Thérapie par le jeu

La thérapie par le jeu, très efficace et accessible pour l'enfant, constitue une méthode de choix. Nancy Boyd Webb (1994) définit la thérapie par le jeu comme une méthode de psychothérapie qui utilise le jeu et la communication verbale dans le but de comprendre et d'aider l'enfant (p.3). Maintes fois j'ai observé que les gestes suppléent au manque de mots ou à la difficulté de dire et qu'ils complètent aussi le dire.

Objectifs de la thérapie par le jeu

La thérapie par le jeu contribue à réaliser trois grands objectifs: (a) établir la relation de confiance entre l'enfant et le thérapeute, en brisant la glace, en apprenant à se connaître et à se familiariser avec l'environnement; (b) évaluer la condition psychologique de l'enfant en entrant dans son monde intérieur qu'il exprime et projette dans le jeu, le développement de l'enfant, sa perception de l'événement traumatisant, sa perception de soi, des autres, du monde et du futur ainsi que ses expériences stressantes vécues antérieurement et ses réactions; (c) traiter en parlant de ses souvenirs de l'abus, ventilant, libérant ses tensions, modifiant le cours des choses dans le processus, faisant l'expérience d'une autre façon de réagir et d'une autre façon de se relier, voyant les choses différemment, se connectant à une autre émotion et finalement, en exprimant un besoin. En bref, nous abordons, à son rythme et selon ses ressources, l'ensemble de son expérience en tenant compte des dimensions comportementale, relationnelle, cognitive, émotionnelle et physique dans le but de faciliter son développement optimal.

Principes généraux de l'approche utilisée

Il y a au moins six principes généraux qui guident le thérapeute dans son travail avec les enfants lors de la thérapie par le jeu:

1. Guider et faciliter le processus thérapeutique sans bloquer la créativité de l'enfant dans l'expression de ses conflits, de ses peurs, de ses émotions, de ses pensées et de ses besoins. Le thérapeute lui donne les moyens de s'exprimer et met du matériel à sa disposition.

2. Accéder à l'expérience traumatique de façon graduelle, selon le rythme de l'enfant et selon ses capacités. Petit à petit, l'enfant sévèrement traumatisé fait face à sa souffrance. En appliquant la notion de Brière (1992), je dirais que l'enfant se désensibilise au traumatisme. Il l'aborde et l'absorbe étape par étape. L'évolution ou la progression de l'expression de l'expérience interne de l'enfant se reflète dans ses dessins, ses peintures, ses modelages et ses mises en scène. Par exemple, au début de la thérapie, une fillette exprime ses peurs secondaires à l'abus comme sa peur du Père Noël et des clowns; par la suite, elle parle de ses rêves où il y a un "monsieur méchant;" plus tard, de ses bébés poupées à qui l'on fait mal et en dernier, de comment un monsieur et une madame (les gardiens) l'ont maltraitée. Dans le cas de jeu post-traumatique où l'enfant répète de façon compulsive et rigide la même scène morbide sans qu'il y ait de résolution naturelle, il est nécessaire de faire des interventions visant à apporter une nouvelle vision

des choses, à bâtir l'espoir ainsi qu'un sens de contrôle sur la vie et le futur afin de ne pas laisser l'enfant dans un état de désespoir, d'impuissance et de terreur (Terr, 1990; Gil 1991).

3. Dégager le thème de l'histoire de l'enfant. Les thèmes développés sont variés tels les thèmes des besoins de protection et de sécurité et les thèmes du danger, de l'impuissance, de la peur, de l'agressivité, de la méchanceté, de la colère, des conflits, des chicanes, du chaos, de l'imprévisibilité, du désespoir et de la honte. Les thèmes principaux constituent la base de la formulation des objectifs thérapeutiques (Meier & Boivin, 1996).

4. Normaliser auprès des parents et auprès de l'enfant lui-même ses réactions au traumatisme. Compte tenu de ce que l'enfant a vécu, il est normal qu'il réagisse ainsi. Normaliser au lieu de "pathologiser" redonne espoir et confiance à l'enfant dans ses capacités et dans l'avenir: les choses peuvent s'améliorer.

5. Déculpabiliser l'enfant et le déresponsabiliser. Faire porter la responsabilité du geste sexuel par l'abuseur.

6. Aider les parents à ce qu'ils soient pour leur enfant une présence stable, forte, calme et supportante, une sorte de refuge où il se sent compris et écouté. Leur expliquer l'impact chez l'enfant de leurs réactions de colère, de désir de vengeance, de chagrin énorme ou de dégoût et les guider vers la modération ou le contrôle de l'expression de leur vécu devant lui. J'ai pu observer la peur qu'éprouve un enfant de perdre son père suite à sa menace d'aller tuer l'abuseur. La crainte que son père aille en prison le faisait regretter d'avoir divulgué l'abus. Un autre enfant niait son histoire dans le but de protéger sa mère en désarroi.

Techniques de thérapie par le jeu

Une variété de techniques de thérapie par le jeu peuvent être utilisées pour faciliter la communication verbale et non verbale. J'ai choisi de présenter celles du dessin et de la peinture, de la mise en situation, du modelage et de la lecture.

Dessin et peinture

Comme les enfants aiment habituellement dessiner et peindre il est assez facile de les engager dans ces activités. Avec le dessin, ils peuvent s'exprimer librement, sans structures, selon leur créativité ou ils peuvent, en réponse à un sujet donné par la thérapeute, représenter une scène d'abus, une image intruse, leur famille, l'image d'eux-mêmes, de l'abuseur, leurs souhaits, et le reste. Souvent un échange verbal suit la production de l'enfant. Parfois, c'est le dessin qui parachève ce que l'enfant vient de dire. II le représente ou l'illustre.

Inhibition face au dessin: Il arrive qu'un enfant ne veuille pas dessiner parce qu'il se dit mauvais en dessin. Je le rassure que ce n'est pas un concours de dessin, qu'il n'y a pas de notes comme à l'école. Souvent, c'est suffisant pour qu'il commence à dessiner. Certains enfants continuent à refuser. Alors je prends une feuille, je fais un paravent avec mon bras pour que l'enfant ne voit pas ce que je dessine et je dis d'un air enjoué quelque chose du genre: "Je fais un dessin que tu pourras regarder lorsque j'aurai fini. Je ne regarderai pas le tien non plus. Tu pourras me le dire lorsque tu auras terminé. Ce sera comme une surprise." Que ce soit avec une fillette de trois ans ou avec un garçon de huit ans, cette approche réussit toujours. Il semble que l'enfant soit engagé par l'effet de surprise, de suspense, de jeu et de complicité.

Dessin ou peinture en parallèle: Un jeune enfant peut demander que je dessine ou que je peigne avec lui. Je vois cela comme une ouverture pour utiliser le dessin comme moyen d'évaluation et de traitement. Je réponds donc au besoin de l'enfant d'être accompagné. Par contre, je veille, en cachant mon dessin, à ce qu'il ne contamine pas le sien. Cela devient aisé lorsque nous pouvons nous installer de chaque côté d'un chevalet à deux ou trois faces.

Illustration de l'utilisation du dessin: Après deux mois de thérapie sur une base hebdomadaire, j'ai utilisé le dessin dans le but d'aider une fillette à surmonter sa peur de dormir dans son lit. Elle était âgée de quatre ans et demi et dormait dans le lit de ses parents depuis qu'elle avait été abusée, deux ans plus tôt. L'enfant ne pouvait pas supporter de s'étendre sur son lit. J'avais travaillé avec la mère auparavant en lui donnant des pistes à savoir comment s'y prendre. Madame avait, selon elle, tout essayé mais la petite venait toujours se coucher avec eux. J'ai alors offert de les visiter à domicile le jour afin d'explorer davantage la situation et l'environnement. Je savais que j'improviserais sur les lieux.

L'enfant était ravie de ma venue chez elle. Elle me fait visiter sa chambre et celle de ses parents où elle couche. Elle me montre plusieurs points d'intérêt dans sa chambre. Dans un effort de désensibilisation, nous nous assoyons toutes les deux sur son lit pour parler et regarder les objets qui lui sont chers. Après ce tour, nous nous installons à la table dans la cuisine pour dessiner. Je dessine le plan de sa chambre qui est adjacente à celle de ses parents ainsi que les portes des deux chambres et le couloir reliant les autres pièces de la maison. Le plan terminé, je raconte l'histoire d'une petite fille qui couche dans son lit, dans une belle chambre. Il y a un mur tout petit qui est magique. De l'autre côté, il y a la chambre de ses parents. II y a aussi deux portes permettant les allées et venues entre les deux chambres. La petite fille dort avec son toutou dans son lit et papa dort avec maman dans leur lit. La réaction de l'enfant à cette histoire a été de prendre immédiatement une feuille de papier pour y reproduire le plan et raconter l'histoire en ses propres mots. Elle était de très bonne humeur. Quatre jours plus tard, l'enfant est très fière de m'annoncer qu'elle dort maintenant dans son lit. Sa mère lui lisait une histoire avant de s'endormir et elle peut rester seule dans son lit.

Au cours de cette session, l'enfant était plus joviale et plus dégagée. Pour la première fois, elle a initié des activités physiques et motrices (sauter sur le matelas, tricycle, etc.) et a demandé mon assistance pour la soulever: premier contact physique du genre. En tricycle, elle jouait à "partir et à revenir" en me quittant pour un voyage de plus en plus long. Pour la première fois aussi, elle s'est ouverte et a raconté son rêve de monstre. Avant elle disait qu'elle rêvait mais elle n'était pas capable d'en parler. II semble donc que l'enfant transigeait alors avec la question de la séparation telle que manifestée par le problème du coucher ainsi que par le jeu "de partir et revenir." Elle a réalisé des gains aux plans de la sécurité et de l'autonomie. Elle a été capable de faire de plus en plus confiance au thérapeute au point de commencer à s'ouvrir sur sa peur et sur son secret et d'être à l'aise avec une plus grande proximité physique. Elle est devenue compétente à s'endormir dans son lit et d'y rester toute la nuit. Cet apprentissage s'est maintenu au moins pendant deux ans.

Modelage

La pâte à modeler sert les mêmes objectifs que le dessin et la peinture. J'offre la pâte à modeler pour varier le mode d'expression et pour engager des enfants que le dessin rebute.

La représentation à trois dimensions d'une scène ou d'une histoire requiert du temps de fabrication. L'enfant s'y investit fort bien en se concentrant et en parlant lors de cette expérience visuelle et sensorielle. Il peut exprimer sa colère. J'ai vu plusieurs enfants écraser et faire ainsi disparaître le personnage de l'abuseur. En ayant le contrôle de la situation, l'enfant se sent puissant. Il arrive que l'enfant me demande de participer au modelage. Afin de ne pas l'influencer, je fais le minimum en lui demandant ce qu'il veut que je fabrique et avec quelle couleur et en vérifiant avec lui si c'est ainsi qu'il le désire. Autrement dit, je le laisse diriger le jeu et développer son histoire. Les enfants plus âgés peuvent être plutôt attirés par l'argile ou par une pâte à modeler plus dure et de couleurs plus nuancées.

En travaillant avec la pâte à modeler, une fille de neuf ans a pris conscience de son double sentiment de tristesse: la douleur que son père lui avait infligée en abusant d'elle et l'emprisonnement de celui-ci. L'activité lui a permis de distinguer les deux sources de sa tristesse et de se rendre compte que si son père était triste d'être en prison qu'il en était le responsable. Cette prise de conscience a permis à l'enfant d'être libérée du poids de la tristesse de son père.

Mise en situation

Dans une mise en situation, l'enfant recrée une scène ou en imagine une en utilisant en toute liberté la maison de poupées avec ameublement et personnages miniatures, les marionnettes ou les animaux miniatures. Il prête vie à ses personnages et parfois demande la collaboration du thérapeute pour manipuler une marionnette ou une poupée. La direction du jeu est laissée à l'enfant. J'interviens dans le but de l'aider à élaborer son histoire. Par exemple, je lui demande: "Que se passe-t-il?" " Que veut le bébé?" ou "Comment l'histoire finira-t-elle?" J'interviens pour le faire progresser dans l'affirmation de soi en disant au personnage abusif: "Tu n'as pas le droit de faire mal au bébé" ou encore j'interviens pour le faire progresser dans le développement d'un sentiment de contrôle et de compétence en disant: "Que peut dire ou faire le garçon pour montrer à X qu'il ne se laissera plus faire?" Il m'arrive d'intervenir pour intensifier l'expression des sentiments: "Qu'est-ce que la petite fille a envie de dire à X (l'abuseur) à papa ou à maman?" ou "Que veut-elle?"

Parfois, je vérifie s'il y a un lien entre l'histoire et sa propre vie: "T'est-il arrivé à toi aussi d'avoir très peur et d'avoir envie de te cacher?" Une intervention ayant comme but de favoriser l'autonomie est, à l'occasion, pertinente. Par exemple, lors d'un repas, une fillette joue le rôle d'une mère qui s'impose à son enfant et qui dit mieux faire qu'elle. Elle m'avait attribué le rôle de l'enfant et j'ai choisi de personnifier une enfant qui valorisait la possibilité de réaliser seule les différentes tâches comme couper sa viande et tartiner son pain.

L'utilisation de l'interprétation comporte des risques puisqu'en interprétant nous risquons de nous aventurer sur un terrain qui ne fait pas encore partie de l'expérience préconsciente ou consciente de l'enfant. En imposant de l'extérieur une connaissance, l'enfant peut se sentir à nouveau contrôlé, trompé, forcé et incompris. Il y a aussi le risque d'être envahissant envers une personne qui souffre déjà de l'intrusion de l'autre. Une approche favorisant la découverte de soi est préférable (Meier et Boivin, 1987).

Dans une autre forme de mise en situation, l'enfant joue lui-même un rôle et en attribue un autre au thérapeute. Différents accessoires peuvent être utilisés pour soutenir l'action. Par exemple, une fillette de trois ans et demi a créé l'histoire suivante en passant spontanément de la pâte à modeler à la dramatisation. Elle raconte d'abord une histoire de loup qui va attaquer le bébé. Elle construit tout un scénario de protection contre l'agresseur avec cachettes et fusil. Tout en faisant cela, elle exprime sa colère, défend le bébé qu'elle trouve impuissant parce qu'il a juste deux petites dents qui ne font pas mal lorsqu'il mord; elle se fâche et réussit à faire peur au loup. Ensuite, elle met en scène les parents à qui elle attribue un rôle de protecteur, le père étant le défenseur principal. Elle m'attribue le rôle du père et lui apporte le bébé sous la table pour qu'il le protège, et elle devient la mère. Elle avait personnifié l'agresseur dans des animaux qu'elle sortait d'une boîte. Elle demande au père de les mettre à la poubelle. Dans un objectif de protection et d'affirmation je fais dire au père: "Vous n'avez pas le droit de faire mal au bébé. Vous n'êtes pas fins!" La fillette, pleinement d'accord, leur dit: "Bye!" et les met à la poubelle. Ensuite, d'un air soulagé, elle réconforte le bébé, le prend dans ses bras, le rassure en étant très douce avec lui. Autant elle avait été animée et expressive durant l'élaboration de son histoire, autant elle était calme une fois l'histoire terminée. Elle a tout simplement passé à un jeu de vaisselle, une activité nourrissante. Il semble qu'un degré de résolution ou de réparation a été atteint.

Lecture

Lire un livre éducatif avec l'enfant peut être utile et efficace au cours des processus de l'évaluation et de l'intervention. Le moment choisi dépendra de l'objectif visé et de l'intérêt de l'enfant.

Un jeune garçon d'environ cinq ans a apporté de lui-même, lors de la quatrième session, un de ses livres qu'il désirait que nous lisions ensemble. J'ai profité de l'occasion pour qu'on regarde aussi un de mes livres. C'était un livre qui illustrait pour l'enfant que son corps lui appartient. À mi-chemin de la lecture, l'enfant divulgue son expérience de touchers qu'il n'a pas aimés recevoir.

En cours de traitement avec une fille de 10 ans qui avait vécu l'inceste, nous avons lu un livre qui s'intitulait: "Moi, je dis non" (Gagnon, Gervais & Potvin, 1987). Un échange a suivi où elle a comparé son expérience à celle de l'enfant dans l'histoire et elle a apporté des nuances pertinentes. Elle a été confirmée dans le fait qu'elle a divulgué tout de suite et dans celui qu'il y a des personnes sur qui elle peut compter.

Il existe des livres conçus pour les enfants et d'autres pour les adolescents qui décrivent et illustrent une situation d'abus sexuel, une situation d'abus physique, la différence entre des touchers OK et des touchers pas OK, et qui promeuvent l'idée que leur corps leur appartient, qu'ils ont le droit de dire non, qu'il y a des secrets qu'il ne faut pas garder, qu'il est bien de se confier et de demander de l'aide. Ces livres sont: "Moi, je dis non" (Gagnon et al., 1987), "L'étrange voisin de Dominique" (1988), "Le secret du petit cheval" (1989), et "I belong to me" (Atkinson, Keller & Pawson,1984). Il y a également des livres spécialisés pour faciliter la préparation de l'enfant à aller à la cour comme la brochure illustrée "Je me prépare pour la cour" conçue par le Ministère de la Justice du Gouvernement du Québec (1989). Le livre "Tu en as parlé" (Ludwig, 1995) explique et illustre le processus d'enquête et les responsabilités de l'appareil judicaire en français, en anglais et en symboles Bliss pour ceux qui ont des difficultés de communication particulières.

Ces quelques vignettes de la thérapie par le jeu avec les enfants donnent une idée de l'art thérapeutique qui sous-tend tout le processus. Les enfants semblent porter en eux l'élan vers la réparation et le mieux-être.

Conclusion

Comme l'enfant est l'adolescent et l'adulte de demain et que nous désirons qu'il grandisse bien et se développe pleinement, il est important que nous tous, peu importe notre rôle et notre rang dans la famille et la communauté, nous ouvrions les yeux et lui tendions la main. L'enfant, ce joyau de la vie, pourra étinceler plutôt que de s'éteindre sous la souffrance du mépris et de l'exploitation de certains, de l'aveuglement et de l'indifférence des autres. Notre compassion à leur endroit ouvrira notre regard et nous motivera à lui tendre la main du mieux possible.

Références

Atkinson, L., Keller, L.K. & Pawson, B. (1984). *I belong to me.* Kelowna, B.C.: Whortleberry Books.

Briere, J. N. (1992). *Child abuse trauma, theory and treatment of the lasting effects.* Newbury Park, CA: Sage Publications.

Conte, J. R., Wolf S. & Smith T. (1989). What sexual offenders tell us about prevention strategies. *Child Abuse & Neglect, 13*, 293-301.

Gervais, J. (1998). *L'étrange voisin de Dominique.* Montréal: Les Éditions du Boréal.

Finkelhor, D. & Browne, A. (1985). The traumatic impact of child sexual abuse: A conceptualization. *American Journal of Orthopsychiatry, 55*, 530-541.

Fondation de la justice pour les enfants (pas de date). *C'est bien de dire non!* Album à colorier. Saint-Lambert, Québec: Édition Héritage.

Gagnon, J., Gervais, M. & Potvin, M. (1987). *Moi, je dis non!* Association d'éducation préscolaire du Québec et Assurance-vie Desjardins-Laurentienne.

Gil, E. (1991). *The healing power of play: Therapy with abused children.* New York: Guilford.

Gil, E. (1993). Sexualized children. Dans E. Gil et T. C. Johnson, *Sexualized children: Assessment and treatment of sexualized children and children who molest* (p.91-99), Rockville: Launch Press.

Klein, M. (1948/1975). On the theory of anxiety and guilt, dans *Envy and gratitude and other works*, 1946-1963, (p.25-42), New York: Delta.

Ludwig, S. A. (1995). *Tu en as parlé.* Conseil d'information et d'éducation sexuelles du Canada, East York, Canada.

Meier, A. & Boivin, M. (1987). Self-discovery approach to counseling, *Pastoral Sciences, 6*, 145-168.

Meier, A., & Boivin, M. (1996). *Theme-analysis: A research method using psychotherapeutic themes to study the change process.* Communication dans le cadre de la 27ième Conférence annuelle de la Society for Psychotherapy Research, Amelia Island, Floride, 19-23 juin.

Ministère de la Justice du Gouvernement du Québec. (1989). *Je me prépare pour la cour. Brochure à l'intention des jeunes témoins.* Québec.

Ministère de la Justice du Canada. (1989). *Le secret du petit cheval.* Ottawa, Ministre des Approvisionnements et Services.

Terr, L. (1990). *Too scared to cry.* New-York: Harper & Row.

Webb, N.B. (1994). *Techniques of play therapy: A clinical demonstration.* New York: Guilford Press.

Wells, M. (1990). *L'exploitation sexuelle des enfants et la législation canadienne. Manuel.* Ottawa, Ontario: Ministère de la Justice du Canada.

Chapter 13

Physical and Sexual Abuse: A Profile of Issues and Treatment*

Frank Landino

Before addressing the issues of abuse, I'd like to present some history regarding my clients and their association with the sex scandal in Alfred, Ontario. Following that, I will describe how I've worked with clients during the last four years. I begin with a brief history concerning these clients and the sex scandal in Alfred.

History

As children, my clients were placed in St. Joseph's Training School for boys located in the town of Alfred, Ontario. Between the years 1935 and 1972, the training school, was run by a group called the Lay Order of Christian Brothers.

Children were sent to this training school for different reasons. Some were placed there because their families could not provide for them. Others were sent there for committing petty thefts, being truant, or for running away from a foster home. Some needed placement because they were hyperactive and unmanageable at home. The children were between 7 and 16 years old

---

*Revision of a paper presented at the First Annual Conference of the Society for Pastoral Counselling held at Saint Paul University, Ottawa, Ontario, May 6, 1994.

when they were sent there. They are now grown men between the ages of 35 and 70.

A few years ago, one of these men decided to come forward and tell the media about his physical and sexual abuse by the Christian Brothers in St. Joseph's Reformatory. He then opened a phone line to locate other victims who went to the same school. Many responded; all claimed that they were abused in the same way.

Together, they formed a committee and took their complaints to the Government of Ontario and to the Archdiocese of Ottawa. They asked to be compensated for their pain and suffering. A compensation package was agreed upon after two years of negotiations. During these negotiations, police investigated the men's allegations of abuse. As a result of the investigation, 700 men came forward with statements and several charges were laid against 18 Christian Brothers.

At this point I became professionally involved with some of these men. In 1990, while working with the Family Service Centre of Ottawa-Carleton, I was asked if I would be interested in counselling a group of men who had been physically and sexually abused as children. I was assigned 20 clients a week for individual counselling, and began co-leading a group of 25 to 30 men on a weekly basis. I also co-lead the wives' group every third week for several years. I am now into my fifth year of this work. Although I recently resigned from the group work, I continue to see 25 clients on an individual basis.

Work Setting

Home Visits

I have been not only a counsellor to my clients, but something of a social worker as well. For instance, I visit their homes to do the counselling. In the beginning, when I saw them in an office, they would often miss their appointments; they found the environment too formal and confining. I decided then to take the counselling to them.

Jail and Hospital Visits

I have visited clients in jails to provide counselling services to those who were charged with crimes of assault, theft, drug possession, and rape. Hospital visits have also been on my agenda. One client for example was taken to the hospital in a straightjacket and locked into a padded cell. Another client was sent to the Royal Ottawa Hospital for attempting suicide. Yet another client went berserk during a drinking binge, beat his wife, and wrecked everything in the house. So home, jail and hospital visits have become a part of my counselling practice.

Court Accompaniment and Hearings

I have also been involved in court accompaniment. By the time I was into my third year of counselling, the court cases had started. At that time, I was called upon to accompany my clients to the trials, to lend them moral support, and to debrief them, before and after each appearance. This went on for over a year. Following that, I spent another year accompanying clients to their hearings with the Criminal Injuries Compensation Board. At these hearings, my clients told their stories of abuse, and the interviewers determined how much money they would be awarded as compensation for their pain and suffering. During these meetings, I reported to the interviewers the issues I had been working on with each client and the impact that the abuse had had on each person's life.

Examples of Abuse

Here is a snapshot of the sort of physical and sexual abuse that occurred in the training school as reported to me by my clients.

One of my clients claimed that he was sodomized three times a week during the three years that he attended the training school. He also claimed that two Christian Brothers molested him at the same time. Apparently, while one held him down, the other sodomized him. Then they simply exchanged positions. The same client also reported that he was forced, on a regular basis, to masturbate and perform felatio on the Brothers. When this client left the training school at age sixteen, he discovered one day as he was passing his stool, that he developed rectal prolapse. It had to be surgically treated. This of course, was a result of all the sodomizing he underwent in the training school.

As for the physical abuse that they experienced in the training school, many clients claimed that they were kicked, punched, and beaten until they were unconscious. Others reported that their noses, jaws and teeth were broken. Many have permanent back injuries as a result of being hit in the back with a large stick. They were also whipped with wide leather straps across the back, legs and buttocks, leaving welts of puss and blood. To this day, their bodies bear the marks of these assaults. These are some examples of what my clients experienced in the training school.

Impact and Issues

What impact did this abuse have on their lives? I will first present a profile of the issues which we dealt with in therapy. Following that, I will share some personal thoughts on the pastoral element in my work.

Reliving Memories of Their Past Abuse

The first issue that came up in therapy for these clients was reliving the memories of their abuse. Some clients were able to give a detailed description of everything that they experienced. Others only had vague memories of what happened to them and of the identities of their abusers. There were a few who were confused as to whether the abuse happened to them or to someone else. Therapy, therefore, began with clients remembering what happened to them. It was like living the abuse all over again and, as a result, their lives were thrown into turmoil.

Sleep Deprivation

As their memories surfaced, clients found themselves unable to sleep at night. They suffered from repeated nightmares, waking in the middle of the night, screaming, yelling, and drenched in sweat. Some flailed their arms and legs while asleep, inadvertently punching their spouse in the face. Others woke up on a regular basis, discovering that they had either urinated or defecated in bed. For over two years now, these clients have only been getting two to three hours of sleep a night.

Issues of Trust

While working through memories and sleep deprivation, other issues emerged. One of those issues was that of trust. All my clients will tell you that they don't trust anyone. They say that their mistrust began when they were betrayed by the Christian Brothers who abused them. And now as adults, they are guarded and defensive with everyone they meet. None of them has ever had a close friend. Somehow, I have become the first person in their life that they have learned to trust. I suppose there are a couple of reasons for this. One is that I have been there consistently for them over a long period of time. Secondly, it seems that I'm one of the few people who ever really listened to them or tried to understand them.

Drug and Alcohol Dependency

Another common issue with my clients is drug and alcohol dependency. They all admit to using drugs and alcohol because it helps them to forget their painful childhood. Most of my clients smoke large quantities of hashish all day long, every day. They claim that it calms them down when they are feeling aggressive and that it prevents them from becoming violent. I've been able to get some clients into a rehabilitation program, and for some, the results were good. A few have stopped drinking and abusing drugs and it has made a difference in their lives. They are becoming more aware of themselves and their feelings. But this in itself is a painful process for them.

Coping With Life After Prison

Nearly all my clients have spent from five to fifteen years of their life in provincial jails and federal penitentiaries. Generally, they were sent to prison for crimes of theft and assault. As a result, they never learned proper lifeskills and were not able to manage their lives once they were freed from prison. Thus they now have to learn how to deal with the outside world.

Struggling with Self-Esteem

Self-esteem is another issue that these clients have had to contend with. In the training school, they were repeatedly told that they were "bad kids" and "retarded imbeciles." It was often said that they would never amount to anything. This made them feel deficient and flawed in some way. Today, as adults, they lack confidence in themselves and feel like misfits on the fringe of society.

Difficulties in Couple Relationships and Parenting

Another issue is their difficulty in couple relationships. Some have been married two and three times. Some have never married, and others have had very limited experience with women. One of the reasons that they have difficulty maintaining relationships is that they are domineering, controlling and aggressive with their partners. They also lack in communication and relationship skills, they don't like to compromise, and it's either their way or no way. Because most of them are only interested in conquering women sexually, these men have difficulties maintaining relationships over the long term. Whenever the woman begins to have expectations of them, they leave and find another person. None of them has ever been sexually faithful to one woman even within their marriages. And all of them have either physically, emotionally or verbally assaulted their partners or children at one time or another.

Depression and Suicidal Tendencies

Depression is another common issue in therapy with my clients. Most of my clients have been suicidal at one time or another in their lives. Many have attempted suicide. For those who are still suicidal, I refer them to a psychiatrist for prescribed medication while they are in therapy with me.

Heightened Anxiety

All of these clients experience heightened anxiety. They live in constant dread and apprehension. They are always expecting something to go wrong. Suspicion and paranoia are their constant companions. As a result, they have great difficulty concentrating on anything for any length of time. Their attention span and tolerance levels are very low. They are easily frustrated, and given to violent outbursts.

Anger

Dealing with anger is a major issue. My clients have had to spend a great deal of time in therapy working through their feelings of anger. Anger is a mild word to use here. What they really experience is rage and violent outbursts. Their anger is like spontaneous combustion. They can lash out in a moment shorter than it takes to snap your fingers. For example, some of my clients have lost their temper at home and have kicked down doors, punched their fists through walls, and thrown TV sets across the room. Others have entered into battles with strangers on the streets or at bars. These clients need to be educated about anger management. Some need to learn how to walk away from situations before they blow up. Eventually, they all need to uncover the source of their rage.

It appears to me that a lot of their rage has to do with their lives having been a series of crises, frustrations and disappointments. And of course, one must not forget the anger they have towards their abusers from the training school. Only after more than three years in therapy have I seen signs of them getting their anger under control. And even then, their behaviour is unpredictable.

Feelings of Shame

My clients have also had to deal with feelings of shame. They don't like to admit that they were sexually abused. To admit this is to bear the stigma that they too might be child molesters. These men are also ashamed to cry in therapy. They think that it's a sign of weakness, that men shouldn't cry.

Confusion about their Sexual Orientation

Many of my clients have reported feelings of uncertainty about their sexual orientation. One man claimed that for most of his life, he felt like a woman inside a man's body and that he wanted a sex change. Many of the others have fears about being homosexual and have had homosexual experiences.

Impoverished Sexuality

Most of my clients view sex as a means of boosting their male ego, or as a mechanism for releasing tension and aggression. They do not experience love and affection during the act of sex. Fifty percent of my clients will admit to having experienced sexual impotency and the other fifty percent will say that they have insatiable sexual desires.

Poverty

Ninety-nine percent of my clients are unemployed. They are unable to keep jobs for long because they resent taking orders, and cannot co-operate with fellow workers. Most of them have been fired for insubordination or for assaulting someone in the workplace. Because of this, nearly all of them are on welfare or disability pension. When their monthly checks come in, they spend it on alcohol, drugs, video rentals, cigarettes, and bingo. They often don't have food in the fridge and sometimes don't eat for days. I've known some who were not able to pay their hydro bill and who had to spend half the winter without heat and electricity. Another client, spent his welfare check on cocaine instead of paying his rent. He was then evicted from his home and had to find shelter with the Union Mission and the Salvation Army. Since he had no money and was cut off from welfare, he began stealing and selling what he had stolen. He was finally caught and sent to jail.

During the last four years, I have spent twenty percent of my time hearing stories of poverty and witnessing how poverty has lead my clients into crime. I have tried to help them by visiting them in jail and negotiating on their behalf with lawyers, parole officers, social workers, Ottawa Housing, and City Living. This entailed writing many reports and making plea bargains with the courts. I didn't realize that I would be doing this kind of social work when I first got involved. I have had to run the gamut of the social and legal systems, including testifying in court on behalf of one of my clients who was being charged for growing crops of marijuana.

Struggling with Religion and Spirituality

Most of my clients are critical of institutionalized religions and would never set foot in a church again. Many disclaim any notion of the existence of God. Others say that they exercise their spirituality through AA by claiming a Higher Power. Most of them are disdainful of clergymen, although some are able to recognize that not all clergymen are child molesters or pedophiles. Others express a wish to believe in God, but feel that their ability to have faith was stolen by the Christian Brothers.

Outcome

In terms of the outcome or success of therapy, only a small percentage of my clients have shown a demonstrable measure of personal growth over the last four years. By this I mean that only a few have gained sufficient awareness of themselves that they can now begin to live life more fully and consciously.

With the rest of them, I do mostly "maintenance" work. That is, I work to prevent them from destroying their lives or someone else's life. Knowing them as I do, I would no be surprised to discover some day that they have either killed themselves, murdered someone, or committed some atrocious crime for which they will spend many more years in prison. Obviously, they require long-term therapy.

Pastoral

What is "pastoral" in the work I do? My answer comes from reflecting on my own life and work experience. For many years while I was a university student, I enjoyed a rather contemplative life, a life of learning, of reading inspirational literature, of meditating and practicing Tai Chi (an ancient Chinese martial art). And then four years ago, I was initiated into this work. Since then, I have taken an equivalent of one month of holidays. I was spending so much time working that I lost my ability to meditate, had no time to read, and spent my entire weekends writing reports. I was so immersed in my work that I began to lose touch with myself. I now understand the true meaning of the term *burnout.* Working was no longer giving me a sense of renewal. It was bringing me stress and exhaustion. I had to do something, otherwise I would have burnt out.

I started making time for myself again: time to meditate, read, practice Tai Chi, visit with friends, and so on. In other words, I had to reclaim my life back. As a result, I've made some good strides towards my own recovery and I'm beginning to feel better again. This was a lesson for me in learning how to take care of myself, and I have come to believe that this is a prerequisite for helping others. When I take care of myself, I am more effective in helping my clients. I have a better sense of what my clients need. I am also able to follow them more attentively, lead them more assertively, and make better use of my creativity in the process of therapy. So for me to be a pastoral counsellor, I must first be pastoral with myself. University has qualified me with knowledge, theories and skills, but only I can qualify my own state of mind by maintaining those things that make me feel sane and whole.

Part Four

Healing in Research

Chapter 14

The Thematic Analytic Research Method and its Application*

Augustine Meier

The topic of my chapter is the Thematic Analytic Research Method and its application to clinical case notes. There are four parts to my presentation. First I will discuss the research domain of pastoral counselling; secondly, I will suggest that the discovery-oriented research is the method of choice for pastoral counselling; thirdly, I will outline the components of a method for organizing and recording clinical material. Finally I will demonstrate how one can use the organized and recorded material for the purpose of informal qualitative research.

Domain of Pastoral Counselling Research

Before I present the Thematic Analytic Research Method to organize and record clinical material, I want to raise and discuss several questions. First, what is the subject matter for pastoral counselling research? That is, what is the research domain or area of pastoral counselling? What are its parameters? When we view some of the other disciplines and professions, we become acutely aware that their subject areas are well-defined. For example, for

*Revision of the Presidential Address given at the 2nd Annual Conference of the Society for Pastoral Counselling Research, Saint Paul University, Ottawa, Ontario, May 13, 1995

the discipline of psychology, the area is the study of human behaviour, for theology, it is the deity, for political science, it is political systems, and for sociology, it is social structures. What is the area of study for pastoral counselling? A simple answer is that which is pastoral. But what is pastoral? What does pastoral mean? One of the more frequent questions that students in the Pastoral Counselling Program ask is "What is pastoral counselling? How does pastoral counselling differ from psychological counselling or psychotherapy?"

Pastoral Counselling Defined

In one of our published papers (Meier, Boivin, Aylward, 1986, p. 22-25) we reviewed the various notions of pastoral counselling put forth by past and current writers. We observed, over the decades, a shift in the way pastoral counselling was defined.

The definitions of the late 1950 and early 1960 conceptualized pastoral counselling as having no goals of its own other than to serve the objectives of the pastoral ministries such as preaching, teaching, and liturgical participation. That is, the goal of pastoral counselling was to help the faithful to be better predisposed to receive the good news and participate in the liturgical celebrations.

In the late sixties and early seventies, pastoral counselling was conceived as a three-way relationship between the client, the counsellor and God. The goal of counselling was to minister to normal persons who have emotional problems that interfere with their use of their inner resources and spiritual functioning.

The more recent writers broadened the notion of pastoral counselling to include not only a nurturing relationship and the treatment of religious and spiritual concerns, but also the application of current psychological concepts and techniques to religious and spiritual concerns. This view is well captured by Clinebell (1984) who describes pastoral counselling as "the utilization of a variety of healing ... methods to help people handle their problems and crises more growthfully and thus experience healing of their brokenness" (p. 26). The Association of Pastoral Counsellors, who accredit pastoral counsellors at various levels, echo this definition by defining pastoral counselling as "a process in which a pastoral counsellor utilizes insights and principles derived from the disciplines of theology and the behavioural sciences in working with individuals, couples, families, groups, and social systems toward the achievement of wholeness and health" (cited by Strunk, 1993, p. 15).

In brief, pastoral counselling is a process comprised of the responses and interventions of the counsellor, the articulation and exploration of the spiritual, religious and/or faith concerns of the client, and the counsellor-client relationship itself. To this process is brought the understanding, knowledge and techniques of theology and the social and/or behavioural sciences.

Pastoral Counselling Experiences as Primary Research Data

I want, now, to turn to the second question: What is the primary data for pastoral counselling research? Based on the current status of pastoral counselling, we can conclude that the most meaningful research will study the pastoral counselling experience itself. To put this in negative terms, research which is based primarily on psychometric data, that is, on data which comes from the administration of standardized questionnaires and inventories, is not sufficient. At the current state of the development of pastoral counselling as a discipline and profession, we need to turn to the experience itself to generate new models and theories. Let me continue with this argument.

When we compare pastoral counselling to other disciplines and/or professions, we are at a disadvantage. We do not have a body of knowledge specific to pastoral counselling. Our knowledge is borrowed from the human sciences, social sciences, theology, and so on. We do not have our own models and theories. These too are borrowed. We do not have specific methods of treatment nor research approaches. Again, these are borrowed from other disciplines. The discipline and/or profession of pastoral counselling does not have much that is its own (Meier, 1990).

When it comes to research, the other disciplines can design theory driven or theory guided research projects that stem from their specific theories, built on the research data that they have collected over many decades. These studies have as their goal to test the theory either by testing a derived hypothesis or by predicting an outcome. Theory guided research assumes that we already have a good understanding of the phenomenon investigated. This method of investigation has serious limitations for pastoral counselling, because we do not have an empirically grounded understanding of the pastoral phenomenon.

This leads us to the conclusion that data generated by theory guided studies, such as outcome studies, are not adequate sources of data for pastoral counselling. This is particularly so since we do not have a pastoral counselling theory with its own set of concepts which can be tested. At this time in the development of pastoral counselling theory, the data from outcome studies is highly limited. The data, however, can be useful when used collectively with data from other types of research.

Discovery-Oriented Research

I believe that the most meaningful research for pastoral counselling at this stage of its development will be based on the pastoral counselling experience itself. Our task as researchers is to identify the components of this experience, that is, the underlying structure of the experiences. These are the latent structures and patterns imbedded within the pastoral counselling experience.

The method best suited for pastoral counselling research is a discovery-oriented approach which has the goal to elicit the understanding of the phenomenon. This approach allows the structure of the experience to be brought to light, to emerge and express itself. These structures form the components of a theory of pastoral counselling.

There are several different discovery-oriented methods that can be used to bring about a greater understanding of the phenomenon under investigation.

Case Studies

First, there are case studies which have as their goal the development of a deeper understanding of a specific phenomenon. For example, Freud used this method to better understand the development of childhood phobia (little Hans), hysteria (Dora), infantile neurosis (Wolfman), obsessional neurosis (rat man), and paranoia (Schreber) (Jones, 1961, p. 533). Pastoral counsellors, I believe, could effectively use the case study method to shed light on phenomenon such as how persons re-establish their trust in people and in God following a trauma wherein their sense of security and trust has been shattered.

Process Studies

Katherine Clarke (1995) presented a research method that uses client experiences to generate data that can serve as the basis for the development of new understanding. The method presented was that of Task-Analysis which was used for the creation of meaning in incest abuse survivors. This is a process-oriented method. Typically in this type of research, the client is asked to perform a task. The client's performance of this task is then analyzed for patterns and/or stages of change. This method can be effectively used by pastoral counsellors to gain a better understanding of the process of resolving guilt feelings, the development of trust in God following a traumatic experience, the forgiveness of those who hurt us, and so on.

Qualitative Studies

One other form of research that uses client experiences as the primary data for analysis is the qualitative approach (Meier & Weber, 1992, p. 162-164). In one of our current research projects, we are studying what aspects of Task-Directed Imagery, Focusing and Contemplative Christian Meditation help persons enhance their trust in God and their trust in a partner. This study will apply an empirical phenomenological approach to the research involving participants' written responses to a questionnaire and to the transcripts of interviews. The qualitative research methods are applicable to host a of pastoral counselling concerns and questions. The qualitative methods use as raw data the pastoral counselling experience itself.

In brief, cases studies, process-oriented methods, and qualitative research methods are able to provide very useful data for the generation of new concepts, models and theories. These methods are particularly suited to pastoral counselling which, at best, is an emerging discipline. As an emerging discipline pastoral counselling must develop its own body of knowledge, concepts, models, theories and research methodologies. I would suggest that the discovery-oriented research methods are preferred over the theory-testing and predictive-oriented methods.

Carrying out discovery-oriented research is very costly and time consuming and requires adequate facilities, personnel, and resources. This type of research is best carried out in an educational setting or in a mental health institution where the necessary support are available.

This being the case, what research possibilities are available to the pastoral counsellor who is working alone in a mental health institution, or in an educational setting, or in a private office? What is available to the individual pastoral counsellor who would like to engage in research but does not have the available resources?

The Thematic Analytic Research Method

I want to present and describe one possible informal method to organize and record material, a method that can be used by the pastoral counsellor for the purpose of research. I will then apply this method to the study of one case.

The method that I am about to describe is an adaptation of a more formal method which students, Micheline, and myself are using here at St. Paul University (Anderson et al., 1994; Meier & Boivin, 1995; Meier, Herring, Sminiski, Tyman, 1995). The major difference between the two approaches is that the formal method uses transcripts of client sessions as the data for analysis, whereas the informal method uses the notes of a therapy session made by the counsellor. Another difference is that the formal method is more specific, whereas the informal method is more global and general. The Thematic Analytic Research Method is phenomenological-oriented and is based on the identification and description of psychotherapeutic themes raised within the context of a counselling session. I will describe how counsellors can organize and record their notes following a counselling session so that the notes are amenable and useful for research using the Thematic Analytic Research Method.

I will present the Thematic Analytic Research Method under three headings: an outline of the content domains, a detailed description of the content domains, and a case illustration.

Outline of Content Domains

The Thematic Analytic Research Method, when applied to the recording of counselling sessions, comprises seven content domains, namely, (a) core psychotherapeutic themes, (b) context of core themes, (c) therapeutic goals, (d) the evolution of the core themes, (e) the nature and quality of interactions, (f) the therapeutic gains, and (g) a summary of the session and recommendations. As can be seen, the central concept is that of the psychotherapeutic theme. In this method, the psychotherapeutic themes are identified, the context from which they emerge is given, the therapeutic strategies to work with the themes are presented, the unfolding of the core theme is described, and the client's therapeutic gains are noted.

Detailed Description of Content Domains

A more detailed description of each of the seven content domains is presented below.

1. *Core psychotherapeutic themes.* Identify the core psychotherapeutic themes which comprise the psychological, interpersonal, spiritual, religious, and/or physical theme(s) presented and addressed in the session. The themes are presented in terms of polarities (e.g., being fearful vs. being courageous; distrust vs. trust; hate vs. love) with one pole representing the current state (distrust) and the second pole representing the goal towards which to work (trust).

2. *Context of the core themes:* The context of the psychotherapeutic theme refers to the situation, incident, happening, event, experience, etc., from which the theme emerged (e.g., fear emerged from exam preparation). The task is to briefly describe the context within which the core themes were experienced.
3. *The therapeutic goals.* The third domain, therapeutic goals, indicates what the therapist and client agreed to do about the theme and how they intended to work with it. Typically the second pole of the bi-polar themes indicates (suggests) the therapeutic goal for a particular session and for the therapy as a whole. Based on the bi-polar themes, the therapist briefly describes the therapeutic goals for that session. The therapeutic goal might be to help the client become more assertive, cope with anxieties, resolve conflicts, clarify feelings, express feelings; make choices, etc.
4. *The evolution of the theme during the course of the session.* The most complex content domain is the fourth domain, which summarizes the evolution of the theme during the course of therapy. Included is a description of the interactive therapist-client process and the shift of the main theme to associated themes. The therapist's interventions and the client's responses to them are recorded. The evolution of the theme(s) is described within context of the therapist-client interaction. The following tasks comprise this domain.
   a) A brief description is included as to how the theme unfolded within the counselling session. If the unfolding process led to other dimensions, these are included as well. Initially the themes tend to be uni-dimensional and simple in composition or structure. As the session and/or therapy unfolds, the psychotherapeutic themes tend to become multidimensional and complex. For example, a client might talk about being bored, only to learn that the boredom stems from his or her driving himself or herself to do things out of a sense of duty or obligation. This may lead to yet other facets indirectly related to boredom such as having high expectations of self, being duty bound, being perfectionistic and being unable to enjoy life. The manner

in which the associated themes emerge and link to each other and influence the person's presenting problems is indicated.

b) The interventions used to address and work with the themes are presented. This includes the use of the usual interviewing skills and the more advanced counselling techniques (e.g., focusing, Gestalt Two-Chair Dialogue, role-reversal, imagery, etc.). The counsellor indicates the purpose for which the technique was used and how he/she proceeded, particularly how the technique was applied to the task that was at hand.

c) The counsellor reports his or her observation as to how the client responded to the use of the interventions. This remains at the level of description without interpretation. If the client did not respond positively to the use of the interventions, the counsellor indicates how he or she attempted to solicit the collaboration of the client.

5. *Gains for the client.* The fifth content domain comprises the gains for the client. These gains can be construed in terms of the client's descriptions and/or in terms of some reference point that the therapist finds useful (e.g., the phases of the counselling process). The counselling gains for the client are briefly summarized. This may include feeling better in having talked about the concerns, greater clarity concerning the presenting problem, insight into the factors underlying the problem, commitment taken to change, actions taken to change, and so on.

6. *Nature and quality of counsellor-client interactions and mood of client.* The quality of the therapist-client relationship and any unusual experiences are recorded in the sixth content domain. Of importance are transferences and countertransferences, broken alliances, etc. The report mentions client mood changes (e.g., depressed, happy) or attitude changes (e.g., negative, positive) that might have occurred during the session or between sessions. Changes that occur in these dimensions are of particular significance.

7. *Summary, recommendation and future work to be done.* Based on the work of this session or on the upgraded assessment, the counsellor specifies the work that needs to be attended to in future sessions. The counsellor may add a note regarding specific interventions that might be useful.

In brief, the focal point of the organizing and recording of data are the psychotherapeutic themes. Of importance are the nature of the themes, the context from which they emerged, how they were treated, their evolution in the course of therapy, and the client gains.

A Case Illustration

An illustration in how to write up a counselling session using the Thematic Analytic Research Method is presented below. (The name, Dennis, is a pseudonym and the summarized data does not represent the material of any actual client. Any resemblance to any real client is purely accidental.) As can be seen, the description of the evolution of the themes comprises the bulk of the report. This is typical particularly when exploratory work is part of the session.

Core themes. Themes included his regret for the lost opportunities of the past versus being content with his response to life's opportunities and feeling loss versus feeling filled.

Context. Dennis related a dream wherein he was with a former girlfriend whom he wanted to marry, but she broke it up without adequate explanation. During and after the dream, he felt regret in not having married her.

Therapeutic goals. The goal was to explore the themes of regret and loss in his current life and in his past life.

Evolution of themes. A focusing exercise was used to help Dennis get in touch with his feelings of regret about lost opportunities in life. There was then a shift to feelings of heaviness, sadness and loss. When asked to get in touch with all of this from a feeling perspective, these feelings shifted to those of worthlessness and low self-esteem. When asked what he needed to comfort these feelings, he said that he needed to be accepted. This feeling was then explored with the therapist asking him by whom he wanted to be accepted. He first thought of his mother, towards whom he felt angry for never having accepted him without conditions related to better performance. Dennis then broadened this to a general feeling that he was not accepted as a person by anyone. In fact, he found it hard to believe that others would accept him unconditionally, yet he yearned for acceptance by the other. An added theme was that Dennis did not let others accept him for fear that he would be rejected, as was the case with his mother.

In brief, the core feelings of regret and loss shifted to include underlying feelings of heaviness, sadness, worthlessness, and low self-esteem. To comfort these feelings Dennis needed to be unconditionally accepted. Despite this need, he feared that he would not be unconditionally accepted.

Nature and quality of interactions. The therapist nudged Dennis carefully but persistently, and in the process Dennis accessed feelings of sadness, hurt, anger, and regret. During the latter part of the session, tears came to his eyes. He followed instructions to enter his feelings and to let the feelings speak for themselves, however, this was hard for him since he tended to distance himself from his feelings.

Therapeutic gains. He found the session helpful because it touched upon many things that were correct for him, even though painful. That is, the session brought him in contact with his truth which had power to liberate him.

Summary and recommendations. This session worked on a greater understanding of Dennis' feelings of regret and loss. This kind of work can continue for some time, but then needs to be complemented by the development of inner resources and skills to deal with problems around closeness, trust, intimacy, regret, etc.

A comment should be made regarding the core themes. The problem pole of the bi-polar theme was stated by the client, and the other pole, the goal towards which to work, was inferred by the therapist. For example, the client expressed regret for the lost opportunities of the past. One could infer that the client wished that in the past he had made better use of opportunities. One could also infer that he wished to make better use of opportunities in the future. The goal towards which to work often is implicitly stated by the client and intuited or inferred by the therapist.

Research Application

Now I want to illustrate how one can use, for the purpose of research, the reports from the counselling sessions which were organized and recorded using the Thematic Analytic Research Method. For this illustration, I have used the reports of the first seven counselling sessions of a middle-aged male client. He was successful at work but was less than successful in his relationships. In fact, his relationships with his parents beginning in childhood and his relationships with peers had been troubled and conflicted. This also applied to his marriage. When he began therapy, he was enraged, depressed, guilt-ridden, suicidal, felt worthless, had low self-esteem, and felt inadequate as a male, husband, and father.

For the purpose of this illustration, I have presented the data from five of the seven content domains. These are summarized in Table 1. As can be seen from the table, I have created a separate category for the interventions used by the therapist. According to the method, the interventions are to be included in the content domain of thematic evolution. Each row on the table represents one therapy session. This arrangement allows one to view the data across the content domains or across the sessions. For the purpose of research, it is useful to view each of the content themes across the sessions and in relationship with each other.

A quick overview of the core themes indicates that feelings of uncontrolled anger, being put down, and being intimidated, were present for the first five sessions. In the last two sessions the themes of vulnerability/inner strength, conflicted/at peace and undecided/decided emerged. Thus the presenting problems changed.

It seems that the change in presenting problems was related to the context from which the theme emerged. The context for the first three sessions was the client's relationships with his par-

Table 1

Results from Application of the Thematic Research Method to a Single Case

Core Themes	**Context**	**Goals**	**Thematic Evolution**	**Interventions**	**Client Gains**
Uncontrolled vs. controlled anger/ rage	Relationships of parents, child-hood peers, adults,	Explore, identify, express, ventilate feelings	Anger/rage> feeling ridiculed> controlled> inadequate> not special	Empathic re-sponses, explor-atory questions, linking statements	Felt understood and accepted, relief
Seething anger/ assertive	Parents, grandparents	Explore and clarify	Belittled/ demeaned> unwanted> worthless> tense/can not play	Same as above	Awareness, linked present emotional states and behaviours to those of childhood
Feeling put down, intimidated, puts self down	Parents, partner	Explore and clarify	Angry> put down> worthless> inadequate	Same as above	Awareness of how he puts himself down, accepted that he has right to his opinions and for affirmation
Anger/acceptance, self- doubt/ self- assurance	Partner, therapist	Explore and clarify feelings	Angry> self-doubt> depressed> needed reassurance	Same as above, focusing	Feeling of release in expressing anger, felt reassured

Table 1 (Cont'd)

Results from Application of the Thematic Analytic Research Method to a Single Case

Core Themes	Context	Goals	Thematic Evolution	Interventions	Client Gains
Angry/happy, hurt/comforted	Partner	Explore feelings underlying anger	Anger>hurt> asserting his needs for privacy, space, and opinions	Empathic responses, linking statements, monologue	Felt affirmed for his needs for respect, space, right to his opinions
Vulnerable/ strong	Partner	Explore options to resolve marital conflict	In a bind> resolution> strong feeling of self	Empathic responses linking statements, exploratory and clarifying questions	Resolution of a couple dilemma
Conflicted/ at peace, undecided/ decided,	Partner	Work towards a decision	Conflicted> anxious> not liked> wants to be at peace with himself	Focusing, same as above	The feeling that he is a good person, more at peace with himself

ents, childhood peers, grandparents, and adults. This shifted then, beginning with the fourth session, to his relationship with his partner.

When we view the interventions used by the therapist, we again notice a change beginning with the fourth session. In the first three sessions, the therapist used, among others, empathic responses, exploratory questions, and linking statements. In the fourth and seventh sessions, focusing was added, and in the fifth, monologuing was added.

There seems to be a relationship between the interventions used and the evolution of the themes. For example, during the first three sessions, when empathic responses, etc. were used, the client explored his feelings of anger, being put down, feeling intimidated and controlled, being worthless, and inadequate. However, in the fourth session, when focusing was introduced, the client expressed self-doubt and requested reassurance. In the fifth session, with the introduction of the monologue, the client became more assertive and added his need for privacy, space, and expression of his opinions. To this was added a feeling of being stronger, which was expressed in the sixth session. There seems to have been yet further progress in the last session, when the client expressed a desire to be at peace with himself.

Lastly, regarding the client gains, there was a movement towards being understood, accepted, a sense of relief, awareness, feeling affirmed, feeling that he is a good person, and being more at peace with himself.

In brief, by using the Thematic Analytic Research Method, one can begin to make links between core themes, therapist interventions, evolution of themes, and client gains. It seems that this method is useful to gain a better understanding of the client and to build a model regarding the working through of a specific problem or concern.

Summary and Conclusions

I have tried to demonstrate the need for discovery-oriented research within the field of pastoral counselling and have proposed that the primary data for this type of research is the pastoral counselling experience itself. Included in my discussion is an informal method for conducting research which uses the therapist session notes organized according to the Thematic Analytic Research Method. Methods such as these make it possible for all professionals to engage in meaningful research, to keep up their research interests and to make a valuable contribution to the discipline and profession of pastoral counselling.

References

Anderson, J., Laronde, M., Kennedy, M., Leblanc, P., McGuinty, E., & Walsh, S. (1994). *Patterns of change emerging from an analysis of therapeutic themes.* Ottawa, Ontario: Saint Paul University. Unpublished M.A. Research Project.

Clarke, K. (1995). *Pastoral counselling approach to trauma: Creation of meaning in incest survivors.* Address given to the Second Conference of the Society for Pastoral Counselling Research, Ottawa, Ontario, May 12.

Clinebell, H. (1984). *basic types of pastoral care and counselling.* Nashville: Abingdon Press.

Jones, E. (1961). *The life and work of Sigmund Freud.* Edited and Abridged in one Volume by L. Trilling & S. Marcus. London: The Hogarth Press.

Meier, A. (1990). Future directions in pastoral counselling I. Constructing theoretical models. *Pastoral Sciences, 9*, 131-152.

Meier, A. (1994). *The research challenges for the professions of pastoral counselling.* Inaugural address presented at the Founding and First Annual Conference of the Society for Pastoral Counselling Research held at St. Paul University, Ottawa, Ontario, May 5 -7, 1994.

Meier, A., & Boivin, M. (1995). *Patterns of change emerging from an analysis of psychotherapeutic themes.* Paper presented at the Eleventh Annual Conference of the Society for the Exploration of Psychotherapy Integration, Bethesda, Maryland, April 6-9.

Meier, A., Boivin, M., & Aylward, C. (1986). The pastoral counsellor: Yesterday and today. *Pastoral Sciences, 5,* 19-46.

Meier, A., Herring, C., Sminiski, J. & Tyman, C. (1995). *Patterns of change emerging from an intensive analysis of counselling themes.* Paper presented at the Second Annual Conference of the Society for Pastoral Counselling Research, Ottawa, Ontario, St. Paul University, May 11-13.

Meier, A., & Weber, W. (1992). Future directions in pastoral counselling: II. Qualitative and quantitative research. In Marc Pelchat (Ed.), *Empirical Approaches in Theology*, Quebec, Canada: University of Laval, 157-182.

Strunk, O. (1985). A prolegomenon to a history of pastoral counselling. In R.J. Wicks, R.D. Parsons, & D. Capps (Eds.), *Clinical handbook of pastoral counselling.* New York: Paulist Press, 14-25.

Strunk, O. (1993). A prolegomenon to a history of pastoral counselling. In R.J. Wicks, R.D. Parsons, & D. Capps (Eds.), *Clinical handbook of pastoral counselling, Volume 1* (Expanded Edition). New York: Paulist Press, 14-25.

Chapter 15

Metaphor and the Appropriation of Peak Religious Experiences*

Peter Sanders

Over the past five years, my graduate students and I investigated peak religious experiences. In one of the research projects, we studied whether storytelling would assist the appropriation of religious experiences (Daniel, Ellis, Frymire, Kuiack, Ling & Lunney, 1989) and in a second project we considered whether the use of symbols facilitated the appropriation of these experiences (O'Keefe & Oxenford, 1992). The findings from these studies confirmed the value of storytelling and the use of symbols to assist persons to better understand, interpret and integrate their religious experiences in their lives.

In this chapter we report the results from our research which evaluated the use of metaphors as a means of appropriating peak religious experiences. We define peak religious experiences, summarize Batson and Ventis' (1982) model of peak religious experiences, present the current theories of metaphor, indicate how metaphors are used in psychotherapy, demonstrate how metaphors might be applied to the appropriation of peak religious experiences, and conclude by presenting the results of our research.

---

*Revision of a paper presented at the 2nd Annual Conference of the Society for Pastoral Counselling Research, Saint Paul University, Ottawa, Ontario, May 12, 1995

Peak Religious Experiences

In his study of self-actualizers, Maslow (1962) observed that they reported a unique phenomenon which he called a peak experience. He described a peak experience as an episodic, brief occurrence in which a person suddenly experiences a powerful transcendental state of consciousness (Maslow, 1962, p. 97; 1970, p. 170; 1978, p. 19). During this state, a person experiences an intense euphoria, an altered perception of time and place, a sense of oneness with the universe and a sense of heightened understanding (Maslow, 1962, pp. 74-96; 1970, pp. 171-178). During peak experiences, persons are "most their identities, closest to their real selves, most idiosyncratic" (Maslow, 1962, p. 103). When considered within the context of religious experiences, Maslow (1970)defined peak experiences as "secularized religious or mystical or transcendental experiences" (p. 170).

In our research, we applied the concept of peak experiences to religious experiences. We refer to these as peak religious experiences. For our research we defined peak religious experiences as "those extraordinary unexpected moments of supreme joy and contentedness in a person's life, experienced through a sudden and enhanced awareness of the transcendent/divinity" (Daniel et al., 1989, p. xiii; Hoven, Lee & Uson, 1994, p. 118). That is, the term refers to those religious experiences that made a difference in a person's life and transformed him or her.

Research on Peak Experiences

Based on their research, Batson and Ventis (1982) developed a four-stage model to track the process leading to a peak religious experience, namely, Existential Crisis, Self Surrender, New Vision, and New Life (pp. 82-85).

By *existential crisis*, Batson and Ventis (1982) mean that an event in the life of a person puts into question the person's total experience or a significant part of the person's experience. The event may be a death in the family, a very troubled marriage relationship, a vocational crisis, a stressful working situation, or some similar experience. This is followed by *self-surrender* wherein the person gives up trying to find a solution to the question or the experience. This is brought on by that person's difficulty to integrate the event into his/her understanding of life, or their inability to cope with this event, or to see a way out. The third stage in this process is the occurrence of a *new vision*. This is signaled by the person having a tremendous emotional experience: hearing a voice, undergoing an action, or understanding a situation in such a manner that he/she sees life in a new way. Life, suddenly, seems manageable, worthwhile, purposeful, understandable, meaningful, and peaceful. A heavy load has been lifted from his/her shoulders. A new vision has occurred. The experience is so powerful that the person is able to undertake new things, know what to do next, understand the meaning of his/her life. The person's life has changed, and a *new life* is begun.

The process that leads to a peak religious experience begins with an event that the person cannot easily integrate. The integration process requires significant reworking of the mindsets that the person established over the years. It demands a new way of thinking, and hence the working-through process takes considerable time. Some people speak of a personal paradigm shift (MacCormac, 1985). If we look at some of the lives of the saints, we discover that they underwent such an experience (e.g., St. Paul, St. Augustine, St. Francis of Assisi). Peak religious experiences are, at times, conversion experiences. A significant number of people have such significant religious experiences (Princeton Religious Research Centre, 1986).

Theoretical Approaches to Metaphor

The notion of metaphor, especially since a publication by Richards in 1935 (cited by Black, 1966, 1980), has undergone an enormous development to the extent that some speak of metaphormania. Thousands of articles and books have been written since then and books of bibliographies on metaphor have been published. There are three fundamental theories regarding metaphor (Gerhart & Russell, 1984).

Substitution theory

This theory was postulated by Aristotle (Gerhart & Russel, 1984). Substitution theory postulates that a metaphor is the transfer of the meaning of one word to another word. Thus, a metaphor is understood as the substitution of one noun for another and as such, it is an ornament to language replaceable by literal translation (Hoven, et al., p. 3). For example, we could say that a person is sly or that the person is a fox. The word fox has the same meaning as the word sly.

Comparison theory

This theory holds that we use a metaphor to better understand something that is new, be it a person, event, or situation. We compare the elements of a metaphor with person, situation, etc. For example, when we call a person a fox, we try to put together the characteristics of the fox with the person. We compare characteristics of the person with the characteristics of the fox, and thereby arrive at a better understanding of the person. The person is viewed through the prism of fox (Gerhart & Russell, 1984).

Interaction theory

Those who subscribe to this theory understand a metaphor as an interaction of one word or phrase with another word or phrase (Black, 1966, 1980; MacCormac, 1971, 1985). The interactive process creates a tension from which arises new meaning. Black (1980) proposes that the thoughts about two subjects interact to produce meaning and in the process both subjects are altered. MacCormac (1971) describes metaphor as "a linguistic device in which words are juxtaposed in such a manner that a literal reading would produce absurdity" (p. 240). For a metaphor to exist, at least two referents which are similar yet dissimilar and an "as if" or hypothetical quality must be present (MacCormac, 1971, p. 240). The combination of the two terms causes an absurdity which in turn causes a tension that is necessary for the creation of a metaphor. According to MacCormac (1971), as a metaphor is formulated, a cognitive process is stimulated; various long-term semantic memories are searched, two referents are found, a meaningful relationship between the two referents is understood and a metaphor is generated (MacCormac, 1971).

The interaction theory, it appears, is best suited for the appropriation of peak religious experiences. It is expected that the use of a metaphor would link the conscious and subconscious elements of the mind and bring about, by their mutual interaction, a new understanding for the person.

The Use of Metaphor in Psychotherapy.

Psychotherapists who consciously use metaphors (Billow, 1977; Atwood & Levine, 1991) can be grouped according to four different approaches. These therapists approach metaphors according to their specific professional orientation without prescribing to a particular theory of metaphor (Lee, 1994).

The interpretative model

According to this model the analyst interprets the client's material using a Freudian theoretical framework. The client presents a metaphor that the therapist then uses to delve more deeply into the person's psyche. The therapist intuits the meaning of the metaphor; then, in collaboration with the client, he/she continues to understand the links that exist between the client's metaphor and the unconscious, and brings these understandings to the level of consciousness. The goal of the therapist is to draw upon the unconscious images, impulses, and motives, and to apply conscious control to ordering and arranging them. There are three stages to this use of the metaphor (Siegelman, 1990; Voth, 1970).

First, the analyst listens carefully for any metaphors that the client may introduce during a session. The analyst selects one metaphor generated by the client and explicitly attends to it. This becomes a determining factor in the process.

Secondly, the analyst works with the client by attending to the underlying perspectives that are present in the metaphor. The client is asked to identify, as closely as possible, with the metaphor and thereby come to the deepest elements of his/her personality.

The final task of the interpretative process belongs to the therapist. It is he or she who determines whether the use of the metaphor has been helpful in the process, whether its use has helped the client to deal with the underlying conflict, and whether the conflict was resolved in such a way that the person can live more fully.

In this approach the client and the analyst work together in order to reach a conscious resolution of the conflict. The use of metaphor itself is not a treatment; rather, it is a tool to be used in the process of interpreting the inner life of the client, to come to a greater awareness of the conflict, and thereby deal with it. It is a preliminary stage leading to more literal statements and understandings, which are deemed to be more useful and accurate (MacCormac, 1985, p. 4).

Cognitive/Behavioural approach

In this approach, there is an attempt to change the dysfunctional thinking or irrational belief system of a person (MacCormac, 1985). A paradigm or way of thinking is replaced with one that expedites learning and more healthy functioning. A person who thinks in terms of black and white, for example, is invited to think more discriminatingly, and hence to explore areas that are more ambiguous. Metaphor, because of its significant place in language and in thinking, can be used appropriately in the process (MacCormac, 1985).

There are four basic stages to this approach:

1. The therapist must know exactly what he or she wishes the client to learn, that is, the concept or paradigm to be developed.
2. The therapist must attend to the language of the client so as to be able to present a metaphor that links with the client's lived experience. For example, using the metaphor of farming would not help a person who has no understanding of farming.
3. The therapist attempts to find an analogous area in the client's life to which the metaphor can be applied. The client is asked

to reflect upon the metaphor and see where the different elements of the metaphor fit in with his or her life. In this process, it is important to be clear and precise so that the concept can become a clear paradigm for the person.

4. The insight must then be acted upon. The new paradigm must manifest itself in behaviour, the goal of a cognitive-behavioural approach.

Existential approach

In this approach, the lived experience of the person is examined in the here-and-now. Gendlin (1979) designed a technique, "focusing," to help a person become aware of deeper issues and to name them using a word, phrase, symbol, metaphor, etc. One can engage in focusing either alone or in conjunction with a therapist. There are six stages to the focusing exercise:

1. The first is to clear a space. The person is asked to relax, to become calm, and to attend to the experience of the body in the here-and-now. He/she is invited to listen to the bodily-felt feeling and get in touch with whatever prevents him/her from feeling content or with what hinders the person's happiness.
2. Next, the person focuses on one particular problem and tries to feel the whole of it. It is a time to feel and listen.
3. A word, phrase or metaphor is allowed to form which describes the bodily-felt feeling. When the person focuses on the word or metaphor, their bodily experience of the problem begins to shift. The word, phrase or metaphor is called the handle and serves as a referent for the bodily-felt feeling.
4. The person moves back and forth between the bodily-felt feeling and the handle so as to get a good fit between the two. The bodily-felt feeling guides this process.
5. The person asks what it is about the whole problem that makes him or her so troubled, or what is needed for things to be better. The person does not give answers to these questions, but waits for the feeling to stir and give him/her an answer.

6. Lastly, the person receives whatever emerges in the exercise. This may be shared between the person and the therapist or with someone else.

Another existential approach is working with a life metaphor (Siegelman, 1990). The person perceives his or her life as a metaphor. This metaphor encompasses the basic orientation of that person's life or an aspect of their life. For example, the metaphor "I am a rock" indicates the person's perception of self as someone who is immovable, hard, unchangeable, cold, static, and impenetrable. By understanding this metaphor, the person may proceed to change it gradually by first perceiving him or herself as a broken-down rock and then as sand. In this way the person experiences self in a new way. The person thereby restructures his or her perception of life.

The communicative approach

In this approach, the therapist communicates a metaphor (e.g., a person, figure, idea, object) which relates to a person's particular problem with the purpose of changing his/her perception of the problem. This approach, which can be thought of as a problem solving approach, has been developed by Milton H. Erickson (Dimond, 1988; Rosen, 1988; Mills & Crowley, 1986).

The approach intends to work at the unconscious level. In defining the unconscious, Erickson includes the learning that is acquired throughout one's life as well as the psychological resources of which one is currently unaware. According to Erickson, the unconscious mind lets its conscious mind know something that it already knows, but doesn't know that it knows (Dimond, 1988; Rosen, 1988). Therefore, there is a communication between the unconscious and the conscious. The more the metaphor is able to connect with the imagining and emotional functioning of the right brain, the more it is able to bring the problem (memory of it) to the left brain and make it explicit in consciousness. In searching the person's stored and imagined experience, new mental images are triggered.

Metaphor is used also to communicate issues that would be more difficult to handle if they were discussed in a conscious and direct manner. The use of metaphors is much less threatening, and therefore it is much easier for the client to handle the question or problem in an indirect manner.

The metaphor is introduced either at the beginning or at the end of a session. If introduced at the beginning of the session, it will give a focus to the total session a metaphor introduced at the end of a session may work in the unconscious between sessions.

Because the approach intends to work at the unconscious level, the metaphor should be introduced when the person is relaxed. Hypnosis or hypnotherapy may be used to create this relaxed position. Through the unconscious processing of the metaphor, the client may be expected to work out new insights at the cognitive and behavioural level.

Research Method

The purpose of our research was to assess whether the use of metaphors facilitated the appropriation of religious experiences. We hypothesized that if the interaction theory about metaphors (Black, 1966, 1980; MacCormac, 1985) was valid, then the metaphorization process would connect with the unconscious parts of the experience and bring these to the fore. In this way the person would be helped to better understand the experience and to put it into a clearer and more coherent perspective. We also attempted to assess whether the working through of the metaphors according to Batson and Ventis' four stages (1982) would help the persons who had peak religious experiences to understand and appropriate these experiences.

For our research, appropriation was defined as "the claiming of the religious experience of oneself, making it a vital part of one's being, and using it to propel oneself to further growth in personhood and faith (Daniel et al., 1989, p. xiii).

Participants

Fifteen people, who indicated that they had had a life changing religious experience that had impacted forcefully upon their lives, were interviewed. For this, we used semi-structured interviews in much the same manner as Batson and Ventis did (1982) to verify their stages. As in previous research, these people were asked to describe their lives before, during, and after the experience. The participants who experienced an existential crisis, resolved the crisis, and were able to get on with their lives in a relaxed, purposeful and peaceful fashion, were invited to the study. That is, the participants whose experiences were consistent with Batson and Ventis' (1982) four stage process model were admitted to the research project.

Instruments

The instruments comprised two semi-structured interviews and a set of guidelines to help participants metaphorize their experiences (Hoven et al., 1994, pp. 176-181). The semi-structured interview used for the first session comprised a series of questions keyed to the participant's life before, during and after the peak religious experience. The second semi-structured interview was used in the second session and comprised questions to assess cognitive insight, emotional impact, and behavioural changes. The guidelines to help participants find a metaphor to express their experiences was used in the last half of the first interview.

Method

The participants who had experienced an existential crisis were invited to join the study. They were interviewed on two different occasions, with two weeks between the interviews. During the first meeting, which used a semi-structured interview, they were asked to tell their life stories as experienced before, during and after the existential crisis. They were also asked to apply a metaphor to their experience for each of the three time frames (before, during and after the existential crisis).

Following a two week period, the participants returned for a second interview. Again, in a semi structured-interview, they were asked to describe the impact that the metaphorization process had had on their understanding of their peak religious experience. They were also asked the following questions: Did they work on the metaphor between interviews? Did they find it difficult to metaphorize? Would they wish to change their metaphor or metaphors into ones that were now thought more appropriate? What did the metaphors do in reference to the peak religious experience? With the consent of the research participants, the interviews were taped.

Results of the Research

Content Analysis

Using the data obtained from the participants' audiotaped reports about their life before, during and after the religious experiences, a word-analysis was applied to ascertain whether these experiences were consistent with Batson and Ventis' (1982) framework of the existential crisis, the self-surrender, new vision, and new life stages.

In the study, participants reported specific words that indicated each of Batson and Ventis' (1982) four stages. The words for each of the four stages were as follows:

Existential crisis: "despairing," "awful," "under a lot of stress," "was about to explode," "anxiety," "turmoil."

Self surrender stage: "Giving up," "not knowing what to do," "suicidal," "saw no way out."

New vision stage: "Absolutely glorious," "turned my life around," "God will see me through situations," "it was the Lord," "it all makes sense now."

New life stage: "A weight has been lifted," "life is so much riche," "freed me up," "I chose Yes," "a complete transformation."

The results from this analysis provide support for Batson and Ventis' (1982) four stages that a person traverses when working through an existential crisis.

Qualitative Analysis

The participants' audiotaped interviews were also analyzed for a more detailed description of their experiences as they worked through an existential crisis. The majority of the participants indicated that they found it helpful to assign a metaphor to their life as experienced before, during and after the peak religious experience. It helped them to see new aspects of their experience, to relive it in a deep fashion, and to relive the emotions of the experience. The metaphor summarized in one symbol the whole experience, it assisted in recalling, organizing and articulating the experience. The following are examples of the participants' comments regarding this experience: "I had difficulty finishing the first interview because the metaphor in a way exploded just as I was sharing it." "The metaphor awakened in me a freshness in my experience, it was almost like taking a breath." "The metaphor can really engage me or even absorb me into it ... it helped me to internalize my experience so that I could not separate myself from it; metaphor has the power to do what we can't do with our language, it helps to put words into our experience." "The metaphors seem to organize my experience ... they make sense of my experience ... organizing it and sort of explaining it to me."

Eleven of the fifteen respondents worked with the metaphor between the interviews. This was not suggested by the interviewers but happened spontaneously with the participants. Some wrote poems, created meaningful rituals, and kept journals about their metaphors, while others sketched their metaphors, worked with their metaphors in therapy, and so on. This spontaneous working was indicative of the power of the metaphor.

Thirteen of the fifteen did not wish to change their original metaphors. The two who did change their metaphors changed only aspects of their original metaphors. For them, the original metaphor captured the basic orientation that they wished to express. One worked with a piece of glass that had shattered and broken into different pieces. In the second interview the same person used the metaphor of a tapestry since it was made up of different parts.

The majority of the participants used only one metaphor for all of the three time frames of the experience, that is, their life experience before, during, and after an existential crisis. They used different aspects of such metaphors as a candle, a pearl, the moon, and the sea.

The peak religious experiences were very profound and sacred moments for the persons. For this reason participants were hesitant to speak about them and to share them unless they felt their disclosures would be received in sacred trust. During the majority of the interviews, some of the persons became teary-eyed while others wept openly. They relived the emotionality of their experience. This even happened to a participant who recounted an experience that had occurred more than twenty years ago.

The participants generally did not experience great difficulty in creating metaphors. Educational background did not seem to make any difference in regard to this ability.

It also became evident that the use of metaphor, because it is such a powerful instrument, must be used with great attention. For this reason, participants must be made aware that in working with metaphors they may make links with emotional experiences that lie deep within their psyche. This study indicates how closely metaphors are related to our past experiences. It further reflects that we are unified individuals and that we cannot compartmentalize our lives.

Since both metaphors and peak religious experiences are complex entities, further research is required. The particular psychotherapeutic approaches could be studied further in regards to the manner in which they can elicit metaphors; this would be useful for the understanding and appropriation of peak religious experiences.

The use of metaphors could also be developed for less intense experiences. The original plan of our research was to find a methodology to help people to live more deeply out of their profound experiences, which usually remain hidden and are not consciously worked with, yet have a great impact upon their lives.

In summary, we believe that the study of metaphors and peak religious experiences is a very important area of research; it assists persons to deal with their experiences not only at the level of rationality, but also at the level of emotions and volition.

References

Atwood, J.D., & Levine, L.B. (1991). Axe murderers, dragons, spiders and webs: Therapeutic metaphors in couple therapy. *Contemporary Family Therapy: An International Journal, 13*(3), 201-217.

Batson, C.D., & Ventis, W.L. (1982). *The religious experience. A social-psychological perspective.* New York: Oxford University Press.

Billow, R. (1977). Metaphor: A review of the psychological literature. *Psychological Bulletin, 84*(1), 81-92.

Black, M. (1966). *Models and metaphors: Studies in language and philosophy.* Ithasca, New York: Cornell University Press.

Black, M. (1980). More about metaphors. In A. Ortony (Ed.), *Metaphor and thought.* Cambridge: Cambridge University Press, 19-43.

Daniel, F., Ellis, K., Frymire, T., Kuiack, R., Ling, P., & Lunney, E. (1989). *Storytelling in the appropriation of peak religious experiences: A partial review of the literature.* Unpublished master's research project, Saint Paul University, Ottawa, Ontario, Canada.

Dimond, R.E. (1988). Ericksonian psychotherapy is the state of the art: Suggestions for a future orientation. In J.K. Zeig & S.T. Laknton (Eds.), *Developing Ericksonian therapy: State of the art.* New York: Brunner/Mazel, 30-38.

Gendlin, E.T. (1979). *Focusing.* New York: Bantam Books.

Gerhart, M., & Russell, A. (1984). *Metaphoric process: The creation of scientific and religious understanding.* Forth Worth, Texas: Texas Christian University Press.

Hoven, W., Lee, B., & Uson, R. (1994). *Metaphor in the appropriation of religious experiences: A partial review of the literature and a preliminary study.* Unpublished M.A. research project, Ottawa, Ontario, Saint Paul University (Research Director: Peter Sanders).

Lee, B. (1994). Uses of metaphor in psychotherapy. In W. Hoven, B.Lee, & R. Uson, *Metaphor in the appropriation of religious experiences: A partial review of the literature and a preliminary study* (pp. 70-123). Unpublished M.A. research project, Ottawa, Ontario, Saint Paul University (Research Director: Peter Sanders).

MacCormac, E.R. (1971). Metaphor revisited. *Journal of Aesthetics and Art Criticism, 30*, 239-250

MacCormac, E.R. (1985). *A cognitive theory of metaphor.* Cambridge, MA: MIT Press.

Maslow, A.H. (1962). *Toward a psychology of being.* Toronto: D. Van Nostrand Company, Inc.

Maslow, A.H. (1970). Religious aspects of peak-experiences. In W.A. Sadler (Ed.), *Personality and religion: The role of religion in personality development.* New York: Harper & Row, 168-179.

Maslow, A.H. (1978). *Religions, values and peak-experiences.* New York: Viking Press.

Mills, J.C., & Crowley, R.J. (1986). *Therapeutic metaphors for children and the child within.* New York: Brunner/Mazel.

O'Keefe, M., & Oxenford, M. (1992). *Symbol in the appropriation of peak religious experiences: A partial review of the literature.* Unpublished master's research project, Saint Paul University, Ottawa, Ontario, Canada.

Princeton Religious Research Center (1986). *Faith development and your ministry.* Report based on Gallop survey conducted for the Religious Education Association of U.S. and Canada. Princeton: Religious Research Center.

Rosen, S. (1988). What makes Ericksonian Therapy so effective? In J.K. Zeig & S.T. Laknton (Eds.), *Developing Ericksonian therapy: State of the art.* New York: Brunner/Mazel, 5-21.

Siegelman, E. Y. (1990). *Metaphor and meaning in psychotherapy.* New York: Guilford Press.

Voth, H.M. (1970). The analysis of metaphor. *Journal of the American Psychoanalytic Association, 18*, 599-621.

Chapter 16

Fundamental Value Questionnaire for Clinical Work and Qualitative Research*

Marie-Line Morin

In previous research, Individual Fundamental Values were extracted from psychological counselling sessions using the method of phenomenological-existential analysis (Giorgi, 1985). This research method requires a considerable amount of time to analyze complete transcripts of sessions and to go through the phenomenological and eidetic reduction processes. To provide clinicians and researchers with a tool to identify Fundamental Values in subjects or clients without having to go through the time-consuming eidetic reduction process, we constructed a questionnaire that would generate a list of values similar to the ones that emerge from an phenomenological-existential analysis. This chapter presents the rationale used in the construction of the questionnaire, called the Fundamental Value Questionnaire (FVQ), and summarizes the results from a study that assessed the internal validity of the instrument.

---

*Revision of a paper presented at the 6th Annual Conference of the Society for Pastoral Counselling Research, Saint Paul University, Ottawa, Ontario, May 15, 1999

The Rationale

The basic principles of phenomenological-existential eidetic reduction and the concept of intentionality (Croteau, 1994) provide the rationale for the construction of the Fundamental Value Questionnaire. They refer to human consciousness that is particularly characterized by its goal towards meaning and purpose. Human beings, therefore, are inherently immersed and situated in a world that becomes meaningful to them (Croteau, 1994). Our goal was to access a subject's set of values similar to the ones identified in previous research using Giorgi's phenomenological-existential procedure. Through this procedure, a subject's Fundamental Value can be inferred from a set of values called "little values." The "little values" are derived from the psychological summary of the subject's responses to a semi-structured interview (Morin, 2001). The phenomenological-existential procedure is based on the principle that an individual's intentionalities are characterized by their subjective way of relating to the world or their way of "being-in-the-world." Humans, as beings, are in relation to the world within themselves (*Eigenwelt*), to the world of relations with others (*Mitwelt*) and to the world around them (*Umwelt*) (May, 1962, pp. 61-65).

The author reviewed the data from a previous research (Morin, 1999) in which Fundamental Values of five subjects were identified using the three ways of being-in-the-world. It was found that the derived values faithfully represented one of the three ways of being-in-the-world. The following summarizes our findings regarding the correspondence between the content of the subject's discourse and the three phenomenological-existential categories presented above. The five subjects generated themes for each of the following categories: *Eigenwelt, Mitwelt and Umwelt.*

Eigenwelt

Eigenweld refers to the world within: thoughts, feelings, desires; self existing in time (present, past and future). The following themes were identified for this category:

Self. Self-control, self-perception, self-concept, feeling loved, feeling isolated, no one to talk to, one's character, one's feeling of self, one's intelligence, being a loser.

Emotions and feelings. Anxiety, pain, bereavement, vulnerability, weakness, depression, shame, shyness, anger, rage, guilt, ways of dealing and listening to feelings, preoccupations, reactions, perceptions, dreams, desires, sexuality, fantasies, suicidal thoughts, wishes to die.

Mitwelt

Mitwelt refers to the world with others: being with others; all of one's interpersonal and social relationships; particularly one's need to be recognized, accepted, confirmed in self-perception. For this category, the following themes were identified:

Relationship with someone. Children, daughter, son, spouse, husband, wife, parents, mother, father, boyfriend, girlfriend, friends, colleagues.

Type of relationship. Intimacy, nurturance, conflictive, confidence, someone who cares for my pain, important persons, close ones, therapeutic relationship, dependence, living together, pregnancy, working relationship.

Needs and desires. Desiring someone, wishing to develop or change attitudes, someone else's wishes, opinion of others, satisfaction (having what one wishes for), appreciating aspects of personality, making changes, having dreams and desires, having sexual desires and fantasies.

Obstacles in relationships. Conflict, incest, adultery, separation, divorce, lack of satisfaction, being abandoned, being angered, frightened, saddened by someone, having secrets, hiding things from close ones or for the public.

Managing relationships. Choosing or being chosen by someone, family reunions, spending time with spouse, supporting one another, declaring one's love, determining the leader and the follower, changing to deal with partner, asking forgiveness, ways of treating others, agreeing or disagreeing, sharing values, sexual differences, character, opening up, revealing oneself, being confident in other, resolving conflict, having initiative, compromising, mistrust, being reserved, ways of communicating, roles in the household and in the family, writing letters.

Attitudes and commitments in relationships. Marriage, choice, responsibility, helping others, children's education, dependency, ambivalence, passivity, maternity, paternity, caring for spouse or for close ones, taking risks, success, study, job.

Relationship with spiritual or religious issues. God, church, spiritual or religious dimension, symbols, myths, metaphors, peak-experiences, para-psychological experiences, listening to one's inner voice, miracles (real or hoped for), beliefs, proverbs, truth, healing.

Relationship with institution. Clergy, religious people, school and education, government, society, culture.

Umwelt

Umwelt refers to the world around: physical space, formed and structured, things from nature; relationship to distance and proximity; strength, instincts and physical, biological and psychological determinism of other humans, subject-body.

The following themes were identified for this category: death, sickness, health, pain, dental care, mistakes, reaction to failure, business, money problems, investments, commercial things, budget, poverty, house, nature, basic needs, food, clothing, house, relaxation, vacations, trips, uncomfortable, dangerous and scary situations, immediacy, shameful and unacceptable situations.

The above list demonstrates that the themes representing the subjects' values could be classified according to the three phenomenological-existential categories representing ways of being-in-the-world. This observation lead us to believe that it would be possible to have access to a subject's values if a questionnaire were constructed to elicit information about their lives which corresponds to the three ways of being-in-the-world. The questionnaire would generate subjects' values reflecting the same three aspects of their unique ways of being-in-the-world.

The principle of intentionality guided the process in operationally defining values. In fact, values give meaning and purpose to life; a person's will-to-meaning is fulfilled through the actualization of values (Croteau, 1994, p. 14). The research also adhered to a tenet of the phenomenological-existential approach — to "go back to the things themselves" as they appear to the subject's conscience and to "bracket," that is, to set aside one's presuppositions and allow the phenomena to reveal its meaning as authentically as possible (Giorgi, 1985). In order to respect both of these principles, we defined values in their simplest form using Aristotle's definition of a value as being a good for which people aim (McKeon, 1941, p. 395). This definition is consistent with our research approach for two reasons: (a) it permits the inference of a subject's intentionality since values reflect that which gives meaning (Frankl, 1969), and (b) it excludes the potential to define values from a psychological or a theological theory that could, if not bracketed, influence the analysis in the direction of a particular school of thought.

A second step in the construction of the questionnaire was to identify questions that could assist people to name the goods for which they aimed. The author's clinical experience shows that such goods are often identified when people are asked what they like or don't like about themselves, about others and about the world around them. The combination of this logic and the need to include all three categories of ways of being-in-the-world led to the conclusion that questions about what people like (value) and don't like (counter-value) on a wide range of things with which they interact or relate would generate the data we needed. It was anticipated that they would provide answers to questions about the goods for which they aimed for a variety of things, situations and people with whom and with which they interact. Our first questionnaire (FVQ), therefore, asked people what they liked and did not like about things, situations and people (including themselves and God) with whom they related. Subjects' values were expected to emerge from these questions in their simplest form while covering all three ways of their being-in-the-world. The questions keyed to the three ways of being-in-the-world were as follows:

a) *Eigenwelt* (being within oneself) was covered by questions such as: what do you like and not like about yourself, about your most frequent feeling, etc..

b) *Mitwelt* (being with others) was covered by questions like: what do you like and do not like about family members, etc.

c) *Umwelt* (being with the world around) was covered by questions such as: what do you like and not like about the environment, about work, about leisure time, etc.

These three categories, although fundamental to describe ways of being-in-the-world, did not seem sufficient in themselves to evaluate the stability of subjects' values. We needed to ensure that the FVQ would identify values that are stable over time. One way to identify these values would be to have subjects respond to a questionnaire at different periods in their lives. Since it is impossible or difficult to meet this condition, we decided to administer the questionnaire to the same subjects at three different times, with each administration keyed to their experiences of either the past, present, and future. In other words, the subjects were asked to respond to the same questions covering the three ways of being-in-the-world on three different occasions, with each occasion keyed to only one of the three time frames: past, present and future. More concretely, after answering how they liked and disliked things, situations and people in their world within, their world with others and the world around them in their present life, subjects were asked similar questions from the perspective of their childhood and from the perspective of anticipating their future. With respect to the subjects' anticipated future, two additional questions were added. One of the questions was borrowed from the Transactional Analysis approach (Stewart & Joines, 1991; James & Jongeward, 1978; Hone, 1988) and the other from the Neuro-Linguistic Programming approach (Walter & Peller, 1992). The two questions were the following: "What would you like to see written on your tombstone?" (Hone, 1988) and "What would be different in your life if a miracle happened?" (Walter & Peller, 1992, p. 73). These questions were chosen because the author's clinical experience shows that they generate powerful information about clients' values as they allow them to project themselves into the future. The inclusion of questions that addressed the subjects' values regarding the past, present and future life, made it possible to assess the stability of values across time. At the same time it provided the possibility for the FVQ to faithfully reflect the subjects' full range of values.

Table 1 illustrates the different categories covered by the FVQ with regards to the past, present and future time frames for the categories of being-in-the-world description.

Table 1

Categories Covered by the Fundamental Value Questionnaire

Being-in-the-world	Past (as a child)	Present (current)	Future (projection)
Eigenwelt	Like and did-not-like questions about world within	Like and do-not-like questions about world within	Would like and would-not-like questions about world within
Mitwelt	Liked and did-not-like questions about world with others	Liked and do-not-like questions about world with others	Would like and would-not-like questions about world with others
Umwelt	Liked and did-not-like questions about world around	Like and did-not-like questions about world around	Would like and would-not-like questions about world around

Eigenwelt, Mitwelt and Umwelt

The comments from the five subjects who completed the FVQ (referred to above) were used to improve the questionnaire, to make corrections to the instrument, to eliminate questions, and to add new questions. A number of general questions were added at the beginning of the questionnaire so that subjects would be introduced gradually to the more personal and taxing questions. For example, instead of starting with "like" and "dislike" questions, which seemed to address more personal issues and which often seemed difficult for subjects to answer at the beginning, it was helpful to first ask subjects questions about their opinions on less personal issues. A brief section on such opinions made it easier for the subject to move gradually to the more personal questions. "Like" and "dislike" questions followed these introductory questions.

A second version of the FVQ was then administered to ten subjects whose responses were used for an internal validation study. Similar to the first study, the subjects were interviewed and asked to speak about one of their concerns. The interviews were audiotaped. Comparison between the results generated through a phenomenological-existential analysis of these interviews and the results generated by the FVQ would provide the data needed to assess the internal validity of the FVQ. The identification of the same Fundamental Value by both methods would be considered to support validity of the FVQ since it demonstrated its capacity to measure what it was supposed to measure: the subject's Fundamental Value.

Our research question may be thus summarized: does the list of values obtained by the administration of the Fundamental Value Questionnaire correspond to the values extracted from an analysis of counselling transcripts using Giorgi's method?

Research Method

The following describes the existential-phenomenological method of analysis, the sample used for the study and the method used to analyze the data.

Methodology

The existential-phenomenological model implies that human beings, closely linked to the world in which they live, experience themselves as beings-in-the-world, as having a consciousness of their own and as being free to make choices and decisions on their own. Unlike animals and inanimate things, human subjects are characterized by what Croteau (1994) calls a *conscience-incarné-au-monde* (consciousness-incarnated-in-the-world) and *conscience-incarné-intentionnelle* (intentional-consciousness-incarnated; author's translations). The world experienced by such a *conscience-incarné* (consciousness-incarnated; author's translation) refers to three modalities of being-in-the-world described by Binswanger (1963): (a) the world around (physical and material things – *Umwelt*), (b) the world with others (people with whom one relates – *Mitwelt*), and (c) the world within (thoughts, feelings, desires revealing how one experiences self – *Eigenwelt*). These categories are used to analyze transcripts of the interviews with subjects so that researchers can identify the essence of the phenomenon – or meaning structure. This essence is then expressed in terms of meaning and purpose originating from the encounter between an aim (something for which the subject aims — *noesis*) and the object itself (the good, the reality, thing aimed at — *noema*) (Croteau, 1994, p. 9). Unlike traditional empirical psychological research, the focus of this method is not to make inferences that can be generalized to a larger population. Its focus is to identify stable laws, fundamental structures and idiosyncratic profiles of invariant structure of meaning in a particular phenomenon. This type of analysis is meaningful in that it produces stable phenomenological meaning structures. A meaning structure is said to be valid if it occurs consistently in repeated interview-based research with people having experienced similar phenomenon. Validity of this method is based on the invariant structures consistently identified in different people experiencing a similar given phenomenon.

The meaning structures are identified using two fundamental principles: phenomenological reduction and eidetic reduction (Croteau, 1994). These principles imply that the researcher, as much as possible, withholds any preconceived ideas, values or theoretical explanations of the interview content. The phenomenological reduction consists in "bracketing" one's natural attitude toward reality and "bracketing" one's theoretical presuppositions about the findings (Giorgi, 1985). This means that the researcher, after identifying his or her theoretical background, chooses not to refer to it while interpreting and describing the content of the interview as it appears to the subject's consciousness-incarnated. The researcher considers the experience as it is understood by the person who describes it, and refrains from defining whether it is measurable or verifiable (Giorgi, 1985) and from making interpretations from preconceived theory. The aim is to focus on knowledge of subjects' meaning structures per se rather than to verify whether the meaning itself is true or false.

Eidetic reduction refers to the process by which the researcher allows a structure of meaning — also called the essence of the phenomenon — to emerge from the interview content (Croteau, 1994). In this procedure, the researcher eliminates all the unnecessary elements of speech in the discourse under study and captures the core essence or the invariable structure of meaning given by that same person in a particular psychic phenomenon.

The technique by which the researcher applies these two principles is called the free imaginary variation (Poupart, Deslauriers, Groulx, Laperrière, Mayer & Pires, 1997, p. 350). Merleau-Ponty describes this technique in the following terms:

> [free imaginary variation is] to allow a concrete experience to float in one's mind so as to let oneself imagine that experience in every possible modified aspect; what remains invariable thereafter is the essence of the phenomenon under examination (Croteau, 1994).

In this process, the researchers, after eliminating peripheral aspects of the person's discourse, identifies with as much accuracy as possible, the "invariable contingents" — that which is constant and relevant to the subjective structure of meaning — describing that person's way of being-in-the-world in relation to a given phenomenon or experience (Giorgi, 1985).

The present research is based on two questions: (a) Can a Fundamental Value be identified from answers to the Fundamental Value Questionnaire, and (b) Does the Fundamental Value identified with the FVQ correspond to the Fundamental Value identified in the phenomenological-existential analysis of the same subjects' interviews?

The Sample

The sample comprised 10 subjects, all students in the Master's degree in Spiritual Anthropology, Sherbrooke University, Québec. There were six women and four men, 28 to 56 years old. Their professions included that of teacher, psychotherapist, social worker and housekeeper. The subjects were from the province of Quebec. Four of the subjects were married, three were living with a partner, one was separated and two were single.

Subjects were asked to complete the Fundamental Value Questionnaire and to share one of their concerns in a one-hour interview with the researcher. They were instructed to share any concern they had and to talk about it at length. The interviewer kept his/her interventions to a minimum to allow the process to flow freely.

The Analysis

The interview transcripts were analyzed, using Giorgi's (1985) phenomenological method, to identify the subject's Fundamental Value. Giorgi's method comprises four steps. The first one involves reading the entire transcript several times in order to achieve a General Sense of the Whole. The second step involves dividing the text into "meaning units," taking values as a basis for this task. This division facilitates subsequent analysis. The third step summarizes the contents of the meaning units in conceptual terms useful for the researcher. These are called "psychological summaries." The word psychological refers to essential psychological aspects retained for the analysis; it does not mean making a psychological interpretation based on any given psychological theory. Researchers can add a sub-step to this step. They can identify, within the psychological summaries, the essential structure emerging from each summary. For this study, this step identified essential values from each psychological summary. In the fourth step the research identifies the structure of meaning and purpose. This is called the Structural Synthesis. In this step, the researcher identifies the stable structure deduced from the analysis of the third step and its subset. For this study, the structure refers to the Fundamental Value emerging from the list of values identified in the subset. To arrive at the Fundamental Value, the third and fourth steps use the principal technique in phenomenological-existential research: the technique of free imaginary variation.

The last step, Structural Synthesis, is the procedure in which the subject's responses were translated in terms of their essential structure: their Fundamental Value. Values and counter-values generated by the FVQ were classified according to their correspondence with the Eigenwelt, Mitwelt and Umwelt categories. Structural Synthesis was then applied to this list of values. A comparison was made between Fundamental Values identified in the interview material to values generated by the FVQ. It is the comparison of the two sets of data that served as the basis to evaluate the internal validity of the FVQ.

Results

The Fundamental Value Questionnaire (FVQ) generated individual Fundamental Values for the subjects who were interviewed. The Fundamental Values identified by the FVQ corresponded to the ones identified through analysis of the same subjects' interviews using Giorgi's method. These findings support the internal validity of the FVQ. The implication is that the FVQ is useful for both qualitative research and clinical work. Table 2 presents the subjects' Fundamental Value identified from the two sources of data. The data from the transcript analysis is summarized in the left column and data from FVQ is summarized in the right column.

Eight of ten subjects showed relatively similar Fundamental Values from the transcript analysis and the Fundamental Value Questionnaire. The ten subjects were asked if the Fundamental Value, identified by the FVQ and by Giorgi's method, corresponded to that which they searched most for in life and whether it described who they were — their deepest identity. Eight had a positive, strong and very significant reaction to the Fundamental Value that emerged from the analysis. They made statements such as "This is exactly who I am," "It says very truly what it is I live for," or "Nothing could describe me better." Subjects also expressed

Table 2

Values Identified in the Transcripts (left column) and the FVQ (right column)*

Transcripts	FVQ
– Strength of her Identity	– Strength to be Herself
– Fullness of Life and Love	– Fullness of Life and Love through Self-Integrity (Blooming of potential)
– Personal Value in Relationship	– Self-Value through Trustworthy Relationships
– Strength to be Free	– Strength to be Free
– *Security* to be Loved for Herself	– Security to be Loved
– Freedom to be Herself through Unconditional Love	– Self-Confidence through Unconditional Love
– Acknowledging one's Self-Value	– Freedom and Fullness of Life through Acknowledgement of Self
– Becoming Self through Harmonious Relationships (family)	– Endless Growth in Life through Harmonious Relationships (family)
– Space to be Self in Relationships	– Strength and Joy in Life through Relationships
– To be Herself with Truth in Relationships	– Truth and Love in Relationships (balance between being Herself — assertive — and Helping Others)

* Values underlined indicate exact correspondence between the two sets of data

feelings of excitement when they realized how correctly the Fundamental Value revealed their deepest identity. One subject did not understand what was meant by the description of her Fundamental Value found through the analysis of her interview and by the FVQ; therefore, she was not sure whether it corresponded to her experience of herself. Another subject agreed with the Fundamental Value only after we explained the meaning of some of the words used to express it. The hesitation of these two subjects may be due to the different usage of words between researcher and subjects and to the fact that Fundamental Values identified were not identical in the transcript analysis to those in the FVQ. The consistency of the findings from the analysis of the two sources of data — the interview and the questionnaire — provides support for the internal validity of the FVQ.

Discussion

The data obtained by this research constitute the first step in the construction and internal validation of the FVQ. More studies that use a larger number of subjects need to be carried out to assess the internal validity of the FVQ. Additional questions might be added to the FVQ to evaluate other being-in-the-world categories. The validation process might include asking subjects to select from the Fundamental Values identified by all of the subjects the one that best represents who they are and that for which they aim in life. The subjects' recognition of their Fundamental Value among a large number of other Fundamental Values would provide greater support to the internal validity of the FVQ. Future research also needs to assess the FVQ's external validity. It would also be interesting to assess if this questionnaire would be useful in contexts other than counselling sessions.

The principal limit to this research is the small number of subjects used to assess the internal validity of the Fundamental Value Questionnaire. Such a limited number of subjects cannot be considered representative of the population. This limit is explained by the fact that using a phenomenological-existential research method to analyze transcripts requires much time. The number of subjects included in this research was limited of budget restraints and by time available. Another limit of this research is that the types of questions used to assess the three categories of being-in-the-world, *(Eigenwelt, Mitwelt and Umwelt)* were not exhaustive. The authors' reflection on the variety of issues associated with three ways of being-in-the-world was the basis on which the questions were selected and formulated. This process of choosing questions was also influenced by the results from the first research comprising five subjects. Thus, certain aspects representing each of the three ways of being-in-the-world may be absent.

The interested reader is invited to contact the author for more information about the Fundamental Value Questionnaire.

References

Binswanger, L. (1963). *Being-in-the-world: Selected papers of L. Binswanger.* New York: Basic Books.

Caron-Bourbonnais, D. (1993). L'expérience vécue du cancer: étude phénoménologique. *Sciences pastorales, 12,* 41-70.

Croteau, J. (1994). *Précis de psychologie phénoménologico-existentielle: initiation à son approche, à sa méthode, à ses techniques d'analyse.* Unpublished Research Manual, Ottawa, Ontario: University of Ottawa.

Frankl, V.E. (1969). *The will to meaning: foundations and applications of logotherapy.* New York: World Publication Company.

Giorgi, A. (1985). Sketch of a psychological phenomenology method. In A. Giorgi

(Ed.), *Phenomenology and psychological research,* Pittsburgh: Duquesne University Press.

Giorgi, A. (1985). The phenomenological psychology of learning and the verbal learning.

In A. Giorgi (Ed.), *Phenomenology and psychological research,* Pittsburgh: Duquesne University Press.

Hone, G. (1988). *Pastoral counselling practicum.* Ottawa, Ontario. Saint Paul University, Institute of Pastoral Studies.

James, M. and Jongeward, D.(1978). *Naître gagnant, l'analyse transactionnelle dans la vie quotidienne.* Paris: InterEdition.

May, R. (1962). Contributions of existential psychotherapy. In R. May, E. Angel, & H.F. Ellenberger (Eds.), *Existence: A new dimension in psychiatry and psychology* (pp. 37-91), New York: Simon and Shuster.

McKeon, R. (1941). *The basic works of Aristotle.* New York: Random House.

Morin, M.L. (1999). Counselling pastoral et valeur fondamentale individuelle: une étude phénoménologique. *Pastoral Sciences, 18,* 25-48.

Morin, M.L. (2001). *Pour une écoute en profondeur, la Valeur fondamentale.* Montréal, Médiaspaul.

Poupart, J. Deslauriers, J.P., Groulx, L.H., Laperrière, A., Mayer, R., & Pires, A.P. (1997). *La recherche qualitative, enjeux épistémologiques et méthodologiques.* Montréal: Gaëtan Morin.

Stewart, I. & Joines, V. (1991). *Manuel d'Analyse Transactionnelle.* Paris: InterEditions.

Walter, J. L. and Peller, J. E. (1992). *Becoming solution-focused in brief therapy.* New York Brunner/Mazel.

Québec, Canada
2003